ADVANCED EMPLOYMENT LAW

Jeffrey A. Helewitz, JD, LLM, MBA

Copyright © 2001
All Rights Reserved.
Pearson Publications Company
Dallas, Texas

Website: Pearsonpub-legal.com

ISBN: 0-929563-60-3

ACKNOWLEDGMENTS

The author wishes to acknowledge the kind assistance of Debbie Santiago-Laracuente, a paralegal and former student, whose thoughtful and concise comments and criticisms were an invaluable help in the completion of this book.

Jeffrey A. Helewitz

We thank Lance Cooper for his contribution to the current edition.

Enika Pearson Schulze
Publisher

TABLE OF CONTENTS

EMPLOYMENT LAW
AND THE PARALEGAL

Advanced Employment Law presents a concise yet informative survey of the various laws governing the employment relationship. The thrust of this text is the impact of federal regulation on employment. Throughout the book, reference is made to the particular federal statute that applies in a given situation. In any instance where reference is not made to federal law, general legal principles are discussed. However, the law in each jurisdiction may vary on these points, and the reader should always refer to the state-specific law whenever the point in question is not federally regulated.

Each topic discussed in the text is deserving of a book of its own, and *Advanced Employment Law* is not intended to replace an in-depth analytical study of each of these fields. This textbook, however, will afford the reader a comprehensive overview of the most important facets of employment law.

Understanding employment law is a practical necessity for the paralegal, both professionally and personally. Professionally, the paralegal may be called upon to assist in the representation of an employee who is charging his or her employer with unlawful employment practices, or the paralegal may assist an employer who is defending a challenge to its employment policies. The paralegal may be asked to draft the initial version of an employment contract, an employee handbook, or an employment document for a human resources department.

On a personal level, a paralegal can be an employee, employer, or independent contractor. The paralegal should be conversant with the law that affects his or her working life. The following case illustrates the types of issues that will be highlighted throughout the text. These issues involve the laws that govern the employment relationship, the necessity for documenting employment practices, and the difficulty of proving employment claims.

STEWART v. BROWNER
67 Fair Emp. Prac. Cases (BNA) Para. 1158 (March 28, 1995)

(The plaintiff, an employee of the United States Environmental Protection Agency, brought suit against her employer for racial discrimination. The EPA moved for dismissal, or alternatively, summary judgment. The court granted the defendant's motion and dismissed the case on the grounds that there was no unresolved issue of material fact that would support the plaintiff's allegations.)

I. Background

The plaintiff was hired by the United States Environmental Protection Agency ("EPA") in 1984. She was initially hired as a temporary GS–7 Freedom of Information Assistant by the EPA's Freedom of Information Office in February 1984. In June 1984, she took a permanent GS–6 secretarial position. The plaintiff subsequently applied, and was selected, for a paralegal specialist position. This position had a promotion potential to GS–11.

On May 1, 1987, the plaintiff filed a formal Equal Employment Opportunity ("EEO") complaint. In her EEO complaint, the plaintiff alleged that despite the fact that her position had a promotion potential to GS–11, the EPA had refused to promote her because of her race (black) and sex (female). She further alleged that the EPA improperly had assigned certain duties to a new white male employee. She also asserted that the Director of the Office of Legislative Analysis had retaliated against her for her prior EEO activity and had harassed her.

In May 1992, an Administrative Judge ("AJ") from the Washington field office of the Equal Employment Opportunity Commission ("EEOC") concluded that the EPA had not discriminated against the plaintiff or retaliated against her. He recommended that the agency issue a decision finding that there had been no discrimination and no reprisal. On March 13, 1992, the EEOC's Office of Federal Operations affirmed the AJ's findings that the EPA had not discriminated against or retaliated against the plaintiff.

On June 13, 1994, the plaintiff, proceeding *pro se*, filed the instant civil action against Carol M. Browner in her capacity as the Administrator of the EPA. The plaintiff also named Ronnie Blumenthal, Director of the Office of Federal Operations of the EEOC, as a defendant. While the plaintiff's complaint is rather unclear, it appears that she is attempting to assert a claim under Title VII of the Civil Rights Act of 11964, 42 U.S.C. § 2000e–16. She appears to claim that the EPA discriminated against her on the basis of her race. She presented no evidence at all. Where, as here, the plaintiff fails to present any evidence from which a trier of fact could possibly infer that the EPA's asserted nondiscriminatory reasons for its action are false or pretextual, summary judgment is appropriate. (Sources Omitted) Accordingly, the Court will grant the defendant's motion for summary judgment on the plaintiff's race and sex discrimination claims.

II. Reprisal Discrimination

The preceding analysis applies with equal force to the plaintiff's retaliation claims. First, the Court notes that it is again unclear whether the plaintiff can establish a *prima facie* case. The AJ stated that the plaintiff established a *prima facie* case of reprisal discrimination, but found that the plaintiff had failed to present any evidence to suggest that the defendant's proffered legitimate nondiscriminatory reasons for its actions were pretextual. The EEOC disagreed with the AJ and found that the plaintiff had failed to establish a *prima facie* case of reprisal discrimination. Once again, the Court does not need to resolve the issue. Even assuming *arguendo* that the plaintiff has established a *prima facie* case of reprisal discrimination, she has failed to present any evidence from which a trier of fact could infer that the defendant's legitimate nondiscriminatory reasons are false or pretextual. Because the plaintiff has failed to present any evidence regarding the pretext issue, the Court must also grant summary judgment for the defendant as to these claims.

III. Conclusion

Although it appears that the plaintiff may have been the victim of an unfortunate administrative error, the Court can find no evidence in the record from which a trier of fact could find that any of the defendant's actions were discriminatory. Assuming *arguendo* that the plaintiff has established a *prima facie* violation of Title VII, the plaintiff has failed to provide the Court with a shred of evidence that the legitimate nondiscriminatory reasons proffered by the defendant are in any way pretextual. Thus, even viewing the facts in the light most favorable to the *pro se* plaintiff, the Court finds that there are no genuine issues of material fact and that the defendant is entitled to judgment as a matter of law.

Accordingly, the Court will grant the defendant's motion for summary judgment and will dismiss this case.

Chapter One

BACKGROUND OF EMPLOYMENT LAW

Chapter Overview

The basis of the American judicial system is the legal relationship that exists between individuals. The law defines, explains, and interprets the legal rights and obligations of people based upon their legal relationships. This concept is especially true in the area of employment law, which, by its very name, describes a specific and special relationship.

Historically, persons were free to hire or fire employees, accept work or quit, and come and go as they pleased. The government imposed few, if any, restrictions on the workplace with respect to employment practices and decisions. This traditional attitude toward employment is known as **employment at will** and, in some states, it is still the backbone of employment law.

Although the parties were free to determine their own work arrangements, they were not able to create a lawless environment. Even under the concept of employment at will, both the employer and the employee were subject to the general rules of contract law with respect to personal services. These arrangements were often formalized by a written agreement between the parties. These agreements could be used by courts to define the parties' rights and obligations.

In addition to the internal legal obligations that might have existed between a worker and an employer, in many instances the employer was held vicariously liable to third persons for injuries caused by the employee while working under the employer's direction or control. An entire body of law developed, generally referred to as the **law of agency**, to deal with situations in which innocent third persons were injured by employees while the employee was fulfilling his or her employment obligations. To reach the presumably deeper pockets of the employer, the injured third person could sue and recover directly from the employer.

Relief was not available, however, to the employee if he or she were injured by a fellow worker. The only remedy that an employee had in such a situation was to sue the fellow employee directly. In most circumstances, this afforded little relief because of the generally poor economic state of the worker.

Consequently, toward the end of the last century, state legislatures, under the prodding of the courts, enacted statutes known today as **workers' compensation statutes.** These provide recovery for workers injured on the job. These statutes help workers by requiring employers to maintain insurance to cover employees' work-related injuries. These statutes form the basis for most of the current laws governing employment and the workplace injuries.

This chapter will discuss three important aspects of employment law:

1. employment at will
2. vicarious liability for employers
3. workers' compensation statutes.

Employment at Will

Traditionally, all persons entered into a work relationship under the concept of employment at will. Employment at will is where an employer and an employee freely enter into an employment relationship, and either party has the right to terminate that relationship at any time.

> **Example:** *A craftsman with highly specialized skills is working for a manufacturer in an employment at will situation. The worker does not like a project he is given and walks off the job at lunchtime, leaving a room full of unfinished work. Under the doctrine of employment at will, the worker is free to leave at any time, and the employer has no recourse.*

In these situations, no reason or justification is needed for the decision to hire or accept employment, and the employee may either quit or be discharged at any time without notice. Generally, employment at will occurs whenever an employee is engaged without any written employment contract.

The doctrine of employment at will does not apply in the following three situations.

1. *Employment Contract*

When an employer and an employee sign a written agreement that spells out their rights and obligations, the agreement prevails over the common law concept of employment at will.

In an employment contract, specific sections, usually entitled "Grounds for Termination" or "Duration," state the situations in which the employment can be terminated. These contracts may also indicate the type and degree of **damages** (monetary relief for injury resulting from a breach of contract) that the injured party may recover. Typically, these provisions provide that adequate notice must be given to the parties, something that is not required under the doctrine of employment at will. Also note that the employment at will doctrine can be incorporated into the agreement.

> **Example:** *This contract may be terminated at any time if one of the following occurs:*
>
> - *failure of a party to fulfill an agreement*
> - *failure of a condition specified in the contract*
> - *dissolution of one or more of parties*
> - *bankruptcy*
> - *death, illness, or disability of one or both of the parties*
> - *destruction of the subject matter*
> - *commission of a felony by one of the parties*

- *commission of a felony by one of the parties*
- *incarceration of one of the parties*
- *change in circumstances as herein specified*
- *upon one month's written notice to the other party for any reason.*

Employment contracts can come in any shape or size, and many courts have held that if a company provides an **employee handbook** that specifies various employment policies and practices, including grounds for termination and benefits provided, that handbook constitutes a contract between the employer and the employees.

Example: Beta, Inc., provides all of its employees with an employee handbook that describes its policies and practices. One of its provisions mandates a specific dress code, indicating that failure to abide by it can result in termination of employment. One of the employees refuses to follow the standards, preferring to be more "casual" in her choice of dress. When she is fired and protests, the employer can defend based on the agreement that exists between them as indicated in the handbook.

For a complete discussion of employment contracts and employee handbooks, *see* Chapters Nine and Ten.

2. *Collective Bargaining Agreements*

As will be discussed in Chapter Two, *The Rise of Labor Unions and Labor Laws*, a specific body of law has been developed for unions and union workers. These relationships are statutorily regulated and have eliminated the employment at will defense for both sides. The collective bargaining agreement is a specialized employment contract.

Example: Gamma, Inc., wants to reduce its overhead by firing ten workers. Gamma is a party to a collective bargaining agreement with a union, and under that agreement, union workers cannot be fired unless certain specified requirements are met. Gamma's desire to reduce overhead without any other proof of necessity is not one of the specified situations under the agreement, and so Gamma cannot fire the workers without violating its union contract obligations.

3. *Civil Service Employment*

Government employment at the federal, state, and municipal level is regulated by statute. Government employees are known as **civil servants,** and the terms and conditions of their employment are governed and regulated by **Civil Service Commissions**. The commissions are agencies that administer government employment. To determine the rights and obligations of civil servants, the appropriate statute must be analyzed.

> *Example: The head of a state agency wishes to hire a friend's child for a position in the office; however, under the provisions of the appropriate statute, the agency can hire only persons who have passed a civil service examination. Also, they must be hired chronologically according to the date of passing the test. Even if the friend's child has passed the exam, if the child was not next on the list by the date of passing the exam, the head of the agency cannot hire him or her. Many private employers also prohibit nepotism (the hiring of relatives) as a matter of policy.*

Limitations on Employment at Will

Over the past hundred years, many statutes have been enacted that limit the employment at will doctrine. Although freedom of employment is still the basis of most work situations, it has been tempered by public policy. The remainder of this text will discuss all of the various enactments that affect the employment at will concept.

The courts have outlined certain standards that apply to cases involving employment at will.

Good Faith and Fair Dealing

Although some courts have stated that even under an employment at will situation the parties must act in good faith and with fair dealing, most courts do not apply this standard unless they find that the employer discharged an employee for a reason that violates public policy.

> *Example: Delta, Inc., fires a worker because it does not want to employ workers of a particular religious persuasion. This firing violates public policy and would be found unlawful by most courts under First Amendment protections.*

Wrongful Discharge

Most courts today hold that it is unlawful for an employer to fire an employee because the employee refused to perform an unlawful act on the employer's behalf. For instance, if the employer fires an employee because the employee refused to commit perjury to further the employer's interests in a lawsuit, the employee may sue the employer for wrongful discharge. Courts do not condone situations that promote illegal conduct.

> *Example: An employer is notified that the company is going to be audited by the Internal Revenue Service. The employer orders the bookkeeper to make fraudulent entries into the company books to avoid IRS sanctions. The bookkeeper refuses and is fired. The employee has been wrongfully discharged.*

Public Policy

Some courts have held that where employment at will governs, an employer is still prohibited from violating public policy in its firing practices; however, these same courts, without statutory mandate, have refused to extend this concept to hiring practices.

> ***Example:*** *An employer refuses to hire a worker who suffers from hepatitis because of dangers to other workers. In this instance, the court would probably find that the employer is within its rights under the concept of employment at will.*

If the doctrine of employment at will does not apply, most courts, absent statutory prohibitions, would still uphold an employer's decision if there is a showing of **just cause**—a legitimate reason for the employer's action. If no just cause can be found, the injured employee may recover lost wages and, occasionally, **consequential damages**—the economic loss suffered as a direct result of the discharge beyond the mere loss of income.

> ***Example:*** *An employee claims wrongful discharge and sues the employer. When the employer cannot justify its actions, the court awards the employee all wages the employee would have received since the discharge, plus the costs the employee incurred in looking for a new job. The job search expenses are consequential damages.*

Note that, because of various laws and judicial decisions, the doctrine of employment at will— although still the foundation of employment law—is now tempered by the many legal restrictions that form the basis of the remaining chapters of this text.

Vicarious Liability

The preceding section discussed the background of the traditional employment relationship. This section covers some of the consequences of that relationship, most specifically the liability to third persons that an employer risks because of the actions of his or her employees. This is known as **vicarious liability**—the legal obligation that one must fulfill through no fault or action of his or her own.

Classically, the basic employment relationship is known as the **master-servant relationship**. A subset of this classification is known as the **principal-agent relationship**. These relationships are discussed below.

Master-Servant

The master-servant relationship exists where one person, known as the servant, is employed by another to render services. The servant must be under the control of the master in rendering the services.

The essential feature of the master-servant relationship is the element of control. The master totally controls and directs the servant's conduct. As a result, the servant has little or no independent discretion. The servant is required to perform the tasks that the master dictates. A typical example of a master-servant relationship would be an attorney and a secretary. The secretary is hired to operate the computer, greet clients, maintain a filing system, answer the telephone, etc. The secretary must perform these duties according to the wishes of the attorney.

> **Example:** *Tired of typing, a secretary decides that on a given day he will do nothing but answer the telephone and file documents. Nevertheless, if the attorney requires the secretary to do data entry, the secretary cannot refuse. The secretary lacks the legal ability to decide which tasks he will or will not perform. His tasks are controlled by the attorney's wishes.*

An **independent contractor** is one who is hired solely for results to be accomplished. The independent contractor is not under the control of anyone else, outside the specifics of the related contractual agreement. A servant could also be an independent contractor.

> **Example:** *As a sideline, the secretary in the above example has his own business as a calligrapher. One day the boss decides that the company needs new stationery and hires the secretary to create the letterhead for a fee of $1,000. In this instance, the relationship of the boss and the secretary has changed from master-servant to client and independent contractor.*

In a master-servant relationship, in addition to the obligation the parties have to each other, the master is held liable for any tortious act committed by the servant in the scope of this employment that injures third parties. A **tort** is a civil wrong, a failure to meet a legal standard of care that results in injury to another person. The doctrine that holds the master liable for a servant's torts is known as *respondeat superior*, meaning "let the master answer." The purpose of this doctrine is to permit the injured third person to recover from the party with the largest monetary resources (or the "deepest pockets").

For the master to be held liable for the tortious acts of his or her servants, it must be shown that the action resulting in the injury was committed by the servant in the course of furthering the master's business. If, conversely, the tortious act was committed by the servant while pursuing his or her own interests, legally known as being on a **frolic of his own**, the master is not held liable, and relief must be sought from the servant individually.

> **Example:** *The owner of a flower shop hires a driver to deliver flowers. One morning the owner sends the driver out in the company van to make deliveries. At 11:45 a.m., the driver realizes that if he can get across town in fifteen minutes he will be able to meet his friend for lunch. While speeding across town, the driver hits a woman who was in a crosswalk. The owner of the flower shop is not liable to the woman because the driver was on a frolic of his own.*

> **Example:** *Assume that at 11:45 a.m. the driver above realizes that he has to deliver floral arrangements for a luncheon banquet. To make the delivery by noon, he speeds across town to get to the banquet hall. While speeding to make the delivery, he hits a pedestrian. In this instance, the master will be liable because the driver was driving negligently to further the master's business.*

The master's liability for the tortious actions of servants committed while furthering the master's business is not absolute. There is an exception to the doctrine of *respondeat superior*, known as the **fellow servant exception**, which holds that a master is not liable for the tortious acts of one servant who injures another servant. This doctrine prevents fellow employees from fraudulently instituting claims against the common employer by collusion.

> **Example:** *A factory worker goes skiing over the weekend, and on the last run down the slopes falls and breaks a leg. The worker's cousin, a doctor who lives in the area, treats the broken leg. That night, while the factory worker and a fellow employee are talking on the telephone, the two decide to pretend that the injury occurred early the next morning at work due to the negligence of the other worker. They plan to sue the employer and split the proceeds. In addition to all of the other legal problems involved in this scenario, they would not be able to maintain a suit because of the fellow servant exception to the doctrine of respondeat superior.*

Be careful to distinguish between situations that give rise to an employer's vicarious liability and those caused by the master's own negligence. For example, if an employee is injured at work because the employer had failed to maintain proper and safe working conditions, the employer is legally responsible for the injuries for failure to meet a legal standard of care.

Furthermore, if a third person is injured by a servant who is unfit for the task assigned, the master might be held liable under a concept of **negligent hiring**. Negligent hiring means that the master hired someone who was likely to injure third parties. This results in the master's personal, not vicarious, liability.

> **Example:** *An employer has a policy of hiring ex-convicts to help their rehabilitation. One of the persons so hired has been in jail on several rape convictions. The employer gives the ex-convict a job in which he meets privately with members of the public in a closed office. Several weeks after the ex-convict starts work, a female customer is raped by the employee in the closed office. The woman sues the employer.*
>
> *This is an example of negligent hiring. Although the employer's motives were good, the ex-convict was placed by the employer in a situation that, because of his background, might give rise to injury to the public. In this instance, the employer may be held liable.*

Even under the doctrine of *respondeat superior*, masters are not held liable for the intentional torts committed by their servants (actions the person specifically intends to take). However, under the doctrine of negligent hiring, some torts that a servant intentionally commits may be considered the legal responsibility of the master, as in the example above.

Principal-Agent

The **principal-agent** relationship is one in which a person, known as the **agent**, acts in the place of another, known as the **principal**, when entering into contracts with third persons on the principal's behalf. In other words, the agent has the legal authority to act on behalf of, and to bind, the principal to third persons by contract. Although an agent may act gratuitously, most agency relationships are supported by **consideration**: the agent is paid for his or her services. Therefore, an agent may be deemed an employee of the principal.

> *Example: A real estate developer wishes to acquire several tracts of land. To make the purchases, she employs someone to find the property, negotiate the price, and sign the contracts for the sale of the land on her behalf. Because the person is hired to enter into contracts on behalf of the real estate developer, the employee is acting as her agent.*

By definition, an agent is authorized to act on behalf of the principal, but that authority is limited to exactly what the principal dictates. In other words, the agent is prohibited from acting beyond the scope of his or her authority.

> *Example: In the preceding example, assume that the real estate developer was interested only in land in Denver and so instructed her agent. If the agent signs a contract for the purchase of land in Tucson on behalf of the principal, this would be beyond the agent's legal authority to act, and the principal would not be bound to the contract.*

Unlike a general servant, an agent has discretion with respect to means and method of carrying out his or her agency—the principal does not control the agent's actions.

> *Example: An employer hires an agent to locate a caterer for the office Christmas party. The employer/principal does not necessarily care which caterer is hired by the agent as long as the food is good and the price is right. The actual choice of caterer is within the discretion of the agent.*

Within a single company, the same two people may be in both relationships: master-servant and principal-agent. The two concepts are not mutually exclusive. One must determine exactly which function the person is performing to determine the potential legal liability of the parties.

> *Example: An attorney hires a secretary to perform general secretarial duties. In addition, the secretary is authorized to purchase office supplies for the company whenever she sees that supplies are running low. In this situation, the attorney is both a master and a principal, and the secretary is both a servant, while performing general secretarial duties, and an agent, while ordering supplies.*

Because the purpose of the agency relationship is to bind the principal contractually to third persons, the principal is held liable for all contracts that the agent enters into on the principal's behalf.

> *Example: In the preceding example, when the secretary orders paper and pens from an office supplier, the company is liable for the cost of the supplies. The contract is one for the purchase and sale of supplies between the company and the supplier, even though it is entered into by the secretary. The secretary merely acts as the conduit to complete the contractual relationship.*

Note the difference in the liability of the parties between master-servant and principal-agent. In the former relationship, the master is liable for the tortious acts that injures third persons committed by the servant while furthering the master's business. In the latter, the principal is liable for the authorized contracts entered into on his or her behalf by the agent. This distinction determines whom the injured party may sue: the master if the basis of the claim is based in tort, the principal if the claim is based on contract.

If an agent negligently injures a third person, only the agent is liable unless a master-servant relationship can be found and the injury occurred while furthering the master's business. It is the act being performed, not the actor, that determines personal or vicarious liability.

How Agency Relationships Are Created

An agency relationship can be created in one of three ways: by agreement, by ratification, or by estoppel.

1. *Agreement.* If two persons agree that one should act as the other's agent, the agency relationship is created. No consideration is necessary to create an agency, but consideration is necessary to create an employment situation.

> *Example: As a favor, one student asks another to buy a book for him from the school bookstore. When the sale is made, the purchasing student is acting as the other student's agent, even though he is not being compensated. If the book turns out to be misprinted, the student who asked for the purchase is the injured party.*

> *Example: A bookstore hires a buyer to acquire inventory for the store. When the buyer purchases the books for the company, she is acting as an agent, and she is an employee because she is paid for her services.*

2. *Ratification.* **Ratification** results whenever the presumed principal accepts the benefits or otherwise affirms the acts of one who purported to act on the principal's behalf. If no agency existed when the contract was entered into, but the presumed principal agrees to the contract, the agency relationship is formed. In other words, the agency is created retroactively.

> *Example: A student knows that his friend is trying to sell her computer. One day he overhears someone talking about buying a used computer. The student, saying he represents the seller, enters into an agreement for the sale of the computer. When the computer owner hears of the agreement and accepts the money, she has retroactively created an agency relationship. Note that if she thought the price too low and declined, the student who made the sale may be personally liable to the buyer because his actions were not authorized.*

3. *Estoppel.* **Estoppel** refers to the court's equitable ability to right a wrong. In agency law, this would occur when one person intentionally or negligently allows a third person to believe that another is his or her agent, and the third person relies to his or her detriment on the appearance of authority in dealing with the presumed agent. In this situation, the law will estop, or bar, the principal from claiming that no agency relationship exists.

> *Example: An appliance store rents in-house space to a repair service and places a sign in the store saying that repair services are available. When a customer brings in a toaster to the repair service to be fixed and the repairs are faulty, the storeowner is liable. Because the owner failed to indicate that the repair service is an independent contractor and not an employee of the store, the owner led the customer to believe that she was dealing with the store in contracting for repairs. As a result, the owner is liable for the breach of contract. Of course, the owner may seek reimbursement from the repair service, but that is the owner's problem, not the customer's.*

Types of Authority

Once it is determined that an agency exists, all contracts entered into by the agent on the principal's behalf are the principal's responsibility, provided that the agent was authorized by the principal to enter into that type of contract. An agent's authority to act is described as either actual, apparent, or by estoppel, depending upon the manner in which the authority is conferred.

1. *Actual Authority.* **Actual authority** results from the principal's acts, words, or directions made directly to the agent regarding the agent's authority to act. Actual authority is either **express** (direct instructions), **implied** (resulting from custom, usage, or the past practices of the parties), or a combination of both. It is the highest form of authority that an agent may possess.

> *Example: A dress manufacturer runs out of a specific fabric and contracts with a converter to find additional fabric. The manufacturer and the converter have worked together for five years, and the converter knows by past practice that any purchases made for this manufacturer are to be billed no sooner than 60 days after delivery. The manufacturer has told the converter exactly how much fabric he needs and agrees to pay the converter a specified fee for his services. In this situation, the converter's authority is both express (for the type and quantity of fabric) and implied (for the billing procedure). [This situation may be modified in different jurisdictions by statute or case law.]*

2. *Apparent Authority*. **Apparent authority** results from the principal's words or behavior toward the third party (not the agent) that the agent has authority to act on the principal's behalf. The agent's authority to act is dependent upon the third party's reasonable belief based on the principal's words or behavior.

> *Example: A storeowner employs a worker whose duties are to clean the store, stock supplies. and make sales to the customers when the owner is away. A farmer enters the store to sell the owner some produce. To get rid of the farmer, the owner tells him that the worker is the person authorized to buy produce for the store. The farmer returns later that day when the owner is out and persuades the worker to buy his produce. The storeowner is bound to pay for the produce because his statements to the farmer gave the worker the apparent authority to buy the produce.*

3. *Authority by Estoppel*. **Authority by estoppel** arises when the principal intentionally or negligently causes or allows a third person to believe that an agent is authorized to do something that the agent is not authorized to do. If the third person is harmed by this, it would be unjust to permit the principal to deny the agency. In this situation, there is no direct manifestation, but the principal has simply permitted a third person to believe that an agency exists, and the third person has detrimentally relied on that appearance. Detrimental reliance generally means economic loss.

> *Example: Assume that in the preceding example the grocery store owner, rather than giving the worker a raise, promotes the worker to "store manager," giving the worker a name tag with that title and other indicia of responsibility. Because store managers are generally permitted to make purchases for the store, if a salesperson persuades the "manager" to buy produce, the storeowner will probably be liable.*

If the agent acted under either actual or apparent authority, the third person may sue the principal for the price negotiated in the contract. If the agent only has authority by estoppel, the third party could recover only his or her actual out-of-pocket loss from the principal.

An agent is considered a **fiduciary** to the principal, meaning that the agent is held to a higher standard than ordinary care with respect to his or her actions toward the principal. The agent, as fiduciary, owes the principal a duty of loyalty and is prohibited from **self-dealing**—that is, making a personal profit that should have gone to the principal.

> *Example: An agent is hired to purchase real estate for a developer. In seeking suitable property, the agent locates a parcel of land that he purchases for himself under a fictitious name. He then buys the land from himself for the principal at a huge profit. This conduct violates the agent's duty of loyalty and prohibitions against self-dealing. The land should have been bought for the principal in the first place.*

Workers' Compensation

One of the earliest efforts to embody the concept of vicarious liability discussed above is the **workers' compensation statutes**. These laws, previously called **workman's compensation** and **workmen's compensation**, resulted from the fellow servant exception noted on page 11.

Workers' compensation is an insurance pool funded by employers who can continue doing business in the event of unexpected injuries to workers. It is a no-fault (no liability) system, totally separate from the above discussions, created not by common law but by statute.

During the Industrial Revolution, many on-the-job accidents occurred. Because of the fellow servant exception to the doctrine of *respondeat superior*, workers who were injured on the job were often discouraged from suing their employers, who could defend on grounds that another employee—not the employer—had caused the accident. Consequently, a worker's only legal remedy was to sue the employee whose negligence caused the accident (but who was probably too poor to pay damages).

To be entitled to relief, the injured worker had to prove that the action of the offending worker was intentional rather than merely negligent. Furthermore, the plaintiff was often precluded from an award of damages if his or her action contributed to the accident. This doctrine, known as **contributory negligence**, also hindered the efforts of injured employees to hold employers financially accountable, especially because judges and juries were often quick to exonerate employers.

Because the courts failed to hold employers financially responsible for their workers' injuries, the public forced legislatures to act. The result was one of the first statutory attempts to redefine the employment relationship.

All states have now enacted workers' compensation laws to protect workers. These statutes enable injured workers to present claims to a **workers' compensation board** that will award recovery to employees who can prove on-the-job injuries. Employers in most states are required to maintain insurance to cover the cost of these claims. In this fashion, the legislatures have mandated that employers take some responsibility for the negligence of their employees, while at the same time statutorily limiting the amount of the recovery.

Most workers' compensation statutes require the worker to be an employee of the employer. The principal test used to determine whether an employment relationship exists is whether the person to whom the service is rendered had the right to control the manner and means of completing the task. Note how this restates the basic definition of the master-servant relationship.

> **Example:** *A retail storeowner employs several salespeople and other workers. Part of one worker's job is to clean the premises. One day the cleaning worker waxes the floor and neglects to put up a sign that the floor is slippery. A salesperson slips on the waxed floor, breaking her arm. The salesperson may either sue the fellow worker who was negligent or file a claim under workers' compensation; she cannot do both.*

Workers' compensation statutes are creations of state law. Because this area of law is state-specific, each state's statutes must be scrutinized to determine what rights and liabilities exist in a given situation.

Chapter Summary

Employment law is generally governed by statutes and judicial interpretation. Because these statutes are a fairly recent development, before they can be analyzed or understood, it is necessary to be aware of the historical background of the law governing employment.

Traditionally, employment was considered to be at will, meaning that both the employer and employee were free to employ or be employed by whomever they wanted and could be fired or resign at any time without cause or notice. This doctrine has been modified by contract, public policy, and statute.

The employment relationship can be categorized as master-servant or principal-agent. In the master-servant relationship, the servant is employed and controlled by the master. The master is therefore liable to third persons for injuries resulting from tortious acts committed by the servant while furthering the master's business. In a principal-agent relationship, the agent is authorized to enter into contracts with third persons on behalf of the principal, thereby rendering the principal liable by contract.

Some of the earliest legislative enactments that modified the historical common law employment relationship were the workers' compensation statutes. These laws provided a statutory remedy for workers injured on the job.

Edited Judicial Decisions

The following cases underscore the concepts discussed in this chapter. The first case, *DiCosala v. Kay*, illustrates the concept of negligent hiring, while *Johnson v. Berkofsky-Barret Productions, Inc.*, highlights a worker's compensation claim.

DICOSALA v. KAY
91 N.J. 159; 450 A.2d 508 (1982)

The primary question raised in this case is whether an employer owes a duty of reasonable care to third persons in the hiring and retention of employees whose aggressive or reckless characteristics or lack of competence in the performance of their employment duties may endanger such third persons.

I.   On August 11, 1973, the plaintiff in this action, Dennis DiCosala, was accidentally shot in the neck by Robert M. Kay. At the time of the accident, the plaintiff was a child of only six years of age. The accident occurred in the living quarters of the plaintiff's uncle, defendant Philip Reuille, which were located on the grounds of Camp Mohican, a Boy Scout camp situated in Blairstown.

Camp Mohican was owned and operated by the Robert Treat Council of the Boy Scouts of America. In spring 1971 Reuille had been hired as a camp ranger by that organization. His duties at the camp included repair work, maintenance chores, and other general work related to the operation of the summer camp. His compensation included the provision of accommodations on the campgrounds. The building in which he lived, Collinmore Lodge, also contained, in addition to Reuille's living quarters, a camp office and meeting hall.

The Boy Scouts claim that the living quarters were regarded as Reuille's private dwelling within which he could entertain private house guests....

On the day of the accident, Kay went to Reuille's home, at the invitation of Benita DiCosala, intending to take her and the plaintiff on a mountain hike. The record is fairly clear that Kay's visit and the planned hike were entirely social and unrelated to Kay's duties as a counselor at the camp. When the plaintiff's mother was unable to leave as planned, she, along with the young boy and Kay, went outside and played hide-and-go-seek for about one-half hour. The three then went into the Reuille living quarters to pass the time.

The young boy and Kay first went into the dining room. While there, they were "playing with a toy pistol and a .22 automatic pistol that he (Robert) had found on top of a cubbard [*sic*] in the dining room." They then moved into the living room, where Kay found another handgun in a holster on the fireplace mantel. He removed it and, despite Benita's warning, pointed it at the plaintiff in play. Kay threatened the boy in jest, saying that he was naughty and if he did not behave, Kay would shoot him. Kay then pulled the trigger, apparently assuming that the gun was not loaded. The boy was struck in the neck by Kay's shot. While the record does not indicate the precise nature and extent of the boy's wound, it seems undisputed that he has suffered severe and crippling injuries.

(The trial court granted a summary judgment for the defendant, and the decision was affirmed by the Appellate Division. The plaintiff appeals.)

II.   In reviewing the dismissal of claims as legally insufficient on a motion for summary judgment, we must accept as true all of the allegations in the pleadings, the affidavits and the discovery submitted on the behalf of the opponent of the motion. We also draw all reasonable inferences most favorable to that party. *Judson v. Peoples Bank & Trust Co. of Westfield*, 17 N.J. 67, 73–75 (1954).

Initially, we consider the plaintiffs' argument that the defendants herein may be liable under the doctrine of *respondeat superior*. Their claim, in essence, is that under that doctrine, an employer may be liable if the actions of its employee either are within the scope of employment or could have been reasonably foreseeable by the employer, whether those actions be criminal or tortious.

The doctrine of *respondeat superior* has traditionally been thought to render the employer liable for torts of one of its employees only when the latter was acting within the scope of his or her employment. *Gilborges v. Wallace*, 78 N.J. 342, 351 (1978); *Wright v. Globe Porcelain Co.*, 72 N.J. Super. 414, 418 (App.Div.1962); W. Prosser, *Law of Torts*, 460–61 (4th ed. 1971). The scope of employment standard, concededly imprecise, is a formula designed to delineate generally which unauthorized acts of the servant can be charged to the master. *Id.* Furthermore, the standard refers to those acts which are so loosely connected with what the servant is employed to do, and so fairly and reasonably incidental to it, that they may be regarded as methods, even though quite improper ones, of carrying out the objectives of the employment. *Id.*

See Roth v. First National State Bank of New Jersey, 169 N.J. Super. 280 (App.Div.), certif. den., 81 N.J. 338 (1979). Conduct is generally considered to be within the scope of employment if "it is of the kind [that the servant] is employed to perform; it occurs substantially within the authorized time and space limits; [and] it is actuated, at least in part, by a purpose to serve the master." *Restatement (Second) of Agency* § 228 (1957). *See also Id.* at § 229 (kind of conduct within scope of employment).

No facts were presented by the plaintiffs to suggest that either Kay's alleged negligence in shooting the plaintiff or Reuille's alleged negligence in leaving a loaded handgun in his quarters on the premises of a Boy Scout camp were within the scope of the employment of either Kay or Reuille. The boy was in the Reuille quarters as part of a purely social visit; Kay's actions toward the boy and his mother were similarly purely socially motivated. Accordingly, we affirm the granting of defendant's summary judgment motion in connection with the plaintiffs' *respondeat superior* claim.

III. As noted, the trial court assumed that there exists a cognizable wrong under New Jersey law regarding the negligent hiring or retention of an employee. In reaching this conclusion, it relied exclusively on a reported case in the Federal District Court of New Jersey. *Nivins v. Sievers Hauling Corp.*, 424 F.Supp. 82 (D.N.J. 1976). Since, as was noted by the *Nivins* court, no New Jersey case has squarely addressed this issue, we turn first to the question of the correctness of the trial court's conclusion that New Jersey recognizes such a cause of action.

A majority of jurisdictions that have addressed this issue have concluded that an employer who negligently either hires or retains in his employ an individual who is incompetent or unfit for the job, may be liable to a third party whose injury was proximately caused by the employer's negligence....

The reasoning that has impelled the recognition of this cause of action in most jurisdictions follows from tort principles of negligence and foreseeability, as well as from firmly established principles of agency and vicarious liability. An employer whose employees are brought into contact with members of the public in the course of their employment is responsible for exercising a duty of reasonable care in the selection or retention of its employees. Comment d to § 213 of the *Restatement (Second) of Agency* discussed these principles in the following manner:

> d. Agent dangerous. The principal may be negligent because he has reason to know that the servant or other agent, because of his qualities, is likely to harm others in view of the work or instrumentalities entrusted to him.

> The dangerous quality in the agent may consist of his incompetence or unskillfulness due to his youth or his lack of experience considered with reference to the act to be performed. An agent, although otherwise competent, may be incompetent because of his reckless or vicious disposition, and if a principal, without exercising due care in selection, employs a vicious person to do an act which necessarily brings him in contact with others while in the performance of a duty, he is subject to liability for harm caused by the vicious propensity....

> Liability results under the rule stated in this Section ... because the employer antecedently had reason to believe that an undue risk of harm would exist because of the employment. The employer is subject to liability only for such harm as is within the risk. If, therefore, the risk exists because of the quality of the

employee, there is liability only to the extent that the harm is caused by the quality of the employee which the employer had reason to suppose would be likely to cause harm.

In short, persons must use reasonable care in the employment of all instrumentalities—people as well as machinery—where members of the public may be expected to come into contact with such instrumentalities.

The tort of negligent hiring addresses the risk created by exposing members of the public to a potentially dangerous individual, while the doctrine of *respondeat superior* is based on the theory that the employee is the agent or is acting for the employer....

Accordingly, the negligent hiring theory has been used to impose liability in cases where the employee commits an intentional tort, an action almost invariably outside the scope of employment, against the customer of a particular employer or other member of the public, where the employer either knew or should have known that the employee was violent or aggressive, or that the employee might engage in injurious conduct toward third persons (citations omitted)....

In sum, the mere fact that the young boy was a private guest of Reuille as opposed to being a client of the Boy Scout Camp does not in itself end the requisite inquiry. Rather, to determine whether the defendants owed a duty to the plaintiff to exercise reasonable care in the selection and retention of their employees, we must inquire whether a reasonably prudent and careful person, under the same or similar circumstances, should have anticipated that "an injury to the plaintiff or to those in a like situation would probably result" from his conduct. *Yaskin*, 75 N.J. at 144. Stated somewhat differently, the question presented is whether the employer, knowing of its employee's unfitness, incompetence or dangerous attributes when it hired or retained its employee, should have reasonably foreseen the likelihood that the employee through his employment would come into contact with members of the public, such as the plaintiff, under circumstances that would create a risk of danger to such persons because of the employee's qualities.

We conclude that the defendants owed a duty to this plaintiff to exercise reasonable care in the hiring and retention of their employees. The present record presents controverted material facts and strong inferences that, if properly adduced at a trial, would provide a basis for liability against defendants.

As previously noted, one requisite predicate for positing liability against defendants in their capacities as employers under the negligent hiring cause of action is their knowledge of the employee's dangerous characteristics and the reasonable foreseeability of harm to other persons as a result of these qualities. *Supra* at 173–174. The second element of the cause of action relates to proximate cause, which involves the foreseeability of the injury that was suffered by the plaintiff.

The record adequately discloses facts indicative of the foreseeability of the accident which actually befell plaintiff and which would support liability.

Defendants knew of Reuille's possession and use of guns. They also provided Reuille with housing on the premises of the Boy Scout Camp in connection with his employment. While it is claimed that these lodgings were not generally accessible to other persons present at the camp, they were part of common facilities that were used by others associated with the camp. In addition, Reuille had frequent contact with such persons, and it was foreseeable that they might be invited to his living quarters. Further, it was foreseeable that Reuille would entertain guests in his home, and the Boy Scouts had actual notice of this. From the standpoint of foreseeability, the status of such guests in Reuille's home would not differ materially from any other person connected with the camp who might be in the same position. Therefore, that the plaintiff here did not have the status of a scout or camper is not determinative. Though plaintiff's presence at Reuille's lodgings was not technically a circumstance within the actual scope of employment or an incident to the performance of employment duties, plaintiff clearly was exposed to the "enhanced hazard" and fell within the "zone of risk" created through defendants' employment of Reuille and the dangerous condition that existed at the Reuille home which was furnished as part of his employment. As such, harm to plaintiff was foreseeable and, therefore, defendants were under a duty to him to exercise reasonable care in choosing to retain Reuille as an employee on their campgrounds.

Under the circumstances, the grant of summary judgment in defendants' favor was in error and must be reversed so that the claims can be resolved in a plenary trial....

Accordingly, we reverse judgment in favor of the defendants and remand the case for trial on the merits.

JOHNSON V. BERKOFSKY-BARRET PRODUCTIONS, INC.
211 Cal. App. 3d 1067, 260 Cal. Rptr. 67 (1989)

Plaintiff and appellant Craig Johnson (Johnson) appeals the summary judgment in favor of defendant and respondent Berkofsky-Barret Productions, Inc. (BBP).

Because the evidence conclusively shows an employment relationship between Johnson and BBP, Johnson is limited to workers' compensation as his sole and exclusive remedy for work-related injuries. Therefore, the trial court properly granted summary judgment in favor of BBP.

FACTUAL BACKGROUND

Johnson, an actor in television commercials, obtained acting jobs through a company called L'Image. Generally, L'Image directed Johnson to the shooting location of the commercial and advised him how to dress. The commercial production company then paid L'Image for Johnson's acting services and L'Image, in turn, paid Johnson after deducting its percentage fee.

On December 3, 1985, L'Image sent Johnson to the filming of an I.B.M. commercial produced by BBP in Lacy Park in San Marino, California. In answer to an interrogatory Johnson described what happened during one of the takes of the commercial as follows: "The scene was a softball game and I played the pitcher. I was instructed to dive for a grounder, miss it, and ham it up. I dove for a ground ball, landing squarely on my shoulder, causing my injuried [sic]."

On July 16, 1986, Johnson filed a civil complaint for personal injury against BBP. Johnson admitted both in answers to interrogatories and at his deposition the director and assistant director of the commercial had supervised him and instructed him how to perform.

On or about June 25, 1987, Johnson filed a claim with the Workers' Compensation Appeals Board (WCAB) against BBP for injuries arising out of the accident.

BBP filed a motion for summary judgment on February 26, 1988, on the theory Johnson was a "special employee" of BBP and therefore limited to workers' compensation remedies for the personal injuries suffered while filming the commercial.

In opposition to the motion for summary judgment, Johnson claimed he was not an employee of L'Image but had hired L'Image as an agent to obtain work for him. He concludes he could not be BBP's "special employee" because he had never been an employee of L'Image.

Although the parties have not supplied a reporter's transcript of the hearing on the motion for summary judgment, Johnson contends, and BBP does not dispute, that the trial court found Johnson's workers' compensation claim constituted an admission he was BBP's employee and granted summary judgment on that basis in favor of BBP.

CONTENTIONS

Johnson claims triable issues of material fact exist as to whether he was an employee of BBP.

DISCUSSION....

3.   The employee/independent contractor distinction.

Labor Code section 3351 defines an employee as "every person in the service of an employer under any appointment or contract of hire or apprenticeship, express or implied, oral or written, whether lawfully or unlawfully employed...."

An independent contractor is "any person who renders service for a specified recompense for a specified result, under the control of his principal as to the result of his work only and not as to the means by which such result is accomplished." (Lab. Code, § 3353.)

"The label placed by the parties on their relationship is not dispositive, and subterfuges are not countenanced. [Citations.] ... [The] principal test of an employment relationship is whether the person to whom service is rendered has the right to control the manner and means of accomplishing the result desired.... [Citations.] While conceding that the right to control work details is the 'most important' or 'most significant' consideration, the authorities also endorse several 'secondary' indicia of the nature of a service relationship." (*S.G. Borello & Sons, Inc. v. Department of Industrial Relations, supra*, 48 Cal. 3d at pp. 349–350.)

To ascertain whether an employment relationship exists, the *Borello* court cautioned that factors in addition to the right to control work must be applied on a case-by-case basis with the salutary purposes of the Workers' Compensation Act in mind.

These secondary factors include the right to discharge at will without cause, whether the alleged employee is in a distinct occupation or business, whether the work is usually done under the direction of the principal or by a specialist without supervision, the skill required, whether the alleged employee supplies tools or the place where the work is to be performed, the duration of the services, whether payment is by time or by the job, whether the work is part of the regular business of the principal and the intent of the parties.

The *Borello* court also reviewed factors used in other jurisdictions to determine whether a worker is an independent contractor. In addition to the right to control the work, these factors include:

(1) the alleged employee's opportunity for profit or loss depending on his managerial skill;
(2) the alleged employee's investment in equipment or materials required for his task, or the employment of helpers;
(3) whether the service rendered requires a special skill;
(4) the degree of permanence of the working relationship; and
(5) whether the service rendered is an integral part of the alleged employer's business. [Citation] (*S.G. Borello & Sons, Inc. v. Department of Industrial Relations, supra*, 48 Cal.3d at p. 355.)

a. Johnson was the employee of BBP.

Here, the primary right of control factor must be determined in favor of BBP. Johnson concedes the operatives of the production company directed and supervised the manner in which he performed in the commercial. Consideration of the great majority of the secondary factors in the context of this fact situation also leads to the conclusion that Johnson was BBP's employee.

BBP had the right to discharge Johnson at will without cause; although acting in commercials might be considered an occupation, it is universally done under the direction of another; Johnson did not supply tools, employ helpers or provide the place the work was to be performed; although acting in the Shakespearean sense requires skill, a far lesser degree of skill is required for acting in commercials; the duration of the services is generally short but payment appears to have been made by the time and not by the job; the filming of the commercial is part of BBP's regular business; and, Johnson had no opportunity for profit or loss depending on his managerial skills nor did he invest in equipment or materials.

We therefore conclude, as a matter of law, Johnson was an employee of BBP at the time of the accident and therefore he is limited to workers' compensation as his sole and exclusive remedy for damages resulting from personal injuries (Lab. Code, § 3602).

4. Workers' compensation remedy is exclusive even construing L'Image as a labor broker.

Finally, we consider whether a different result is required if L'Image is viewed as a labor broker or agent.

This question was discussed in *Riley v. Southwest Marine, Inc.*, (1988) 203 Cal. App. 3d 1242 [250 Cal. Rptr. 718]. The *Riley* court concluded: "Extensive nationwide case law ... hold[s] the 'special employment' or 'borrowed servant' doctrine applies to the labor brokerage situation and bars an employee who is injured while on assignment from a labor broker, such as Manpower, from bringing a tort suit against the assigned employer. [Citations.]" (*Id.* at pp. 1251–1252.)

We perceive no reason to deviate from the *Riley* rule in this instance. Although the accounting of proceeds between Johnson and L'Image might not have mirrored the manner in which other temporary personnel providers operate, the concept remains the same. L'Image provided BBP with short-term employees from its labor pool in a fashion nearly identical to the way in which other employment agencies, such as Manpower, Employers' Overload, etc., furnish temporary personnel services.

The *Riley* court also rejected the argument that a tort remedy should be permitted to temporary employees because they receive lower pay and fewer benefits. Although this equitable exception has appeal, its logic also applies to part-tine and probationary employees and "would significantly alter and contradict the intent of the workers' compensation statutory scheme." [*Riley v. Southwest Marine, Inc.*, *supra*, 203 Cal. App. 3d at p. 1259; *See, e.g., Laeng v. Workmen's Comp. Appeals Bd.*, *supra*, 6 Cal. 3d 771 (an injury sustained during a "'tryout'" for an employment as a refuse crew worker compensable under workers' compensation as a matter of law).]

Thus, we agree with the conclusion reached by the *Riley* court and limit Johnson to a workers' compensation remedy.

CONCLUSION

Johnson's concession that BBP controlled and directed every aspect of his employment and our consideration of secondary determining factors render Johnson an employee as a matter of law. As such, Johnson's exclusive remedy for his work-related injury is workers' compensation.

DISPOSITION

The judgment is affirmed.

Glossary

actual authority – agent's ability to act resulting from direct manifestations to the agent by the principal

agency by estoppel – agency created when a person intentionally or negligently causes or allows a third person to believe that another is his or her agent

apparent authority – agent's ability to act resulting from the principal's manifestations to third persons about the agent's authority

civil service – government employment

Civil Service Commission – government agency with authority over government employment

consequential damages – monetary remedy above the standard measure for unusual losses resulting from a breach of contract

employee handbook – employer-generated document regarding employment policies and procedures disseminated to employees

employment at will – common law right of freedom of employment

express authority – subset of actual authority arising out of specific instructions by the principal to the agent

fellow servant exception – a master is not liable for the tortious acts of one servant who injures another servant

fiduciary – one who is held to a higher standard of care than ordinary care

frolic of his own – a master is only liable for a servant's tortious acts that injure third persons if the servant was furthering the master's business and not acting on the servant's own devices when the negligent act took place

implied authority – actual authority resulting from custom and usage

just cause – legitimate business reasons for discharging an employee

law of agency – common law rules that define an aspect of the employment relationship

master-servant – the basic employment relationship in which the master controls the activities of the servant

negligent hiring – an employer hiring someone unsuitable for the job whose unsuitability results in injuries to third persons; the master is personally liable

principal-agent – relationship in which one person is legally empowered to contract on behalf of another

ratification – method of creating an agency relationship retroactively by accepting the benefits of an unauthorized contract

respondeat superior – a master is liable for the tortious act of a servant who injures third persons

vicarious liability – being held legally accountable for actions committed by other persons

workers' compensation – formerly workmen's compensation; statutes granting recovery to workers for injury in the performance of their duties

wrongful discharge – terminating employment without just cause

Exercises

1. Read and analyze your state's workers' compensation statute.

2. Is an attorney an agent for her clients? Discuss.

3. Discuss why workers' compensation statutes limit recovery and prohibit suing both the wrongdoer and filing a workers' compensation claim.

4. Discuss the benefits and drawbacks of employment at will.

5. Discuss the difference between vicarious liability and negligent hiring.

Chapter Two

THE RISE OF LABOR UNIONS
AND LABOR LAWS

Chapter Overview

The rise of trade unionism at the turn of the twentieth century directly affected employment law. During the latter part of the nineteenth century, the law was overwhelmingly in favor of employers in situations where workers attempted to band together to achieve better wages and working conditions. Under the common law, such activity was considered a criminal conspiracy. To prove the organized activity was illegal, the employer merely had to show that the union was formed for an illegal purpose. This burden was easily met by a showing of "intentional infliction of economic distress," and the courts typically found in the employer's favor.

At the end of the last century and into the first part of this century, after the passage of various antitrust statutes, beginning with the **Sherman Act of 1890**, courts held that union activity constituted an illegal restraint on trade and competition. This allowed employers to seek injunctions in the federal courts against union activity. This use of the antitrust laws to hinder union activity by granting injunctive relief to employers continued until 1932 when Congress passed the **Norris-LaGuardia Act**. This Act, sometimes referred to as the "anti-injunction act," curtailed the power of the federal courts to grant injunctions in nonviolent labor disputes. The Norris-LaGuardia Act opened the way for further and more far-reaching legislation that would come about as part of the New Deal (*see* Chapter Three).

In 1935, Congress passed the **National Labor Relations Act**, also known as the **Wagner Act**, which supported the concept of unionism and collective bargaining. The Wagner Act established the **National Labor Relations Board (NLRB)** to administer the provisions of the statute and to determine which activities of employers would be considered "unfair labor practices."

After World War II, because of the increasing strength of unions and what was viewed as union abuses arising from their increased powers, the federal government enacted the **Taft-Hartley Act (the National Labor Relations Act),** which prohibited certain union activities as being unfair to employers.

In 1959, Congress passed the **Labor Management Reporting and Disclosure Act (the Landrum-Griffin Act).** The Landrum-Griffin Act has been considered a "bill of rights" for union members. The act requires disclosure of union finances by union officials, establishes procedures for the election of union officers, and provides civil and criminal sanctions for enumerated abuses by union officials.

The area of law dealing with labor disputes, known as labor law, has come full circle within a relatively short period. From first outlawing union activity, the law then fostered and protected unions, which resulted in abuses by unions of their newfound powers. This, in turn, resulted in legislation to regulate union activity.

Labor law is an extremely important subset of employment law because of the significant number of American workers who are union members. Labor law has eroded the common law concepts of employment at will and freedom of contracting.

The Rise of Trade Unionism: The Norris-LaGuardia Act of 1932

The Norris-LaGuardia Act defined as public policy the right of workers to form a union free from employer interference. This statute totally reversed the body of judicial law, which had uniformly found union activity to be illegal. The Norris-LaGuardia Act limited the court's ability to enjoin union activity that was nonviolent. Nonviolent union activity was now permitted and federally protected.

> *Example: In 1930, immediately after the initial impact of the stock market crash, a group of workers banded together to attempt to obtain higher wages from their employer. To prevent this movement, the employer went to court and received an injunction prohibiting the workers from forming a union to demand higher wages. Three years later, the workers again formed a union to seek more pay. Now, when the employer sought injunctive relief, it was denied because of the passage of the Norris-LaGuardia Act. The union activity was nonviolent and, therefore, injunctive relief was no longer available to stop the workers from organizing.*

The immediate effect of the Norris-LaGuardia Act was threefold:

1. The statute specifically rejected the use of injunctions as a remedy available to employers in labor disputes.
2. The act declared that the federal courts were not the proper agency for formulating substantive labor law (but federal courts retained the power to *interpret* federal legislation creating labor law).
3. The statute specifically enunciated a policy of government neutrality in labor disputes.

At first blush, it might appear that the Norris-LaGuardia Act gave free rein to unions and union activity, but such was not the case. Even though the statute gave legitimacy to unions and prohibited employers from obtaining injunctions against nonviolent union demonstrations, certain union activities still violated antitrust laws. Concerted action by unions and employers to obtain a competitive edge in the marketplace, as well as the use of secondary boycotts (to be discussed in detail below), were determined by the Supreme Court to be prohibited by the antitrust laws.

> *Example: An employer and its union agree to limit or reduce wages for a period of time drive competitors out of the market by reducing the price of a product manufactured by union labor. Once the company acquires a specified market share, the employer and the union have agreed that the workers' wages will automatically increase to a predetermined level. This activity violates antitrust law because it uses activity to drive out market competition.*

The Norris-LaGuardia Act was the first federal legislation that gave legal recognition to union activity. It was shortly followed by the Wagner Act.

The National Labor Relations Act of 1935

The National Labor Relations Act (the Wagner Act) came quickly on the heels of the Norris-LaGuardia Act in the first wave of New Deal legislation. The Wagner Act is the basis of all modern labor law, and its importance can be seen in the statute's three main provisions:

1. It established the National Labor Relations Board to administer and oversee the provisions of the statute.
2. It defined certain activities as "unfair labor activities" by both unions and employers.
3. It established standards for collective bargaining negotiations between employers and unions.

Each of these aspects of the Wagner Act will be discussed in turn.

The National Labor Relations Board (NLRB)

The NLRB was established to administer the Wagner Act and to prevent what the Act decreed to be "unfair labor practices." The NLRB is composed of five members, each of whom is appointed by the president to serve a staggered five-year term. **Staggered terms** means that, although every member serves a full five-year period, only a portion of the board is appointed at one time.

> *Example: This year, the president appoints a new member to the NLRB. This new member serves for five years; the remaining four members of the NLRB also serve for five years, but their current terms expire in one, two, three, or four years, depending upon when each was appointed.*

The NLRB also has an appointed general counsel, various regional directors, and **administrative law judges** (ALJs), who hear disputes and render decisions on matters concerning the NLRB system, separate from the civil justice system. The NLRB has jurisdiction over businesses that do at least $50,000 a year in interstate commerce.

> *Example: A multi-million-dollar company employs members of various unions. The employer conducts all of its business exclusively within one state, including all purchases of supplies. If a labor dispute arose, the NLRB would not have jurisdiction because the employer does not do the requisite dollar business in interstate commerce.*

The NLRB has original jurisdiction over disputes that come within the purview of the statute. The parties may only seek judicial relief once all of the procedures established by the NLRB have been exhausted.

> *Example: A union claims that an employer who meets the jurisdictional requirements of the NLRB is engaging in an unfair labor practice. The union files suit against the employer in the appropriate federal district court. The court must refuse jurisdiction; the dispute must first be brought to the NLRB.*

The procedures that have been established by the NLRB for deciding disputes are as follows:

1. The **charging party**, the person claiming the violation of the Wagner Act, must file a charge of unfair labor practices in the regional office of the NLRB within six months of the alleged unfair practice.

2. The Regional Office of the NLRB will investigate the claim. If the office finds some indication that an unfair labor practice has taken place, the office will issue a **complaint**. If the office does not find sufficient grounds for issuing a complaint, the charging party may appeal the decision to the NLRB's general counsel.

3. If a complaint is issued, an attorney working for the Regional Office will gather evidence and attempt to work out a settlement between the parties. Statistically, 80 percent of all disputes are settled at this stage.

4. If the parties cannot settle the matter, a hearing takes place before an ALJ sitting either in the District of Columbia or San Francisco. The ALJ is appointed under procedures established by the Civil Service Commission to ensure impartiality.

5. The ALJ will issue recommendations based on his or her findings. If no challenge is made to them, these recommendations become final.

6. If one of the parties to the dispute disagrees with the ALJ's recommendations, the party can file an **exception** to the findings. The matter is forwarded to the full NLRB sitting in Washington, D.C., for a final determination. Once the NLRB issues a final decision, all administrative remedies are exhausted. If the parties disagree with the result, they may now seek judicial relief.

7. Once a final decision is reached, either by the ALJ or the full NLRB, the decision may be challenged in the federal Court of Appeals.

8. After a decision by the federal Court of Appeals, the parties may appeal to the United States Supreme Court.

The Wagner Act specifies four remedies that are available to the parties:

1. *Post Notices*. The NLRB can require that notices be posted in the place of employment to alert all persons to activities that are considered unfair labor practices, along with a summary of employee rights under the law.

> **Example:** *The NLRB has found, subject to a complaint, that an employer is refusing to permit its workers to engage in lawful union activities. One of the remedies ordered by the NLRB is to require the employer to post notices in prominent areas informing the workers of their right to engage in lawful union activity.*

2. *Award **Back Pay**.* For cases in which the NLRB determines that a union member has been unlawfully discharged, the NLRB may award the worker back pay. Back pay includes all lost wages, benefits, and paid holidays. The employer is also liable for interest on all back pay. The discharged employee, however, has the duty to **mitigate damages** and attempt to find work in the interim to lessen the amount of his or her lost back pay, which will be reduced by the amount of the interim earnings.

Example: The NLRB has determined that an employer unlawfully discharged an employee for engaging in lawful union activities. The total back wages to which the employee is entitled is $10,000; however, it was discovered that the employee was offered and refused comparable work during the period of discharge that would have brought the employee $8,000 in wages. Consequently, the NLRB will award the employee a net of $2,000: $10,000 of back pay less the $8,000 the employee could have earned to mitigate damages.

---

3. *Set Aside Elections.* If the NLRB decides that there has been some inequity in the union elections, the election will be set aside and a date for new elections will be established.

4. *File a Private Suit.* An employer is permitted to file a private suit for damages it suffered because of unlawful union activity.

Example: The NLRB determines, based on an employer complaint, that a union has engaged in unlawful union activity, and the NLRB orders the union to desist. The employer, because of this unlawful union activity, has suffered a $3 million loss to its business. The employer may now file a private suit against the union to recover the loss occasioned by the unlawful union activity.

The preceding describes the procedures and remedies specified under the Wagner Act for the settlement of labor disputes under the National Labor Relations NLRB.

Unfair Labor Practices

Just what constitutes an "**unfair labor practice?**"

The National Labor Relations Act specifies certain unfair labor practices. These activities are applicable to both employers and unions and are spelled out in Section 8 of the Act.

Employer Unfair Labor Practices. Under Section 8(a) of the Wagner Act, five particular practices are deemed unfair labor practices by employers. These activities are:

1. 8(a)(1): "To interfere with, restrain, or coerce employees in the exercise of their right to unionize." This means that any activity on the part of an employer that prohibits or has a chilling effect on its workers' right to form a union is illegal.

Example: An employer, afraid that its workers are planning to unionize to force higher wages and increased benefits, threatens to close its facility and dissolve the business if the workers form a union. This is a violation of Section 8(a)(1) of the Wagner Act.

---

2. 8(a)(2): "To dominate or interfere with the formation or administration of any labor organization or contribute financial or other support to a labor organization." The Act is intended to avoid a conflict situation in which an employer influences or controls the union's activities by means of financial support.

> *Example: An employer believes that a particular candidate for union office is favorable to management and finances his election campaign. This would constitute an unfair labor practice because unions and employers are meant to be separate and independent.*

3. 8(a)(3): "To discriminate with regard to hiring or firing, or any other form of activity used to encourage or discourage union membership." The Wagner Act applies only to discrimination with respect to union participation. Employment discrimination based on race, sex, religion, national origin, etc., is covered separately by Title VII of the Civil Rights Act. *See* Chapter Four.

> *Example: An employer wants to hire several new workers. On the employment application, the applicants are asked about their union affiliations. Later it is shown that the employer consistently fails to hire any applicant who indicates union membership. This is an unfair labor practice.*

4. 8(a)(4): To discharge or discriminate against any employee who has filed a complaint under the Act. The statute specifically prohibits retaliation by employers against employees who file charges of unfair labor practices.

> *Example: An employee files a charge of unfair labor practices against her employer with the NLRB. The employer immediately fires the worker as a "troublemaker." This constitutes an unfair labor practice.*

5. 8(a)(5): To refuse **collective bargaining**. Collective bargaining is a requirement for employers and unions under the Act and will be discussed in detail in the next section of this chapter.

> *Example: The current union contract is expiring, and the union wishes to negotiate a new contract for its members. The employer refuses to "come to the table," but simply states what it is willing to do under a new agreement. This is deemed an unfair labor practice because the employer is refusing to negotiate.*

An employer practice that violates Sections 8(a)(2), (3), (4) or (5) automatically violates Section 8(a)(1). This is called a **derivative violation**. Conversely, a violation of Section 8(a)(1) that does not violate another subsection of Section 8(a) is called an **independent violation**. Any violation by an employer of Section 8(a) of the statute enables the union to file a complaint against the employer for unfair labor practices under the NLRB procedures discussed above.

Union Unfair Labor Practices. Unfair labor practices on the part of the union are covered in Section 8(b) of the Wagner Act are as follows:

- 8(b)(1)(A): To restrain or coerce employees in their right under Section 7 of the Act (the right to organize). Just as employers are prohibited from coercing employees not to organize, so are unions prohibited from coercing employees to join the union.

> **Example:** *Employees at a factory are all independent workers. The workers have an extremely good relationship with their employer, and they are very well treated. A union representative attempts to get the workers to join a union. When they refuse, the representative attempts to harass and threaten them into joining. This is an unfair labor practice on the part of the union.*

- 8(b)(1)(B): To restrain or coerce employees in the selection of representatives. Neither the employer nor the union may unduly influence the workers in their election process.

> **Example:** *A union election is coming up, and the current officers wish to retain their positions. They start to harass the workers in an attempt to be reelected. This violates Section 8(b)(1)(B) of the Act.*

- 8(b)(2): To encourage an employer to discharge an employee, except for the employee's failure to tender his or her union dues. The Wagner Act prohibits unions from trying to influence employers, in any manner, to discriminate against employees.

> **Example:** *The union wants a factory to be a completely union shop. The union attempts to influence the employer to fire all nonunion employees by threatening to force a boycott (see below). This attempt to get an employer to discriminate based on union membership is illegal.*

- 8(b)(3): To refuse to bargain in good faith. As stated previously, the Wagner Act requires both employers and unions to negotiate their relationship; the failure to do so in good faith constitutes an unfair labor practice. *See* below.

- 8(b)(4): To engage in strikes, boycotts, and other specified activities used to compel an employee to join a labor organization or to engage in **secondary boycotts**. Strikes, picketing, and boycotts will be discussed in detail in a separate section of this chapter.

- 8(b)(5): To charge its members excessive dues or fees. This section of the statute specifies an unfair labor practice by a union against its own members rather than against employers. This section may be considered as the forerunner of the Landrum-Griffin Act mentioned in the introduction to this chapter.

- 8(b)(6): *Featherbedding.* **Featherbedding** is forcing payment for work that is not actually performed. This might include demanding that an employer maintain a position for a task that no longer exists.

> *Example:* A computerized factory no longer uses typewriters, but the union is demanding that the employer continue to employ a "typewriter repairman" even though that function is no longer necessary. This violates Section 8(b)(6) of the act as featherbedding.

Collective Bargaining

The third major area covered by the National Labor Relations Act deals with the issue of collective bargaining. Recall that under the common law concept of employment at will, both the employer and the employee were free to negotiate an employment agreement, or not, at their own discretion. Under the Wagner Act, an employer and a union are *required* to negotiate the terms of employment with one another; failure to do so constitutes an unfair labor practice. Take careful note that the requirement of contract negotiation only exists for employment situations involving unions—the right is not extended to independent employees. Labor laws were enacted to protect a particular class of worker: members of a union.

Good Faith Bargaining. Under the statute, good faith bargaining means that an employer must negotiate in good faith with the representatives of the union. Before the bargaining can take place, the union representative must be determined to be the *exclusive* representative of the employees. Once that has been determined, the employer and the representative must meet at reasonable times, confer, and incorporate the results of their negotiations into a union contract.

> *Example:* A union representative charges an employer with refusing to bargain in good faith. An NLRB investigation discovers that there is a power struggle going on within the union to determine officers. As a consequence, no one individual or group is capable of speaking on the union's behalf. Under these circumstances, the employer is not acting in bad faith by refusing to negotiate with a person who may not be the "exclusive" representative of the union.

The statute defines "good faith" as negotiating with an open mind and with the sincere purpose of reaching an agreement. The NLRB, in ascertaining whether this standard has been met, will look at the *quality* of the bargaining as a whole, not just an isolated incident.

> *Example:* During contract negotiations, the union representative continues to ask for greater benefits and wages than the union has negotiated with similar employers over the past few months. The representative claims to be looking out for the union's best interests; however, on investigation, it is learned that the representative is facing reelection against stiff competition. The representative hopes that by reaching an unusually favorable agreement, he will bolster his chances of reelection. The representative is not bargaining in good faith; he is attempting instead to further his own private interests.

The obligation to bargain in good faith arises whenever

- a union is recognized for the first time
- a representative is certified by the NLRB
- a union contract is up for renegotiation.

During the negotiation process, both parties are required to provide proof to document their positions, and the opposing side may demand explicit proof of the opposition's position. The right to see the supporting information is not absolute. The parties' right to information is limited to a showing of a legitimate need for the documentation. Furthermore, neither side is permitted to undertake unilateral action.

Example: The employer is claiming that it cannot meet the total wage increases the union is demanding because of stagnant sales. The union demands company financial statements to prove the sales figures. This is a legitimate request for proof. If the employer counteracts by demanding to see wages and benefits paid to union officials, this is not a legitimate request because it has no relevance to the issue being negotiated.

The National Labor Relations Act enumerates three categories of issues that may or may not be subject to collective bargaining. These three categories are:

1. *Wages, hours, and other conditions of employment.* These issues are deemed mandatory concerning collective bargaining.

2. *Notice about the predicted sale of the business.* This may be the topic of collective bargaining, but it is not mandatory. The issue of the sale of the business is deemed permissive with respect to collective bargaining.

3. *Items that must be included in the final agreement*, such as certification of the union.

These items are totally nonbargainable because they are specified in the statute.

The refusal of either side to bargain on an issue included in the mandatory category is *per se* an unfair labor practice, but it is not an unfair labor practice to refuse to bargain over permissive issues.

The Bargain

The result of the collective bargaining process is intended to be a **collective bargaining agreement** (i.e., the contract between the employer and the union). This final contract is similar to all employment contracts (*see* Chapter Nine) with certain provisions that pertain specifically to labor unions. Some of these provisions are:

- *Recognition of the Union.* As mandated by the National Labor Relations Act, once the union has been properly and legally formed, the employer is required to recognize the union as its members' representative, and this recognition is required to appear in the contract. This provision gives the union the legal right to represent its members in any problem arising from the collective bargaining agreement.

- *Obligation of the Successors in Interest.* To protect both the union and the employer, all collective bargaining agreements contain provisions that bind all successors in interest who acquire that interest during the term of the agreement. A **successor in interest** is any person or company who takes over from the employer or the union representative.

- *Protection of the Union Shop*. The agreement contains a provision that recognizes that the shop, or workplace, is a union shop, meaning that all nonexempt employees *must* be union members.

- *Work Preservation Clauses*. These provisions state that the employer will use its best efforts to maintain the business and preserve the same number of employees without a reduction in force.

- *Grievance Procedures*. The union contract typically specifies exact procedures to be followed should there be a claim of breach of any part of the contract. Specific procedures that must be followed streamline the process, and so, delays are avoided. *See* Chapter Ten.

- *No Strikes or Lockouts*. This clause makes it a contract violation if the union calls a **strike** or the employer initiates a **lockout** under any circumstances that such action may not be permitted under the contract. Strikes and lockouts will be discussed in detail in the next section.

The Act provides several methods for enforcing the terms of the collective bargaining agreement:

- The parties may seek specific performance of the contract in a federal court; if remedies are sought in a state court, the state court is required to apply federal law.
- The dispute may be settled by arbitration. Note that the decision of an arbitrator is final and binding, and in most cases, it cannot be challenged in court (*see* page 42).
- The employer may seek damages for losses resulting from unauthorized worker action such as a **wildcat strike** (a strike called by the workers not authorized by the union).

Pickets, Boycotts, and Strikes

Strikes and boycotts are detailed in Sections 8(b)(4) and (7) of the National Labor Relations Act; pickets are not mentioned in the Act, nor are they specifically defined. All three of these activities are used by unions to bring attention to their position. Employers are not permitted to use these activities to bring attention to their concerns.

Pickets

Picketing means to patrol the workplace, usually with placards, to publicize a dispute or gain support for union activity. With respect to labor law, there are generally five reasons that a union will picket a workplace:

1. to force the employer to recognize the union
2. to obtain specific economic benefits from the employer

> ***Example:*** *The employer is attempting to change the insurer of the employees' health insurance. The union feels that this new insurer will not provide the same benefits as the previous insurer and pickets to force the employer to stay with the current insurer.*

3. to protest unfair labor practices

> ***Example:*** *The union has discovered that an employer is discriminating in hiring by hiring nonunion workers over union members. To protest this unfair labor practice and to bring public attention to the problem, the union pickets the employer.*

4. to alert the public to a labor dispute

> ***Example:*** *During the collective bargaining process, the employer is stalemating. To alert the public to the employer's failure to act in good faith and attempt to foster public opinion in its favor, the union forms a picket line outside the place of negotiations.*

5. to protest the total package of employee benefits.

> ***Example:*** *The contract proposed by the employer is well beneath union demands and desires. To protest against this proposal, the union members form a picket line.*

Boycotts

A **boycott** is a concerted refusal to work for, purchase from, or handle products of an employer. There are two categories of boycotts: primary and secondary. A **primary boycott** is an action directed against the employer specifically involved in the dispute. A **secondary boycott** is an action against a neutral employer to force that employer to exert influence on the primary employer to change its policies or cripple the primary employer by drying up a critical source of supplies.

> ***Example:*** *A nonunionized employer is attempting to keep unions from coming into its plant. To get public support for the union, the union calls for a boycott of the employer's product to force it, through loss of sales revenues, to permit unionization of its workplace. This is a primary boycott.*

> ***Example:*** *In the above example, after several weeks of boycotting the primary employer without any success, the union asks its members who are employed by a company that supplies the primary employer with raw materials to boycott the supplier company, which, when its sales are down, may influence the first employer to permit unionization. This is a secondary boycott.*

Strikes

A strike is probably the most dramatic action a union can take against an employer. A **strike** is a refusal to work. The Wagner Act recognizes three legitimate grounds for calling a union strike:

1. to protest economic conditions, such as poor wages, benefits, pensions, etc.
2. to protest against unfair labor practices enumerated in the statute
3. to protest against abnormally dangerous working conditions.

Under an amendment to Section 8 of the Wagner Act, healthcare workers may not go on strike for ten days after a strike (a **cool down period**). This provision was enacted to protect the welfare of the patients who are under the care of the union workers.

> *Example: The unionized employees of a nursing home have been working without a contract for six months, and negotiations have broken down. The union wants to go on strike, but under the Wagner Act, it must wait a ten-day period after serving notice of its intention to strike before it walks out. This period gives the nursing home the opportunity, if necessary, to make provisions for the care of the patients if the strike should in fact take place.*

The above methods of bringing attention to labor problems are available only to the union. The methods available to employers are more limited. An employer always has an absolute right to close its business, but this means that everyone loses: there are no more jobs for the workers and no more income for the owners. There are some situations, however, in which terminating the business is the only viable solution.

> *Example: An employer's sales have been steadily declining over the past few years, but under the terms of its union contract, the workers' wages and benefits are increasing. It is no longer financially feasible to continue the business, so the employer goes out of business.*

Despite the foregoing, an employer may not close one operation and then immediately open up a new operation as a method of creating a nonunion workplace. This type of activity is called a **runaway shop** and is a violation of Section 8(a)(3) of the Wagner Act as an unfair labor practice.

> *Example: An employer is tired of dealing with constant union demands and closes its facility. The next month the same employer opens up a "new" facility under a new name in a nearby community. If this can be proved an attempt by the employer to force out the union, it will be deemed a runaway shop and a violation of the Wagner Act.*

If the union is the party engaging in the unfair labor practice, as by refusing to commit to collective bargaining, the employer is permitted to stage a lockout. A **lockout** is a practice used by employers to force the union to come to the bargaining table. During the lockout, the employer may hire temporary replacements for the union workers it has locked out, but it cannot hire permanent replacements.

> *Example: During the collective bargaining process, the union is making unfair demands and appears to be unwilling to bargain in good faith. To force the union to adhere to the provisions of the Wagner Act, the employer locks out the union employees from its workplace. Until the union changes its position and the lockout is called off, the employer may hire workers to replace the union workers and keep the business going.*

Mediation and Arbitration

Effective grievance procedures minimize complaints, pickets, boycotts, strikes, and lockouts. Most collective bargaining agreements contain provisions for handling grievances that arise between employers and employees. Mediation and arbitration are the final steps in the grievance procedure.

A **mediator** is an independent person who assists the parties in resolving the dispute. The mediator's purpose is to enable the parties to arrive at a solution they create and can live by.

> *Example: During the collective bargaining process, the union and the employer have been deadlocked on an issue concerning pension benefits. After several weeks of unsuccessful negotiations, the parties call in a neutral third person who will hear each side's position and then make suggestions to help the parties arrive at a mutually agreeable solution. The neutral third party is called a mediator.*

Conversely, an **arbitrator** is a neutral third person to whom the parties defer for the final solution. Unlike the mediator, the arbitrator does not try to get the parties to resolve the problem themselves, but instead renders a decision for them. The role of an arbitrator is similar to the function of a judge or jury in court. An arbitrator's decision is final and is called an **award**.

> *Example: In the example above, after the mediator is unsuccessful in helping the parties resolve the problem, they agree to submit the matter to an arbitrator. An arbitrator, selected by both parties, hears both positions and renders a decision.*

Because the decision of an arbitrator is final and binding, the matter cannot then be litigated in the court system. The mediator facilitates, but the arbitrator decides. Parties frequently opt for binding arbitration because it is faster and less expensive than litigation. One of the drawbacks of arbitration is that there is no right of appeal (unless some illegality can be found in the arbitration process itself).

> *Example: In the situation above, after the arbitrator makes her award, the union is still unhappy and wants to litigate the matter. This is not possible. The decision of the arbitrator is final and binding.*

Chapter Summary

Over the past century, the labor movement has tremendously impacted the workplace and employment law. For those occupations that are subject to unionization, the body of law that has developed has, for the most part, replaced the common law concept of employment at will.

Various federal statutes have recognized workers' rights to organize to better their working conditions. The statutes have specified certain conduct that must be adhered to by both employers and unions in dealing with employment matters. Congress has established the National Labor

Relations Board to hear and settle labor disputes between unions and employers. The board has also established standards for determining which activities are considered unfair labor practices.

It must be borne in mind, however, that these statutes only pertain to the union-employer relationship. The union and the employer are still subject to all other federal statutes that affect employment issues, such as the Civil Rights Act of 1964 and the Americans with Disabilities Act, which will be discussed later in the text. Labor law is merely one subset of the general topic of employment law and is limited to issues of organized workers under collective bargaining agreements.

Edited Judicial Decisions

The two edited judicial decisions presented below highlight some of the issues detailed in the chapter. *Shaw's Supermarkets v. NLRB* addresses the NLRB's following its own procedures and precedents. *United Paperhangers Int. Union v. Misco, Inc.* concerns the arbitration provisions of a collective bargaining agreement, arbitrator's ward, and appeals.

SHAW'S SUPERMARKETS, INC. v. NATIONAL LABOR RELATIONS BOARD
884 F.2d 34 (1st Cir. 1989)

The National Labor Relations Board (the "Board") found that Shaw's Supermarkets ("Shaw") violated the National Labor Relations Act ("NLRA") § 8(a)(1), 29 U.S.C. § 158(a)(1), during a representation election held at Shaw's Wells, Maine, distribution facility in January 1987. In the election, 71 votes were cast for no union, 46 votes for a Teamsters local, and one vote for an independent union. The finding of violation rested primarily upon the fact that, five days before the election, a Shaw vice president told the employees at the plant that if they were to turn their affairs over to a third party [i.e., a union], the employees "would be guaranteed minimum wages and workmen's comp[ensation] and that's where our collective-bargaining process would begin."

The Board decided that this statement, taken in context, constituted a "threat of reprisal" against collective organizing, an illegal threat that NLRA §§ 8(a)(1) and 8(c) make illegal. 29 U.S.C. §§ 158(a)(1), 158(c). *See NLRB v. Gissel Packing Co., Inc.*, 395 U.S. 575, 618, 23 L. Ed. 2d 547, 89 S.Ct. 1918 (1969). The Board ordered a new election. The Board now asks us to enforce its order.

We have examined the Board's decisions in this case and in prior cases on this subject; however, in comparing those prior cases with the facts of the present case, we conclude that the Board's findings here are inconsistent with what it has held before. That is to say, past precedent would require the Board to find in the employer's favor here. Although the Board is not permanently bound by its precedent, when it wishes to deviate from well-established precedent as significantly as it has done here, it must, at least, explain the reasons for its deviation. Because the Board has not explained its inconsistent decision in this case, we shall not now enforce its order, but instead we shall remand this case to the Board.

I.   Background

A.   Labor law. The basic principles of labor law that govern this case are well established. Under NLRA § 7, employees have the right to "self-organization, to form, join, or assist labor organizations, to bargain collectively through representatives of their own choosing...." 29 U.S.C. § 157. Employers may not "interfere with, restrain, or coerce employees in the exercise of" those rights. NLRA § 8(a)(1), 29 U.S.C. Sec, 158(a)(1). Moreover, the NLRA expressly states that a "threat of reprisal or force or promise of benefit" does not constitute otherwise protected "express[ion]." NLRA § 8(c), 29 U.S.C. § 158(c). Thus, the NLRA prohibits employer speech during an election campaign, which contains a "threat of reprisal," and thereby "interfere[s] with, restrain[s] or coerce[s]" employees in the exercise of their rights to "form, join or assist" labor unions. *See NLRB v. Gissel Packing Co., Inc.*, 395 U.S. 575, 618, 23 L.Ed. 2d 547, 89 S.Ct. 1918 (1969).

Whether any particular employer speech amounts to such a "threat of reprisal" depends upon the context in which the speech is uttered. *Wyman-Gordon Co. v. NLRB*, 654 F.2d 134, 145 (1st Cir. 1981); *Belcher Towing Co.*, 265 NLRB 1258, 1268 (1982); *Plastronics Inc.*, 233 NLRB 155, 156 (1977); *Wagner Industrial Products Co.*, 170 NLRB 1413, 1413 (1968). And, as a general rule, the law gives the Board, not the courts, the authority to examine the circumstances, to find the facts, and to decide whether the remarks, in context, amounted to an unlawful threat. *See NLRB v. Marine Optical, Inc.*, 671 F.2d 11, 18 (1st Cir. 1982) ("Generally, courts will defer to the Board's special expertise on the impact of employer statements to employees."). *See also, Universal Camera Corp. v. NLRB*, 340 U.S. 474, 95 L.Ed. 456, 71 S.Ct. 456 (1951); 5 U.S.C. § 706(2)(E) (agency's fact findings must be supported by "substantial evidence"). But, as we shall discuss shortly, the Board's findings must be consistent with its own rules and precedents or the Board must explain the deviation.

B.   Facts. In January 1987, in the midst of a union representation campaign, and five days before the election, Charles Wyatt, Shaw's vice president for distribution, held three meetings with three different groups of employees. In response to questions at the first meeting, Wyatt said that if a union won, "the employees would be guaranteed minimum wages and workmen's comp and that's where our collective bargaining process would begin." He made the same statement to the other two groups of employees. Wyatt also told all the employees that "typically the art of collective bargaining is a give and take process and that ... we would start with minimum wages and workmen's comp and build from that point." Wyatt referred to a union as a "third party." He also said that "the first contract is generally the toughest or hardest to negotiate ... and that generally it could take up to a year." Wyatt's audience contained both full-time employees, then earning up to $11.70 an hour, and part-time employees, then earning about $5.00 an hour; the federal minimum wage at that time was $3.55 an hour.

The Board found no other unfair labor practices committed by Shaw during this election campaign. We can find nothing else in the record that might sharpen the details or color the background of the "context" of the bargaining campaign, either in the Board's or the company's favor. And as Board counsel told us at oral argument, neither can the Board.

II.   The Problem of Inconsistency

Were the Board writing on a blank slate, were there no set of Board cases on the subject, we should likely find sufficient basis in the record to sustain the Board's conclusion. Statements like those at issue here—that the company will "begin" its bargaining at "minimum wages and workmen's comp," that it will "build from that point"– might, depending on the context, innocently represent a legal truth about how the collective bargaining process works, legitimately remind employees that a union might trade certain payments or benefits that many workers now enjoy to obtain other payments or benefits, or improperly constitute a threat that, if the union wins, the employer will strip benefits back to the minimum, forcing the union to struggle even to keep the status quo. In deciding how to react to these statements, a court must recognize that the Board is expert, not simply about the factual context of the individual case, but also about how employees are likely to understand certain forms of words in the mine-run of cases. Thus, if the Board were to conclude that it should always assume that employees would reasonably take words of the sort at issue here as threats of regressive bargaining in the absence of added employer explanation to the contrary, we believe (though we need not, and do not decide) that a court could not easily say the Board was acting outside the authority that the law grants it.

The problem in this case for the Board, however, is that (a) it is not writing on a blank slate, but has written on the subject often in the past; (b) the Board has not said that it wishes to depart from its several prior cases on the subject; yet (c) as we shall discuss below, the prior cases dictate a result in Shaw's favor.

The law that governs an agency's significant departure from its own prior precedent is clear. The agency cannot do so without explicitly recognizing that it is doing so and explaining why. As Professor Davis has pointed out, "the dominant law clearly is that an agency must either follow its own precedents or explain why it departs from them." 2 K. Davis, *Administrative Law Treatise* § 8:9 at 198 (1979). The agency has a duty to explain its departure from prior norms. *Secretary of Agriculture v. United States*, 347 U.S. 645, 653–54, 98 L.Ed. 1015, 74 S.Ct. 826 (1954). The agency may flatly repudiate those norms, deciding, for example, that changed circumstances mean that they are no longer required to make congressional policy. Or it may narrow the zone in which some rule will be applied, because it appears that a more discriminating invocation of the rule will best serve congressional policy. Or it may find that, although the rule in general serves useful purposes, peculiarities of the case before it suggest that the rule not be applied in that case. Whatever the ground for departure from prior norms, however, it must be clearly set forth so that the reviewing court may understand the basis of the agency's action and so may judge the consistency of that action with the agency's mandate....

[If] the agency distinguishes earlier cases[, it must] assert distinctions that, when fairly and sympathetically read in the context of the entire opinion of the agency, reveal the policies it is pursuing. *Atchison, Topeka & Santa Fe Railway Co. v. Wichita Board of Trade*, 412 U.S. 800, 808–09, 37 L.Ed. 2d 350, 93 S.Ct. 2367 (1973) (plurality opinion) (emphasis added).

It is, of course, true that the Board is free to adopt new rules of decision and that the new rules of law can be given retroactive application. Nevertheless, the Board may not depart *sub silentio* from its usual rules of decision to reach a different, unexplained result in a single case. As this court held in *Mary Carter Paint Co. v. FTC* [333 F.2d 654, 660 (5th Cir. 1964) (Brown, J., concurring), rev'd on other grounds, 382 U.S. 46, 15 L.Ed. 2d 128, 86 S.Ct. 219 (1965)], "there may not be a rule for Monday, another for Tuesday, a rule for general application, but denied outright in a specific case." "An inadequately explained departure solely for purposes of a particular case, or the creation of conflicting lines of precedent governing the identical situation, is not to be tolerated." *NLRB v. International Union of Operating Engineers, Local 925*, 460 F.2d 589, 604 (5th Cir. 1972) (citations omitted). *See also Massachusetts Dep't of Education v. United States Dep't of Education*, 837 F.2d 536, 544–45 (1st Cir. 1988) (once an agency "builds a body of precedent ... it cannot thereafter lightly disregard" that precedent, but must follow, distinguish, or overrule it); *National Black Media Coalition v. FCC*, 249 U.S. App. D.C. 292, 775 F.2d 342, 355

(D.C. Cir. 1985) ("it is also a clear tenet of administrative law that if the agency wishes to depart from its consistent precedent it must provide a principled explanation for its change of direction."); *Baltimore Gas & Electric Co. v. Heintz*, 760 F.2d 1408, 1418 (4th Cir.) ("It is a well-settled proposition of administrative law that when an agency deviates from established precedent, it must provide a reasoned explanation for its failure to follow its own precedents ... when an agency treats two similar transactions differently, an explanation for the agency's actions must be forthcoming.") (Citations omitted.)

III. The Board's Departure from Precedent

The Board says that Wyatt's statements fell within a category it calls "bargaining from scratch." It has held the making of such statements unlawful when, in context, a reasonable employee would take them as a coercive threat that an employer will engage in "regressive bargaining," by removing wages and benefits if the union wins. The Board has distinguished lawful from unlawful "bargaining from scratch" statements by ascribing importance to the varying elements of the factual contexts embodied in its past precedent. *See NLRB v. Cable Vision, Inc.*, 660 F.2d 1, 5–6 (1st Cir. 1981); *Wyman-Gordon*, 654 F.2d at 145; *Beverly Enterprises-Indiana, Inc.*, 281 N.L.R.B. 26, 30 (1986); *Histacount Corp.*, 278 N.L.R.B. 681, 689 (1986); *Plastronics, Inc.*, 233 N.L.R.B. at 156; *Wagner Industrial Products*, 170 NLRB at 1413.

The relevant "bargaining from scratch" precedents are of two sorts. First, in several cases the Board has found that a "bargaining from scratch" statement did not violate § 8 (a)(1), because it did not amount to regressive bargaining. In reverse chronological order.(these cases omitted). In many of these cases, the statements in context seem to us just as threatening (if not more so) than those in the present case. We do not see how, after reading the record in this case and the opinions in the cases we have just mentioned, one could reasonably find no violation in those earlier cases yet find a violation in this case. Wyatt used language virtually identical to that used in the cases just listed.

The Board, in its brief, attempts to distinguish these precedents by arguing that this case involved a statement by a high company official, who said that the first contract would be the "toughest to negotiate" and could "take up to a year," and who did not explicitly state that the company would not engage in regressive bargaining. But several of the cases finding no violation involved high-ranking officials, *see, e.g., La-Z-Boy* (personnel manager); *Campbell Soup Co.* (plant manager); *Ludwig Motor Corp.* (president of company); *White Stag* (vice president of manufacturing); one of these cases involved an employer who said bargaining would take "years," *see Histacount Corp.*, 278 NLRB at 686, 689; *see also Clark Equipment Co.*, 278 NLRB at 499 (no violation where employer said "bargaining with a union can be a complicated and time-consuming process"); and several other of these cases involved no explicit offsetting promise to bargain in good faith, *see, e.g., Campbell Soup*; *Computer Peripherals*; *Wagner*. The Board decision here (though not its brief) also said that employers were attempting in past cases to respond to employees' potential belief that the union would necessarily raise benefits, but the record here shows that Shaw's employees asked questions reflecting the same idea; and it said that Wyatt's reference to the union as a "third party" was inaccurate and pejorative, but prior case law does not support reliance on that factor. *See Campbell Soup*, 225 NLRB at 225 (use of term "third party" for union not found to violate 8(a)(1)).

The record does not reveal any other elements suggesting regressive bargaining. Indeed, Board counsel at oral argument simply stated that he "did not know" just what it was in the context of the prior cases finding no violation that "made these same statements" benign there, yet harmful here. Counsel's statement, in our view, honestly reflects the circumstances, for we do not see how one can distinguish prior cases in which the Board found "no violation."

Of course, there are other cases in which the Board found that a "bargaining from scratch" statement violated the law. But these cases are more distant from the present case. (Cases omitted.)

In almost all these cases, the "bargaining from scratch" speech was accompanied by other serious unfair labor practices, such as the discriminatory treatment of labor organizers. *See Beverly Enterprises-Indiana, Inc.*, 281 NLRB at 29 (statement "was made following the discriminatory transfer of the principal union activist"); *Mississippi Chemical Corp.*, 280 N.L.R.B. 413 (several other unfair labor practices); *Belcher Towing Co.*, 265 N.L.R.B. 1258 (same). Here there were no other unfair labor practices committed. And, in the cases finding violations, the language and context suggested, far more strongly than here, a threat to eliminate benefits before bargaining. Compare *Mississippi Chemical Corp.*, 280 NLRB at 417 (statement that the result of a union victory would be to "knock down" all wages and to "take all their benefits" was an "express threat" that bargaining "would start only after employees had been reduced to 'minimum wage' and all their benefits taken away."); *Belcher Towing Co.*, 265 N.L.R.B. at 1268 ("ground zero" comment, in the context of several other unfair labor practices, meant that employer would reduce benefits if the union won); and *Plastronics, Inc.*, 233 NLRB at 156 (violation when comments "established unequivocally" that existing wages and benefits "would be lost" before bargaining began), with *Histacount Corp.*, 278 NLRB at 689 (these comments, in context, did not indicate that the employer would "unilaterally discontinue existing benefits if the employees selected union representation, but rather that existing benefits may be lost as a result of bargaining."); *Campbell Soup Co.*, 225 NLRB at 229 (no violation because there was no evidence the employer would itself reduce benefits upon a union victory, but only that through bargaining the union might decide to trade existing benefits for other benefits); *Computer Peripherals, Inc.*, 215 NLRB at 294 (no violation on the grounds that the employer had not threatened "that all existing benefits would unilaterally be eliminated if the union were successful" and "no implication that any benefits would be taken away unilaterally ... rather the emphasis was on the possible results of lawful bargaining ... benefits depended on the give and take of bargaining."). Here Wyatt's language in context does not suggest "unilateral" reductions, so much as it suggests "give and take" of the sort that the Board, in earlier cases, has approved. *See, e.g., La-Z-Boy,* 281 N.L.R.B. at 340; *Plastronics*, 233 N.L.R.B. at 156; *Computer Peripherals*, 215 N.L.R.B. at 294.

In sum, the cases draw a boundary between the lawful and unlawful. And, given that boundary, this case is not borderline, but, rather, lies tucked well within the boundary of the lawful. In finding the Board's decision in this case inconsistent with its precedents, we do not intend to impose upon the Board the time-consuming obligation of microscopically examining prior cases; nor to encourage counsel to examine past precedent with an eye towards raising hosts of legalistic arguments and distinctions. Here, however, the past cases trace a relatively clear line. Nor do we believe that past cases are a straitjacket, inhibiting experimentation or change. But, as we have explained, the Board remains free to modify or change its rule; to depart from, or to keep within, prior precedent, as long as it focuses upon the issue and explains why change is reasonable. *See Atchison*, 412 U.S. at 808; *Baltimore Gas & Electric Co.*, 760 F.2d at 1418; *Operating Engineers*, 460 F.2d at 604. Unless an agency either follows or consciously changes the rules developed in its precedent, those subject to the agency's authority cannot use its precedent as a guide for their conduct; nor will that precedent check arbitrary agency action. *See Atchison*, 412 U.S. at 808–09; *Local 777*, 603 F.2d at 872; *Contractors Transport Corp. v. United States*, 537 F.2d 1160, 1162 (4th Cir. 1976).

For these reasons, we decline to enforce the Board's order, and we remand the case to the Board. *See Atchison*, 412 U.S. at 822 (remand is appropriate remedy); *Secretary of Agriculture*, 347 U.S. at 655 (same); *Operating Engineers*, 460 F.2d at 604–05 (same).

UNITED PAPERWORKS INTERNATIONAL UNION v. MISCO, INC.
484 U.S. 29, 108 S.Ct. 364, 98 L.Ed. 2d 286 (1987)

Respondent employer's collective-bargaining agreement with petitioner union authorizes the submission to binding arbitration of any grievance that arises from the interpretation or application of the agreement's terms, and reserves to management the right to establish, amend, and enforce rules regulating employee discharge and discipline and setting forth disciplinary procedures. One of respondent's rules listed as causes for discharge the possession or use of controlled substances on backseat of someone else's car in respondent's parking lot with marijuana smoke in the air and a lighted marijuana cigarette in the front seat ashtray. A police search of Cooper's own car on the lot revealed marijuana gleanings. Upon learning of the cigarette incident, respondent discharged Cooper for violation of the disciplinary rule. Cooper then filed a grievance which proceeded to arbitration on the stipulated issue whether respondent had just cause for the discharge under the rule and, if not, the appropriate remedy. The arbitrator upheld the grievance and ordered Cooper's reinstatement, finding that the cigarette incident was insufficient proof that Cooper was using or possessed marijuana on company property. Because, at the time of the discharge, respondent was not aware of, and thus did not rely upon, the fact that marijuana had been found in Cooper's own car, the arbitrator refused to accept this fact into evidence. However, the District Court vacated the arbitration award and the Court of Appeals affirmed, ruling that reinstatement would violate the public policy "against the operation of dangerous machinery by persons under the influence of drugs." The court held that the cigarette incident and the finding of marijuana in Cooper's car established a violation of the disciplinary rule that gave respondent just cause for discharge. ...

OPINION BY: WHITE

A. Collective-bargaining agreements commonly provide grievance procedures to settle disputes between union and employer with respect to the interpretation and application of the agreement and require binding arbitration for unsettled grievances. In such cases, and this is such a case, the Court made clear almost 30 years ago that the courts play only a limited role when asked to review the decision of an arbitrator. The courts are not authorized to reconsider the merits of an award even though the parties may allege that the award rests on errors of fact or on misinterpretation of the contract. "The refusal of courts to review the merits of an arbitration award is the proper approach to arbitration under collective bargaining agreements. The federal policy of settling labor disputes by arbitration would be undermined if courts had the final say on the merits of the awards." *Steelworkers v. Enterprise Wheel & Car Corp.*, 363 U.S. 593, 596 (1960). As long as the arbitrator's award "draws its essence from the collective bargaining agreement," and is not merely "his own brand of industrial justice," the award is legitimate. *Id.*, at 597.

"The function of the court is very limited when the parties have agreed to submit all questions of contract interpretation to the arbitrator. It is confined to ascertaining whether the party seeking arbitration is making a claim which on its face is governed by the contract. Whether the moving party is right or wrong is a question of contract interpretation for the arbitrator. In these circumstances, the moving party should not be deprived of the arbitrator's judgment, when it was his judgment and all that it connotes that was bargained for.

"The courts, therefore, have no business weighing the merits of the grievance, considering whether there is equity in a particular claim, or determining whether there is particular language in the written instrument which will support the claim." *Steelworkers vs. American Mfg. Co.,* 363 U.S. 564, 567-568 (1960) (emphasis added; footnote omitted). *See also AT&T Technologies, Inc. v. Communications Workers,* 475 U.S. 643, 649-650 (1986).

The reasons for insulating arbitral decision from judicial review are grounded in the federal statues relating labor-management relations. These statutes reflect a decided preference for private settlement of labor disputes without the intervention of government: The Labor Management Relations Act of 1947, 61 Stat. 154, 29 U.S.C. § 173 (d), provides that "[f]inal adjustment by a method agreed upon by the parties is hereby declared to be the desirable method for settlement of grievance disputes arising over the application or interpretation of an existing collective-bargaining agreement." *See also AT&T Technologies, supra,* at 650. The courts have jurisdiction to enforce collective-bargaining contracts' but where the contract provides grievance and arbitration procedures, those procedures must first be exhausted and courts must order resort to the private settlement mechanisms without dealing with the merits of the dispute. Because the parties have contracted to have disputes settled by an arbitrator chosen by them rather than by a judge, it is the arbitrator's view of the facts and of the meaning of the contract that they have agreed to accept. Courts thus do not sit to hear claims of factual or legal error by an arbitrator as an appellate court does in reviewing decisions of lower courts. To resolve disputes about the application of a collective-bargaining agreement, an arbitrator must find facts and a court may not reject those findings simply because it disagrees with them. The same is true of the arbitrator's interpretation of the contract. The arbitrator may not ignore the plain language of the contract; but the parties having authorized the arbitrator to give meaning to the language of the agreement, a court should not reject an award on the ground that the arbitrator misread the contract. *Enterprise Wheel, supra,* at 599. So, too, where it is contemplated that the arbitrator will determine remedies for contract violations that he finds, courts have no authority to disagree with his honest judgment in that respect. If the courts were free to intervene on these grounds, the speedy resolution of grievances by private mechanisms would be greatly undermined. Furthermore, it must be remembered that grievance and arbitration procedures are part and parcel of the ongoing process of collective bargaining. It is through these processes that the supplementary rules of the plant are established. As the Court has said, the arbitrator's award settling a dispute with respect to the interpretation or application of a labor agreement must draw its essence from the contract and cannot simply reflect the arbitrator's own notions of industrial justice. But as long as the arbitrator is even arguably construing or applying the contract and acting within the scope of his authority, that a court is convinced he committed serious error does not suffice to overturn his decision. Of course, decisions procured by the parties through fraud or through the arbitrator's dishonesty need not be enforced. But there is nothing of that sort involved in this case.

B.   The Company's position, simply put, is that the arbitrator committed grievous error in finding that the evidence was insufficient to prove that Cooper had possessed or used marijuana on company property. But the Court of Appeals, although it took a distinctly jaundiced view of the arbitrator's decision in this regard, was not free to refuse enforcement because it considered Cooper's presence in the white Cutlass, in the circumstances, to be ample proof that Rule II.1 was violated. No dishonesty is alleged; only improvident, even silly, fact-finding is claimed. This is hardly a sufficient basis for disregarding what the agent appointed by the parties determined to be the historical facts.

Nor was it open to the Court of Appeals to refuse to enforce the award because the arbitrator, in deciding whether there was just cause to discharge, refused to consider evidence unknown to the Company at the time Cooper was fired. The parties bargained for arbitration to settle disputes and were free to set the procedural rules for arbitrators to follow if they chose. Article VI of the agreement, entitled "Arbitration Procedure," did set some ground rules for the arbitration process. It forbade the arbitrator to consider hearsay evidence, for example, but evidentiary matters were otherwise left to the arbitrator. App. 19. Here the arbitrator ruled that in determining whether Cooper had violated Rule II.1, he should not consider evidence not relied on by the employer in ordering the discharge, particularly in a case like this where there was no notice to the employee or the Union prior to the hearing that the Company would attempt to rely on after-discovered evidence. This, in effect, was a construction of what the contract required when deciding discharge cases: an arbitrator was to look only at the evidence before the employer at the time of discharge. As the arbitrator noted, this approach was consistent with the practice followed by other arbitrators. And it was consistent with our observation in *John Wiley & Sons, Inc. v. Livingston,* 376 U.S. 543, 557 (1964), that when the subject matter of a dispute is arbitrable, "procedural" questions which grow out of the dispute and bear on its final disposition are to be left to the arbitrator.

Under the Arbitration Act, the federal courts are empowered to set aside arbitration awards on such grounds only when "the arbitrators were guilty of misconduct...in refusing to hear evidence pertinent and material to the controversy." 9 U. S.C. § 10(c). *See Commonwealth Coatings Corp. v. Continental Casualty Co.,* 393 U.S. 145 (1968). If we apply that same standard here and assume that the arbitrator erred in refusing to considerer the disputed evidence, his error was not in bad faith or so gross as to amount to affirmative misconduct. Finally, it is worth noting that putting aside the evidence about the marijuana found in Cooper's car during this arbitration did not forever foreclose the Company from using that evidence as the basis for a discharge.

Even if it were open to the Court of Appeals to have found a violation of Rule II.1 because of the marijuana found in Cooper's car, the question remains whether the court could properly set aside the award because in its view discharge was the correct remedy. Normally, an arbitrator is authorized to disagree with the sanction imposed for employee misconduct. In *Enterprise Wheel,* for example, the arbitrator reduced the discipline from discharge to a ten-day suspension. The Court of Appeals refused to enforce the award, but we reversed, explaining that though the arbitrator's decision must draw its essence from the agreement, he "is to bring his informed judgment to bear in order to reach a fair solution of a problem. his is especially true when it comes to formulating remedies." 363 U.S. at 597 (emphasis added). The parties, of course, may limit the discretion of the arbitrator in this respect; and it may be, as the Company argues, that under the contract involved here, it was within the unreviewable discretion of management to discharge an employee once a violation of Rule II.1 was found. But the parties stipulated that the issue before the arbitrator was whether there was "just" cause for the discharge, and the arbitrator, in the course of his opinion, cryptically observed that Rule II.1 merely listed causes for discharge and did not expressly provide for immediate discharge. Before disposing of the case on the ground that Rule II.1 had been violated and discharge was therefore proper, the proper course would have been remand to the arbitrator for a definitive construction of the contract in this respect.

C.   The Court of Appeals did not purport to take this course in any event. Rather, it held that the evidence of marijuana in Cooper's car required that the award be set aside because to reinstate a person who had brought drugs onto the property was contrary to the public policy "against the operation of dangerous machinery by persons under the influence of drugs or alcohol." 768 F. 2d, at 743. We cannot affirm that judgment.

A court's refusal to enforce an arbitrator's award under a collective-bargaining agreement because it is contrary to public policy is a specific application to the more general doctrine, rooted in the common law, that a court may refuse to enforce contracts that violate law or public policy, *W.R. Grace & Co. v. Rubber Workers*, 461 U.S. 757, 766 (1983); *Hurd v. Hodge*, 334 U.S. 24, 34–35 (1948). That doctrine derives from the basic notion that no court will lend its aid to one who founds a cause of action upon an immoral or illegal act, and is further justified by the observation that the public's interests in confining the scope of private agreements to which it is not a party will go unrepresented unless the judiciary takes account of those interests when it considers whether to enforce such agreements. *E.g., Mullen v. Hoffman*, 174 U.S. 639, 654–655 (1899); *Twin City Pipe Line Co. v. Harding Glass Co.*, 283 U.S. 353, 356–358 (1931). In the common law of contracts, this doctrine has served as the foundation for occasional exercises of judicial power to abrogate private agreements.

In *W.R. Grace*, we recognized that "a court may not enforce a collective-bargaining agreement that is contrary to public policy," and stated "the question of public policy is ultimately one for resolution by the courts." 461 U.S., at 766. We cautioned, however, that a court's refusal to enforce an arbitrator's interpretation of such contacts is limited to situations where the contract as interpreted would violate "some explicit public policy" that is "well defined and dominant, and is to be ascertained 'by reference to the laws and legal precedents and not from general considerations of supposed public interests.'" *Ibid.* (*quoting Muschany v. United States*, 324 U.S. 49, 66 (1945). In *W.R. Grace*, we identified two important public policies that were potentially jeopardized by the arbitrator's interpretation of the contract; obedience to judicial orders and voluntary compliance with Title VII of the Civil Rights Act of 1964. We went on to hold that enforcement of the arbitration award in that case did not compromise either of the two public policies allegedly threatened by the award. Two points follow from our decision in *W.R. Grace*. First, a court may refuse to enforce a collective-bargaining agreement when the specific terms contained in that agreement violate public policy. Second, it is apparent that our decision in that case does not otherwise sanction a broad judicial power to set aside arbitration awards as against public policy. Although we discussed the effect of that award on two broad areas of public policy, our decision turned on our examination of whether the award created any explicit conflict with other "laws and legal precedents" rather than an assessment of "general considerations of supposed public interests." 461 U.S., at 766. At the very least, an alleged public policy must be properly framed under the approach set out in *W.R. Grace*, and the violation of such a policy must be clearly shown if an award is not to be enforced.

As we see it, the formulation of public policy set out by the Court of Appeals did not comply with the statement that such a policy must be "ascertained 'by reference to the laws and legal precedents and not from general considerations of supposed public interests.'" *Ibid.* (*quoting Muschany v. United States, supra*, at 66). The Court of Appeals made no attempt to review existing laws and legal precedents in order to demonstrate that they establish a "well-defined and dominant" policy against the operation of dangerous machinery while under the influence of drugs. Although certainly such judgment is firmly rooted in common sense, we explicitly held in *W.R. Grace* that a formulation of public policy based on "general considerations of supposed public interests" is not the sort that permits a court to set aside an arbitration award that was entered in accordance with a valid collective-bargaining agreement.

Even if the Court of Appeals' formulation of public policy is to be accepted, no violation of that policy was clearly shown in this case. In pursuing its public policy inquiry, the Court of Appeals quite properly considered the established fact that traces of marijuana had been found in Cooper's car. Yet the assumed connection between the marijuana gleanings found in Cooper's car and Cooper's actual use of drugs in the workplace is tenuous at best and provides an insufficient basis for holding that his reinstatement would actually violate the public policy identified by the Court of Appeals "against the operation of dangerous machinery by persons under the influence of drugs or alcohol." 768 F. 2d, at 743. A refusal to enforce an award must rest on more than speculation or assumption.

In any event, it was inappropriate for the Court of Appeals itself to draw the necessary inference. To conclude from the fact that marijuana had been found in Cooper's car that Cooper had ever been or would be under the influence of marijuana while he was on the job and operating dangerous machinery is an exercise in fact-finding about Cooper's use of drugs and his amenability to discipline, a task that exceeds the authority of a court asked to overturn an arbitration award. The parties did not bargain for the facts to be found by a court, but by an arbitrator chosen by them who had more opportunity to observe Cooper and to be familiar with the plant and its problems. Nor does the fact that it is inquiring into a possible violation of public policy excuse a court for doing the arbitrator's task. If additional facts were to be found, the arbitrator should find them in the course of any further effort the Company might have made to discharge Cooper for having had marijuana in his car on company premises. Had the arbitrator found that Cooper had possessed drugs on the property, yet imposed discipline short of discharge because he found as a factual matter that Cooper could be trusted not to use them on the job, the Court of Appeals could not upset the award because of its own view that public policy about plant safety was threatened. In this connection, it should also be noted that the award ordered Cooper to be reinstated in his old job or in an equivalent one for which he was qualified. It is by no means clear from the record that Cooper would pose a serious threat to the asserted public policy in every job for which he was qualified.

The judgment of the Court of Appeals is reversed.

So ordered.

Glossary

administrative law judge – servant who renders decisions at administrative agency hearings

arbitration – the process of having a dispute resolved by an independent person outside the court process

boycott – union action to bring attention to its position by refusing to work for or buy from a particular employer

charging party – person bringing a complaint before the NLRB

collective bargaining – process of contract negotiation between unions and employers

cool down period – period before union action may be taken

derivative violation – violation of Section 8(a)(2), (3),(4) or (5) of the Wagner Act

featherbedding – requiring pay for work not actually performed

good faith – showing a clear willingness to bargain

independent violation – violation of Section 8(a)(1) of the Wagner Act

Labor Management Reporting & Disclosure Act (Landrum-Griffin Act) – federal statute requiring unions to disclose financial information to their members

lockout – employer keeping union workers out of the workplace to protest the union's unfair labor practice

mediation – form of negotiation that is assisted by an impartial third party called a mediator

mitigation of damages – legal obligation of injured party to lessen the amount of the award the injuring party will have to pay

National Labor Relations Act (Wagner Act) – major federal statute regulating union activities

National Labor Relations Board (NLRB) – agency established to administer the Wagner Act

Norris-LaGuardia Act – first federal statute to legitimize unions

picket – standing in front of a workplace with signs to bring attention to a labor problem

primary boycott – boycott of the employer against whom the union has a complaint

runaway shop – employer closing one facility, then opening up a similar facility to de-unionize

secondary boycott – boycott of an employer not in conflict with the union in hopes that the second employer will force the first employer to give in to union demands

Sherman Act – first United States – antitrust act

staggered term – appointment procedure for NLRB members; each member serves a five-year term, but each is appointed in different years

strike – union action of refusing to work for a particular employer

Taft-Hartley Act – continues the Labor Relations Act and in addition provides for an 80-day injunction against strikes

unfair labor practice – activities specified in the Section 8 of the Wagner Act as violative of labor relations

wildcat strike – strike by union members not authorized by the union

Exercises

1. According to the Supreme Court in the *Misco* case, may a court review an arbitrator's decision because it feels that the arbitrator has misinterpreted the facts of the case or the terms of the contract involved? Why or why not?

2. Which common law doctrine would permit a court to refuse to enforce an arbitrator's award? Cite your authority from the *Misco* case.

3. Research the state statutes that affect labor law in your jurisdiction.

4. Find three cases that discuss situations in which a lockout has been determined to be an appropriate or inappropriate employer action in a labor dispute.

5. Members of labor unions have been singled out for special treatment under federal law. What is your opinion of special treatment being afforded to a specific group of workers? Explain.

Chapter Three

THE DEPRESSION AND EARLY FEDERAL REGULATION

Chapter Overview

The twentieth century has seen the greatest output of legislative enactments affecting employment law in the history of the modern legal system. Three great events caused this regulation:

1. the rise of trade unionism at the turn of the century as the result of the Industrial Revolution
2. the Great Depression of the 1930s
3. the civil rights movement of the 1960s.

These three events have revolutionized society and public policy in many ways, including the common law concepts of freedom of employment and employment at will. This chapter will focus on the early legislation that resulted from the Depression. The following two chapters will discuss the impact of labor law and the Civil Rights Act respectively.

The major problem facing society after 1929 was how to protect citizens from the ravages of economic chaos and provide them with a means of earning a decent livelihood. One of the first long-term enactments emanating from the New Deal was the creation of the **Social Security Act**. This statute was developed to ensure that people who work all of their lives will not find themselves destitute in their later years, living by the support of family or public charity. Social Security was intended to provide income to people in their retirement sufficient to provide the necessities of life. As an additional benefit, Social Security induced people to retire, making jobs available for young people trying to enter the work force.

A few years after the enactment of the Social Security Act, Congress passed the **Fair Labor Standards Act**[1], which mandates a minimum wage scale and maximum work hours. Once again, the concept behind the statute was twofold: one, it provided a basic living wage for workers who were not covered by specific employment contracts; and, two, by limiting work hours, created employment for additional workers.

Finally, in 1963, Congress passed the **Equal Pay Act**[2], a statute that may be considered a natural outgrowth of the Fair Labor Standards Act resulting from the civil rights movement. The impact of the Equal Pay Act is to guarantee that workers performing the same tasks, for the same employer, at the same facility are paid the same wage. This statute combined all of the policy determinants of both the Social Security Act and the Fair Labor Standards Act and paved the way for the Civil Rights Act and all of its descendants.

The three statutes discussed in this chapter—the Social Security Act, the Fair Labor Standards Act, and the Equal Pay Act—constitute early legislative responses to a change in society's attitude

---

[1] 29 U.S.C. § 213(a)
[2] 29 U.S.C. § 206(d)

toward work and employment: namely, fairness to the employee with respect to income and economic security.

The Social Security Act

The Social Security Act of 1935[3] was one of the first of the New Deal measures designed to combat the Great Depression. The purpose of the Social Security Act was to fund a program of retirement and service benefits for persons who had worked a sufficient number of years. Under the Social Security Act, which comprises a small portion of the federal law regarding retirement, the government levies a tax on an employee's wages. This tax is imposed on both the employee and the employer—both contribute to the plan. The law is administered by the **Social Security Administration**, and the funds collected are used to provide retirement and disability benefits, as well as healthcare payments in the form of Medicare, Medicaid, and certain child health programs.

> *Example: A paralegal is employed by a law firm. When the paralegal receives a salary, a portion is withheld and paid into the Social Security fund for the paralegal's benefit. The law firm pays taxes to the Social Security fund for the benefit of the paralegal as well. Funding Social Security is a joint effort of employers and employees.*

Requirements to Qualify for Social Security

In order to qualify for Social Security retirement benefits, the employee must meet two primary requirements: (1) he or she must be "fully insured" and (2) at least 62 years old. **Fully insured** means that the employee seeking benefits has worked a minimum number of quarters during which the Social Security tax was withheld. A quarter consists of a consecutive three-month period, and the minimum number of quarters to qualify is 40.

> *Example: An employee wishes to retire. He has only worked for eight years, which equals 32 quarters. The employee has not met the requirement of being "fully insured" and therefore would not qualify for retirement benefits.*

The 40 quarters do not have to be consecutive. Periods of unemployment may occur throughout the employee's work life. For Social Security retirement benefits, there simply must be a total of forty quarters of employment.

> *Example: An attorney had worked for five years when she earned a multi-million-dollar fee. She quit work and spent the next several decades spending the money. When the money ran out, she returned to work for an additional five years to be eligible for Social Security retirement benefits.*

In addition to the employee receiving retirement benefits, Social Security also provides benefits for the contributor's dependents, including the spouse, surviving spouse, children, and dependent parents. A spouse who is not entitled to Social Security benefits may be entitled to benefits earned

---

[3] 42 USC § 301, *et seq.*

by his or her spouse. This may be true even if the couple has been divorced, provided that the spouse seeking benefits was not insured.

> *Example:* A couple was married for more than 30 years when they divorced. The husband worked only two years before the marriage, and the couple decided early on that, because the wife earned more money, the husband would stay home and take care of the house and the children. The wife was the husband's sole means of support. Now they are divorced, and the wife is retired. Since they were married more than ten years, the ex-husband, who has not remarried, may be entitled to spousal Social Security retirement benefits.

Widows and widowers of contributors to Social Security who were supported by the deceased spouse are entitled to survivors' benefits under the Social Security Act if they were married to the deceased spouse for at least ten years.

> *Example:* After 40 years of marriage, a husband dies leaving a widow he had supported her entire adult life. The widow may be entitled to Social Security benefits as a surviving spouse.

Surviving spouses are entitled to receive benefits once they reach the age of 60 or, if they are disabled, at the age of 50. Children of a deceased contributor to Social Security are entitled to benefits if they are unmarried, under the age of 18, or—if they are students—under the age of 19. They may also be entitled to survivors' benefits if they were disabled before they reached the age of 21.

> *Example:* A contributor to Social Security dies, leaving a widow and two minor children. The widow and the children are all entitled to Social Security benefits as survivors of the contributor.

Finally, Social Security also permits parents of the contributor to receive benefits as survivors if:

- the parent is at least 60 years old
- the parent received at least one-half of his or her support from the deceased wage earner
- the parent does not marry or receive benefits in his or her own right.

> *Example:* A paralegal is the sole support of his widowed mother. His deceased father had not worked long enough to qualify for Social Security benefits. The paralegal predeceases his mother. If the mother is over 60 years of age, she would be entitled to Social Security benefits as the surviving dependent of her son.

Social Security also applies to persons who are self-employed, provided that they work a sufficient number of quarters and make payment to the plan at the rate determined for self-employed individuals.

> *Example: An attorney operates as a sole practitioner. Every quarter she pays taxes into the Social Security fund as a self-employed individual. When she retires, she will be eligible for Social Security benefits.*

To qualify for benefits, the wage-earning contributor must file for benefits with the Social Security Administration and present evidence of earnings and contributions. To document citizens' and legal immigrants' employment records, the Social Security Administration issues **Social Security numbers** as identifying marks that are used on all of the employees' employment records to verify employment income and taxes withheld.

The exact amount of a person's benefits is dependent upon the person's earnings during his or her work life and the amount of the contributions paid to the plan. These benefits may be increased if the person works beyond the minimum retirement age without receiving benefits and continues to contribute to the Social Security fund. Conversely, if a person works and also collects Social Security benefits, the amount of benefits will be reduced to reflect the employee's continuing income from employment.

> *Example: A paralegal retires at age 65 and begins to collect Social Security benefits. Three years later she is bored and returns to work on a part-time basis. If she earns more than the statutory minimum for extra earned income, her current benefits will be reduced, but her future benefits, when she stops working, will be increased because of her additional contributions to the plan.*

Payment benefits are limited for persons who are incarcerated.

Effect of Social Security

The effect of Social Security retirement and survivor benefits (as well as disability benefits, which are not discussed here) is to provide employees with some peace of mind with respect to the future financial security of themselves and their dependents. Although the Act may be considered somewhat paternalistic, by forcing people to prepare for their futures, it has had the effect of making the majority of people more financially secure than they have been at any other time in U.S. history.

Social Security was the one of the first major acts that had a direct effect on employment, requiring both the benefit recipient and the employer to contribute to the fund. Social Security creates an additional expense for the employer for each person employed. It also imposes certain tax withholding obligations on the employer. Although suspicious at first, people have come to rely on Social Security. The current fear is that the Social Security fund may go bankrupt before the current contributors become eligible for benefits.

The Fair Labor Standards Act

The **Fair Labor Standards Act (FLSA)** was enacted in 1938, shortly after the Social Security Act. The FLSA required employers to pay their employees a minimum hourly wage and to fix the maximum number of hours that an employee could work without overtime pay. A minimum wage creates a minimum benefit that an employee will eventually receive from Social Security, because benefits are tied to wages.

Requirements of the Fair Labor Standards Act

The FLSA is administered by the Department of Labor. To come within the purview of the FLSA, an employer must have a business whose income exceeds $500,000 per year. All employees of the employer, including independent contractors, are covered under the Act, with certain exceptions enumerated below. The minimum wage is statutorily established and adjusted every few years. Most states also have statutory minimum wages for persons not covered by the federal statute.

> *Example: A law firm generates an income in excess of $10 million per year. Under the Fair Labor Standards Act, the firm must pay its entire nonprofessional staff the minimum wage established by the statute.*

Under the FLSA, the maximum number of hours that an employee may work at the minimum wage is 40 hours per week. The 40 hours are computed on a full seven-day basis, and the hours do not have to be in any particular sequence. The number of hours simply must total no more than 40 hours in any seven-day period. If the employer requires the worker to work over 40 hours, the worker must be paid 1½ times the minimum wage for each hour after the first 40 in the seven-day period.

> *Example: A law firm pays its copy clerk, who is covered under the FLSA, the minimum wage for working a 40-hour week from Monday through Friday. When the law firm becomes inundated with extra work, the clerk is asked to come in on Saturdays for several weeks. The firm must pay the clerk 1½ times the minimum wage for every hour worked during the weekend.*

Under the FLSA, four categories of employees are exempt from the statutory wage requirements. The criteria used to define exempt employees include their duties, responsibilities, and amount of their salaries. All three criteria must exist for the employee to be exempt. The four exempt categories are:

1. *Executives.* The FLSA defines an "executive" as a person whose primary duty is to oversee the management of the business or one of the business' divisions. In addition, an executive is someone who controls two or more employees and has the ability to hire and fire staff, and who spends 20 percent of his or her time on nonmanagerial duties (40 percent for service or retail businesses). An executive's salary must be at least $155 per week.

> *Example: For administrative reasons, a large wholesaler has divided the country into seven regions. Each region is headed by a regional manager who directly controls a work force of 20 people. Each regional manager, who is paid a base salary of $24,000 per year, is expected to spend 20 percent of his or her time selling. These managers are exempt from FLSA requirements as executives.*

2. ***Administrative Personnel.*** An "administrator" is defined as one who performs nonmanual work related to general policies or operations or responsible work related to education or training. This person must exercise independent discretion and judgment and regularly assist an executive or administrator. Twenty percent of an administrator's time may be spent on nonadministrative duties (40 percent for service or retail businesses), and an administrator must be paid a salary of at least $155 per week.

> ***Example:*** *A law firm hires a paralegal coordinator to assist in the hiring, training, and supervising of the firm's paralegal staff. The coordinator receives a salary of $210 per week. The coordinator is exempt from the FLSA provisions as an administrator.*

3. ***Outside Salespersons.*** An "outside salesperson" is one who regularly works out of the place of business selling the business' goods or services. There is no minimum salary requirement for this category, and up to 20 percent of the salesperson's time may be spent on the type of work usually performed by nonexempt employees.

> ***Example:*** *A manufacturing company employs ten salespersons whose job is to travel in specific geographic areas selling the company's products. The salespersons do not receive a salary but are paid by commission (a percentage of the dollar volume of their sales). These salespersons are considered exempt employees under the FLSA.*

4. ***Professionals.*** A "professional" is defined under the FLSA as one who has acquired advanced knowledge or training, is a certified teacher or recognized instructor, or is a creative artist in a recognized artistic field. This person's work is predominantly intellectual, rather than routine or mechanical, and he or she regularly exercises independent discretion. Up to 20 percent of this person's time may be spent on nonprofessional functions, and the person must receive a minimum salary of $170 per week.

Recently courts have determined that various computer-related jobs qualify the employee who performs such work as a professional and, consequently, exempt from the FLSA overtime provisions. Courts have stated that computer operators, computer programmers, and system analysts may possess special knowledge or skill that renders them exempt professionals. Because of the increase in office technology, this has become a "hot topic" with respect to interpretation of this statute.

> ***Example:*** *A paralegal is employed by a law firm. The paralegal is not, by law, permitted to exercise independent discretion in the performance of his or her duties, and is regularly supervised by a licensed attorney. The paralegal is not considered an exempt employee. If, however, the paralegal is performing administrative functions or is responsible for training programs at the firm, the paralegal may be exempt as an administrator.*

Being defined as an exempt employee means that the employee may be required to work more than 40 hours per week without receiving any additional compensation above his or her salary.

Effect of the Fair Labor Standards Act

Congress enacted the FLSA to ensure that workers will not be exploited by their employers. The government requires all employees to receive a minimum wage, calculated to be adequate to live on, and to receive additional compensation if they work more than 40 hours in any given seven-day period. This statute is an example of public policy overriding the common law concept of freedom of contract and employment at will.

The Equal Pay Act

The **Equal Pay Act**, which is an outgrowth of the civil rights movement, is a more modern application of the FLSA. In 1963, Congress enacted the Equal Pay Act under Title 26 of the United States Code. The Equal Pay Act prohibits employers from paying workers of one gender a different wage than members of the other gender when they are both performing jobs that require "equal skill, effort and responsibility," performed under the same working conditions.

Requirements of the Equal Pay Act

To maintain a claim under the Equal Pay Act, an employee must meet three specific tests:

- proof that the work is equal work
- proof that the work is performed at the same establishment
- proof that a differing pay rate is paid to workers of the opposite sex.

1. *Equal Work*. Under the Act, equal work does not necessarily mean performing identical functions, but rather that the jobs are "substantially equal." To demonstrate this equality, the law focuses on the duties rather than the job title. **Equal work** is defined by the statute as "jobs, the performance of which requires equal skill, effort, responsibility, and which are performed under similar working conditions." "**Skill**" refers to the ability to perform the prescribed task, "**effort**" can be either physical or mental, and "**responsibility**" refers to the worker's accountability (i.e., his or her supervisory, decision-making powers, or compensation attributable to the job performance).

> *Example: A law firm hires a woman as an executive assistant to the senior partner and a man as a paralegal. Both employees are certified paralegals, and each has two years' job experience. The woman performs legal research, edits memos, and writes and speaks to clients. The man performs the same functions. In this instance, despite the title differentiation, these two jobs would be considered equal work.*

Equal work also refers to the physical surroundings—where the job is performed. If one employee works in a clean, modern facility, and the other works in an older facility with inadequate heat and light, the differing work conditions might permit a pay differential. Be aware, however, that all workers in the same facility performing equal work must be paid the same.

If the basic work performed is the same, a pay differential may be permitted if one worker performs additional, secondary, duties as well as the "equal work." These additional duties must
- actually be performed
- be a regular and recurring part of the job
- be substantial
- be such that duties of a comparable nature may not be regularly assigned to lower-paid workers
- be commensurate with the pay differential.

Simply stated, an employer may not assign fictional or minor duties to discriminate in pay between employees of opposite sexes performing equal work.

> *Example: A law firm employs two paralegals, a man and a woman, who perform similar functions. The firm pays the man $100 a week more than the woman because, when the firm is open after 5 p.m., it asks the man to sit near the front door as a security measure. This "additional" work would not justify the pay differential.*

2. *Same Establishment*. The **same establishment** refers to the physical location of the facility, not to different areas within the same facility. As indicated above, different physical locations may warrant unequal pay if working conditions are substantially different, but different offices in the same facility are not different establishments.

> *Example: A law firm employs a male and a female as paralegals. The office operates on five floors of the same office building. The male paralegal works on the main floor, whereas the female works on one of the other, less attractive floors. The woman cannot receive additional compensation for working in a different establishment.*

3. *Unequal Pay Rate*. In determining the equality of the pay, the Equal Pay Act looks at all aspects of the compensation paid to the employees: base salary or wage, pension, fringe benefits, leave, etc. All of these factors are considered to determine whether the pay is equal between the sexes. In making the comparison, the determination may be made based on the average rate paid to workers performing equal work, or may be particular, focusing on the pay paid to one named individual. If the totality of the pay rate is unequal for equal work performed at the same establishment, the Equal Pay Act has been violated.

> *Example: A female secretary claims that a male secretary in her office is being paid more than she in violation of the Equal Pay Act. In evaluating the pay rate, it is discovered that, although the male is paid a salary of $100 a week higher than the female, the female is given car service and meals when she works late, a regular function of both employees, and has one week more annual vacation than the male. Both secretaries have worked at the office for the same length of time. In this instance, it may appear that they are in fact receiving equal pay.*

An employer who is charged with violations of the Equal Pay Act may defend its position by demonstrating some of the following factors:

- *A shift differential.* There may be a pay differential for workers who work on different time shifts. For example, an employer may give increased pay to workers who work on the night shift versus the day shift.

- *A "red circle" rate.* Red circle refers to temporary assignments that would create a need for a *temporary* pay differential.

- *Temporary or part-time workers.* An employer may differentiate in pay between full-time workers and those who are only temporary or part-time and who do not receive regular employee benefits, such as health insurance.

- *Salary matching.* An employee with the higher wage was recruited from a different company where he or she was already earning more than other employees of the new employer, and the employer agreed to match the higher salary to acquire the services of this employee.

- *Extra training.* If the higher-paid employee has greater training or experience than the person complaining of unequal pay, the employer can justify paying the better-qualified employee a higher wage. Be alert to the fact, however, that the employer cannot discriminate in paying for employees to acquire additional training to justify the pay differential. *See* Chapter Four, "The Civil Rights Act and the ADEA."

Effect of the Equal Pay Act

The Equal Pay Act ensures that workers performing the same job for the same employer are not discriminated against on the basis of gender with respect to pay. Note that the Equal Pay Act does not refer to the economic needs of the worker, but is focused exclusively on the work performed. Therefore, an employee who is the sole support of a family cannot be paid more than a worker of the opposite sex who is performing the same job and whose income is supplemental to his family's primary support.

Just as with the Fair Labor Standards Act, the Equal Pay Act adds social and ethical dimensions to the common law concept of employment at will.

Chapter Summary

The three federal statutes discussed in this chapter—the Social Security Act, the Fair Labor Standards Act, and the Equal Pay Act—are all governmental responses to the need to provide workers with adequate and fair wages throughout their work lives and during their retirements. These laws, which relate directly to wage earning, demonstrate the government's early response to changes in the social climate of the country. They reflect the government's responsibility to protect the welfare of the citizens. These statutes form the basis of all modern employment law legislation.

Edited Judicial Decisions

The following two cases underscore some of the concepts discussed in this chapter. *Thomas v. Sullivan* discusses who may qualify as a "surviving spouse" for Social Security benefits, and *Dole v. Shenandoah Baptist Church* highlights certain provisions of the Fair Labor Standards Act.

THOMAS V. SULLIVAN
922 F.2d 132 (2d Cir. 1990)

I.   BACKGROUND.

Gertrude Thomas ("Gertrude") lived with Joseph Thomas ("Joseph") for 47 years, from 1938 until his death in 1985, and they had ten children together. They lived together in Atlanta, Georgia, for many years until they moved to New York. Georgia law recognizes common-law marriages. Although New York law does not, it gives full faith and credit to such marriages that are valid under the laws of other states.

In October 1978, Gertrude applied for wife's insurance benefits ("wife's benefits") under Section 202(b) of the [Social Security] Act, 42 U.S.C. § 402(b) (1988), stating that she and Joseph had married on January 25, 1943. In support of that application, Joseph submitted a signed statement to the Social Security Administration ("SSA"), identifying Gertrude as his wife, certifying that they had been married by a "clergyman or authorized public official," and stating that his previous marriage to one "Janie Mills" had ended with Janie's death in 1940. Thereafter, Gertrude received wife's benefits, which were converted to widow's benefits when Joseph died in May 1985.

In July 1985, a woman identifying herself as Janie Thomas ("Janie") applied for benefits as the widow of Joseph Thomas. In support of her application, she submitted a marriage certificate showing that she and Joseph had married in September 1918. Janie stated in her application that although she and Joseph had separated in 1933, they had never been divorced and she had never been notified of any attempt by Joseph to obtain a divorce. SSA notified Gertrude that her widow's benefits might be terminated as a result of Janie's claim and gave her an opportunity to present evidence to prove her own entitlement.

A search by SSA turned up no record of a divorce in any of the places where Joseph or Janie had lived since 1933. As a result, SSA determined that Janie was Joseph's lawful widow and that Gertrude's marriage to Joseph was not valid. It notified Gertrude that she would no longer receive widow's benefits. Gertrude promptly requested reconsideration, contending that she was entitled to those benefits, having been told by Joseph that he was divorced and having gone through a marriage ceremony with him. In support of her request for reconsideration, she submitted a statement that in October 1942 she had obtained a marriage license in Decatur, Georgia, and that, shortly thereafter, she and Joseph had been married by a minister in Atlanta. She also stated, "my husband had told me that he was previously married and divorced. But, he never gave me any details about the first marriage.... He never wanted to discuss anything about his first marriage."

In a March 1986 "Reconsideration Determination," SSA indicated that it had searched the marriage records of Decatur and had found no record of a marriage of Gertrude and Joseph, and that it had separately searched for any record of issuance to them of a marriage license, also without success. As a result, SSA concluded that "since Gertrude Thomas was not validly married to Mr. Thomas," and since "no evidence of a ceremonial marriage has been submitted or located," Gertrude was not eligible for widow's benefits. Gertrude timely requested and received a hearing before an Administrative Law Judge ("ALJ"). At the hearing, she testified that she had obtained a marriage license and she and Joseph had been married by a minister in 1938. She said the only witnesses to the wedding had been members of the minister's family, whom she did not know. Her own family was informed of the wedding a few days thereafter; none of the family was still alive at the time of the hearing. Gertrude testified that after the ceremony, the minister "told us that he was going to mail the license in so it could be recorded, and mail us our marriage certificate, which he never did." She explained that her failure to verify that the marriage had been recorded was a result of her youthful trust in Joseph:

[Gertrude]: I didn't follow up as I should have, because I was quite young at the time and I just took what he said to be true, and at the time I was 21 and he was 45, so I can see now where I could have been very much easy to lead, to be led by what he said and I was in love with him and I just accepted what he told me, thinking everything was okay.

ALJ: It happens when you are in love.

[Gertrude]: Oh, yes sir. But I can see my mistake now. It's just too late.

After giving Gertrude more time to attempt to produce additional evidence, the ALJ found that because Joseph had remained married to Janie until his death, he "was under a legal impediment preventing him from entering into a valid marriage with Gertrude," and that Gertrude "has not supplied any evidence of a ceremonial marriage with Joseph Thomas and therefore cannot be considered as a 'deemed widow' within the meaning of section 416(H)(1)(B)." ALJ Decision dated September 20, 1986....

The district court, in an opinion published at 713 F.Supp. 114 (1989), rejected Gertrude's constitutional challenge to section 416(h)(1)(B), finding that there was a rational basis for the statute's distinction between invalid ceremonial marriages and invalid common-law marriages. Noting that the legislative history of section 416(h)(1)(B) was sparse, the court found principally that Congress might well have considered claims based on invalid marriages to be "inherently suspect," and that it could rationally have decided to exclude such claims as it believed could more easily be falsified.

(The District Court upheld the denial of benefits, and Gertrude appealed.)

II. DISCUSSION.

Section 216(h)(1)(A) of the [Social Security] Act provides that for purposes of deciding an application for, *inter alia*, widow's benefits, the Secretary will recognize as valid a marriage that would be recognized as valid by the courts of the state in which the wage earner was domiciled. 42 U.S.C. § 416(h)(1)(A). Where there is no valid marriage, section 216(h)(1)(B) of the [Social Security] Act requires the Secretary to "deem" the applicant for benefits to be a widow in certain cases where she has in good faith gone through a marriage ceremony. The latter section (the "deeming rule") provides, in pertinent part, as follows:

in any case where ... an applicant is not the ... widow of an ... insured individual ... but it is established to the satisfaction of the Secretary that such applicant in good faith went through a marriage ceremony with such individual resulting in a purported marriage between them which, but for a legal impediment not known to the applicant at the time of such ceremony, would have been a valid marriage, and such applicant and the insured individual were living in the same household at the time of the death of such insured individual[,] ... such purported marriage shall be deemed to be a valid marriage.... For purposes of this subparagraph, a legal impediment to the validity of a purported marriage includes only an impediment (i) resulting from the lack of dissolution of a previous marriage, or (ii) resulting from a defect in the procedure followed in connection with such purported marriage. 42 U.S.C. § 416(H)(1)(B).

For the reasons below, we conclude that this provision does not violate principles of equal protection.

There is no fundamental right to the receipt of benefits from the government. *See generally Dandridge v. Williams*, 397 U.S. 471, 485–86, 25 L.Ed. 2d 491, 90 S.Ct. 1153 (1970). In deciding an equal protection challenge to a statute that classifies persons for the purpose of receiving such benefits, we are required, so long as the classifications are not suspect or quasi-suspect and do not infringe fundamental constitutional rights, to uphold the legislation if it bears a rational relationship to a legitimate governmental objective. *See Weinberger v. Salfi*, 422 U.S. 749, 769–70, 45 L.Ed. 2d 522, 95 S.Ct. 2457 (1975); *Schweiker v. Wilson*, 450 U.S. 221, 234–5, 67 L.Ed. 2d 186, 101 S.Ct. 1074 (1981). In seeking to determine whether there is such a relationship and objective, we consider not only contemporaneous articulations of legislative purpose but also any legitimate policy concerns on which the legislature might conceivably have relied. *See, e.g., Exxon Corp. v. Eagerton*, 462 U.S. 176, 196, 76 L.Ed. 2d 497, 103 S.Ct. 2296 (1983); *Minnesota v. Clover Leaf Creamery Co.*, 449 U.S. 456, 464, 66 L.Ed. 2d 659, 101 S.Ct. 715 (1981). We will uphold the legislation if we can ascertain that the classifications Congress has created can be explained on the basis of factors relevant to the administration and purposes of the particular benefit program, and are not "merely an unthinking response to stereotyped generalizations" about the excluded group. *Califano v. Jobst*, 434 U.S. 47, 54, 54 L.Ed. 2d 228, 98 S.Ct. 95 (1977). "As long as the classificatory scheme chosen by Congress rationally advances a reasonable and identifiable governmental objective, we must disregard the existence of other methods of allocation that we, as individuals, perhaps would have preferred." *Schweiker v. Wilson*, 450 U.S. at 235.

Where the legislation grants rights to a segment of a class that as a whole had theretofore been denied benefits, our assessment of the rationality of Congress' scheme should be even more generous. In lifting a barrier to benefits, Congress should not be "required to take an all-or-nothing approach," but should be allowed to "proceed more cautiously" where "it had valid reasons for doing so." *Bowen v. Owens*, 476 U.S. 340, 347, 90 L.Ed. 2d 316, 106 S.Ct. 1881 (1986); *see also id.* at 348 ("A constitutional rule that would invalidate Congress' attempts to proceed cautiously in awarding increased benefits [under the Act] might deter Congress from making any increases at all."); *Mathews v. De Castro*, 429 U.S. 181, 185, 50 L.Ed. 2d 389, 97 S.Ct. 431 (1976); *Califano v. Jobst*, 434 U.S. at 57–58. Congress is generally entitled to adopt prophylactic rules as a means of reducing the possibility of fraudulent claims upon the public treasury. Though the lines drawn may not perfectly exclude all abusers and include all nonabusers, they are to be upheld if Congress could rationally have concluded (a) that the general classification would provide some protection against abuse, and (b) that the expense and other difficulties of making individual determinations justified the inherent imprecision of the exclusion of a group.

The question raised is not whether a statutory provision precisely filters out those and only those, who are in the factual position which generated the congressional concern reflected in the statute. Such a rule would ban all prophylactic provisions.... Nor is the question whether the provision filters out a substantial part of the class which caused congressional concern, or whether it filters out more members of the class than nonmembers. The question is whether Congress, its concern having been reasonably aroused by the possibility of an abuse which it legitimately desired to avoid, could rationally have concluded both that a particular limitation or qualification would protect against its occurrence, and that the expense and other difficulties of individual determinations justified the inherent imprecision of a prophylactic rule. *Weinberger v. Salfi*, 422 U.S. at 777.

In analyzing section 416(h)(1)(B) in the present case, we are aided little by the legislative history. Prior to 1957, social security benefits to spouses were awarded in accordance with state laws of succession. *See* 42 U.S.C. § 416(h)(1) (1952). In 1957, Congress enacted ' 416(h)(1)(A), which premised rights to such benefits on state laws with respect to marriage. Pub. L. 85–238, § 3(h)(1), 71 Stat. 518, 519 (1957). Thus, until 1960, widow's benefits were available only to applicants whose marriages to the wage earner were valid. Section 416(h)(1)(B) was added in 1960 because Congress recognized that it is sometimes difficult for an individual to determine, *inter alia*, whether or when a prior marriage has been validly ended. *See* S. Rep. No. 1856, 86th Cong., 2d Sess. 22, reprinted in 1960 U.S. Code Cong. & Admin. News 3608, 3629 ("since the State laws governing marriage and divorce are sometimes complex and subject to differing interpretations, a person may believe that he is validly married when he is not"). Though those who aspire to a common-law marriage may find it equally difficult to determine whether a prior marriage has been validly ended, the legislative history is silent as to why Congress excluded such aspirants from those who should be "deemed" valid widows. *See id.*; *see also* H.R. Rep. No. 1799, 86th Cong., 2d Sess. 16 (1960).

Congress may have modeled section 416(h)(1)(B) after the civil-law doctrine of "putative marriages." Under this doctrine, some states recognize an invalid marriage as valid when one or both parties have a good faith belief in the validity of a marriage and were ignorant of the legal impediment that makes the marriage invalid. *See generally* H. Clark, *The Law of Domestic Relations*, § 2.4, at 55–56 (2d ed. 1988). Traditionally, this recognition was not given unless the participants had gone through a ceremonial marriage, a requirement imposed to demand proof of their good faith, albeit mistaken, belief in the validity of their marriage. *See, e.g., Smith v. Smith*, 1 Tex. 621, 628–29 (1846) (ceremony prerequisite to the granting of relief to a putative spouse is relevant to applicant's good faith); Comment, The Requisite of a Marriage Ceremony for Putative Relationships, 4 Baylor L. Rev. 343, 346 (1952). In more recent years, some states have extended the putative-marriage doctrine to recognize common-law marriages. *See, e.g., Hupp v. Hupp*, 235 SW 2d 753 (Tex. Civ. App. 1950); Minn. Stat. § 518.055.

Though Congress gave no explanation in the legislative history for its decision to limit the deeming rule of section 416(h)(1)(B) to applicants who have gone through ceremonial marriages, it is inferable that the decision to continue to deny benefits to invalidly married persons who had not gone through such ceremonies had two purposes. First, Congress may have sought a means of reducing the incidence of fraudulent claims. In these modern times, many couples, with or without uncertainty as to the dissolution of a prior marriage, decide to cohabit without marrying. Congress may have envisioned the possibility that an unlimited deeming provision would invite fraudulent claims from such persons. Further, Congress may have adopted the more traditional view that a willingness to go through a formal marriage ceremony constitutes some objective evidence of a good-faith belief in the dissolution of any prior marriages. It could rationally have believed that persons who have doubts about whether a prior marriage has been validly ended will be more reluctant to go through a marriage ceremony than they will to enter into an informal cohabitational relationship, perhaps from fear of public criticism, or from fear of having word get back to the prior spouse, or from fear of violating laws against bigamy.

Second, since section 416(h)(1)(B) requires the applicant to show that but for the unknown impediment there would have been a valid marriage, Congress may have sought to establish a criterion that is entirely objective and normally susceptible to documentary proof in order to limit the administrative cost of determining whether that prerequisite is met. If the deeming rule had been made applicable to invalid common-law marriages, the applicant would have to show that all of the prerequisites to common-law marriage were met. Traditionally, the two fundamental requirements for a common-law marriage imposed by the states that have recognized such marriages were (1) the parties' express agreement to be husband and wife, and (2) their holding themselves out to the world as married. *See* H. Clark, *The Law of Domestic Relations,* § 2.4, at 48. The first requirement has been eroded somewhat by rulings that have allowed the existence of the required agreement to be inferred from the fact that the couple has lived together "for all intents and purposes" as husband and wife. *Id.* 2.4, at 49 & n. 31. Whichever test is applied, however, the focus is on the parties' intent. Thus, establishment of a purported common-law marriage would generally require proof of an element that is ultimately subjective.

A ceremonial marriage, on the other hand, is an objectively observable event occurring at a defined place and time. Proof of such a marriage will normally be available through documentary evidence such as the original marriage certificate, a certified copy of a public record of marriage, or a certified copy of a church or synagogue record of marriage. *See generally* SSA Program Operations Manual System ("Manual") § 00305.075. Such documentary evidence is normally accepted by the Secretary as conclusive proof that there was a marriage ceremony. By extending benefits only to those invalidly married persons who can prove that they went through such a ceremony, Congress has made it possible for the Secretary to make a determination in part on the basis of one objective, rather than subjective, criterion, and on the basis of documentary, rather than testimonial, proof.

To be sure, the marriage ceremony requirement in the deeming rule does not relieve the Secretary of all need to assess subjective factors or testimonial evidence. First, there is the statutory requirement that any applicant demonstrate to the Secretary's satisfaction that she went through the marriage ceremony "in good faith." This element, of course, requires a subjective assessment.

... Thus, even where there has been a ceremonial marriage, there remains at least one subjective component to be dealt with by the Secretary....

Further, under the Secretary's procedures, the marriage ceremony itself may be proven by secondary evidence where "primary proof" of a marriage by a certificate or official record is not available. Such secondary proof might consist of the testimony of witnesses who attended the ceremony. Where the claimant relies on secondary evidence, the Secretary will not deem that evidence conclusive but will conduct further inquiry. *See* Manual § 00305.090 ("Secondary proof of marriage ... cannot be treated as conclusive but must be considered in the light of other information in the file.... This is particularly significant in claims involving a deemed marriage.") Thus, in some cases even the marriage-ceremony requirement will not spare the Secretary the burden of taking testimony on all of the elements of the applicant's claim.

Nonetheless, in most instances, the ceremonial marriage requirement does lessen the Secretary's administrative burden by eliminating the need to receive and assess testimonial evidence on one element, and it is therefore rationally related to the goal of reducing administrative costs. In these circumstances, the fact that the line drawn does not lessen the burden in all instances is unimportant.

In sum, though the result of the deeming rule structured by Congress may seem harsh in the present case, we conclude that it is rationally related to legitimate governmental objectives and may not be overturned.

CONCLUSION

For the foregoing reasons, we affirm the judgment dismissing the complaint.

DOLE V. SHENANDOAH BAPTIST CHURCH
899 F. 2d 1389 (4th Cir. 1999)

The dispute underlying this appeal arose when the federal government sought to apply certain provisions of the Fair Labor Standards Act (the Act or the FLSA) to the Roanoke Valley Christian Schools (Roanoke Valley) operated by the Shenandoah Baptist Church. The church and twenty-one intervening employees (Shenandoah) urge that the district court erred in awarding back pay for teachers (for equal pay violations) and for nonprofessional support staff (for minimum wage violations). Shenandoah asserts that Roanoke Valley is not covered by the FLSA; that application of the Act violates the free exercise and establishment clauses of the First Amendment and the equal protection guarantee of the Fifth Amendment; and that, even if the Act does apply, the damages were improperly calculated. The government cross-appeals, contending that the trial court abused its discretion in declining to award prejudgment interest and in refusing to grant injunctive relief. We affirm the decision of the district court in all respects.

Applicability of the Fair Labor Standards Act

Shenandoah urges that the strictures of the Fair Labor Standards Act do not apply to Roanoke Valley. We disagree. Two conditions are necessary for the FLSA to apply. The first is that Roanoke Valley be an "enterprise" within the definition of the Act; the second is that the teachers and support staff be "employees." *See* 29 U.S.C. §§ 203(r) & (e); *Tony & Susan Alamo Found. v. Secretary of Labor*, 471 U.S. 290, 295, 105 S.Ct. 1953, 1958, 85 L.Ed. 2d 278 (1985). We begin with the question of enterprise.

When the FLSA was amended in 1961 to cover enterprises as well as individuals, nonprofit religious and educational organizations were exempt, provided they were not engaging in ordinary commercial activities. *See Alamo* 471 U.S. at 297–97, 105 S.Ct. at 1959. However, Congress amended the statute again in 1966 to include public and private schools in the definition of enterprise. The amended statue explicitly states that nonprofit schools are within the scope of the Act: "Enterprise" means the related activities performed (either through unified operation or common control) by any person or persons for a common business purpose, and includes all such activities whether performed in or more establishments or by one or more corporate or other organizational units.... For purposes of this subsection, the activities performed by any person or persons—(1) in connection with the operation of ... a preschool, elementary or secondary school, or an institution of higher education (regardless of whether or not such ... school is public or private or operated for profit or not for profit) ... shall be deemed to be activities performed for a business purpose. 29 U.S.C. § 203(r); *see also* 29 U.S.C. § 203(s)(5).

Shenandoah urges that this amendment does not demonstrate a clear "affirmative intention" by Congress that the Act apply to church-operated schools. *NLRB v. Catholic Bishop*, 440 U.S. 490, 501, 99 S.Ct. 13131, 1319, 59 L.Ed. 2d 533 (1979).

The conclusion that church-operated schools are encompassed within the Act's definition of enterprise is supported by subsequent legislative action. Cf. *Andrus v. Shell Oil Co.*, 446 U.S. 657, 666, 100 S.Ct. 1932, 1938, 64 L.Ed. 2d 593 (1980); *see also 2A Sutherland Statutory Construction* § 49.11 (Sands 4th ed. 1984). In 1977, Congress again amended the FLSA to create an exemption for "religious or nonprofit educational conference center(s)." 29 U.S.C. § 213(a)(3); *see also* 123 Cong. Rec. 32724–26 (1977). Such an exemption would not have been necessary if church-operated facilities had been excluded under the statutory definition of "enterprise."

Inclusion of church-operated schools under the protective umbrella of the Act is also consistent with Supreme Court precedent construing the FLSA "liberally to apply to the furthest reaches consistent with congressional intention." *Alamo*, 471 U.S. at 296, 105 S.Ct. at 1959 (quoting *Mitchell v. Lublin, McGaughy & Assocs.*, 358 U.S. 207, 211, 79 S.Ct. 260, 264, 3 L.Ed. 2d 243 (1959)).

We therefore hold that the history of the statute demonstrated an affirmative intention by legislators to treat church-operated schools as enterprises. *Accord Marshall vv. First Baptist Church*, 23 Wage & Hour Cas. (BNA) 386, 1977 WL 1755 (DSC 1977); *see also Ritter v. Mount St. Mary's College*, 495 F.Supp. 724 (D. Md. 1980) (holding to the contrary), rev'd in relevant part, 738 F 2d 431 (4th Cir. 1984). The Ninth Circuit implicitly acknowledged this principle in *EEOC v. Fremont Christian School*, 781 F.2d 1362, 1367 (9th Cir. 1986), applying the equal pay provisions of the FLSA to a church-operated school which provided health insurance only for heads of households. *See also Russell v. Belmont College*, 554 F.Supp. 667, 670–76 (M.D. Tenn. 1982) (denying college's motion for summary judgment); *Marshall v. Pacific Union Conference*, 23 Wage & Hour Cas. (BNA) 316, 1977 WL 885 (C.D. Cal. 1977) (denying conference's motion for summary judgment); cf. *Archbishop of Roman Catholic Apostolic Archdiocese v. Guardiola* 628 F.Supp. 1173, 1178–79 (D.P.R. 1895) (holding lay Catholic Church employees are covered by the Puerto Rico Minimum Wage Act, which is modeled on the FLSA).

Shenandoah urges nevertheless that Roanoke Valley should not be covered by the statute because it is inextricably intertwined with the church. It argues that school employees are really church employees and therefore not covered by the FSA. Shenandoah asserts that the church and school share a common physical plant and a common payroll account, that the associate pastor for school ministries reports to the pastor, that the pastor hires all teachers, and that school staff must subscribe to Shenandoah's statement of faith. Shenandoah insists, "The school is the church."

Shenandoah relies on *Corporation of Presiding Bishop v. Amos*, 483 U.S. 327, 107 S.Ct. 2862, 97b L. Ed. 2d 273 (1987), and *Forest Hills Early Learning Center v. Grace Baptist Church*, 846 F.2d 260, 263–64 (4th Cir. 1988) cert. denied, __ U.S. __; 109 S.Ct. 837, 102 L.Ed. 2d 969 (1989), for the proposition that the government should be required to accept the church's characterization of Roanoke Valley as an inseverable part of the church. Shenandoah's reliance is misplaced. These cases only considered whether legislators could exempt religious organizations from certain statutory provisions without running afoul of the First Amendment. They concluded that such exemptions were constitutionally permissible; they did not hold that they were mandatory. *See County of Allegheny v. Pittsburgh ACLU*, 492 U.S. ___, 109 S.Ct. 3086, 3105 n. 51, 106 L.Ed. 2d

472 (1989). The case *sub judice* presents an entirely different question—whether Congress intended the FLSA to *include* (not exclude, as in *Amos* and *Forest Hills*) church-operated schools. We hold that Congress affirmatively intended the Act to apply to such schools.

Shenandoah also asserts that the second criterion for application of the Fair Labor Standards Act is not present here because Roanoke Valley teachers are not "employees." It urges that they are ministers and therefore covered by the "ministerial exemption" from the Act. This exemption is derived from the Congressional debate excerpted above and delineated in guidelines issued by the Labor Department's Wage and Hour Administrator:

Persons such as nuns, monks, priests, lay brother, ministers, deacons and other members of religious orders who serve pursuant to their religious obligations in the schools ... operated by their church or religious order shall not be considered to be "employees." *Field Operations Handbook*, Wage and Hour Division, U.S. Dept. of Labor, § 10b03(b) (1967).

Shenandoah states that Roanoke Valley teachers consider teaching to be their personal ministry. It urges that all classes are taught from a pervasively religious perspective, and that teachers lead students in prayer and are required to subscribe to the Shenandoah statement of faith as a condition of employment.

Shenandoah contends that the characterization of Roanoke Valley teachers as ministers is consistent with this court's holding in *Rayburn v. General Conference of Seventh-Day Adventists*, 772 F.2d 1164 (4th Cir. 1985), cert. denied, 478 U.S. 1020, 106 S.Ct. 3333, 92 L.Ed. 2d 739 (1986). In *Rayburn*, we explained that the ministerial exemption in Title VII depended upon the function of the position, not simply on ordination. *Id.* at 1168. But the facts of *Rayburn* are far removed from those of the case at bar. There the claimant, whom we ultimately characterized as clergy, was a woman who held the degree of Master of Divinity form the church's theological seminary and who sought appointment to the seven-person pastoral staff as one of the denomination's largest congregations.

The teachers in the present case perform no sacerdotal functions; neither do they serve as church governors. They belong to no clearly delineated religious order. Shenandoah insists that there is not cognizable difference between its teachers and nuns who teach in church-affiliated schools, but it has failed to adequately support this assertion. Cf. *Fiedler v. Marumsco Christian School*, 631 F.2d 1144, 1153 (4th Cir. 1980); *Triple "AAA" Co. v. Wirtz*, 378 F.2d 884, 887 (10th Cir.) cert. denied, 389 U.S. 9959, 88 S.Ct. 338, 19 L.Ed. 2d 364 (1967).

This is not to minimize the vocation of the Roanoke Valley teachers or the sincerity which they bring to it. But "[e]xemptions from the Fair Labor Standards Act are narrowly construed," *Hodgson v. Duke Univ.*, 460 F. 2d 172, 174 (4th Cir, 1972), and as the district court has observed, the exemption of these teachers would "create an exception capable of swallowing up the rule." *Shenandoah I, 573 F.Supp.* at 323. We therefore decline to give the ministerial exemption the sweeping interpretation Shenandoah seeks. The Supreme Court has explained "[t]he test of employment under the Act is one of 'economic reality." *Alamo*, 471 U.S. at 301, 105 S.Ct. at 1961. The economic reality in this case is that the Roanoke Valley teachers are employed as lay teachers in a church-operated private school.

We therefore hold that Congress intended church-operated schools such as Roanoke Valley to be covered by the Fair Labor Standards Act, and that their teachers and support staff are employees under the Act. We next consider the constitutional challenges raised by Shenandoah Baptist to application of the statute.

[The arguments regarding free exercise of religion, establishment of religion and equal protection are omitted.]

To summarize, we conclude that Congress affirmatively intended the Fair Labor Standards Act to apply to church-operated schools and that application of the Act to Roanoke Valley does not violate the First or Fifth Amendment rights of the church of the intervenors in this action. We affirm the district court award of $16,818.46 back pay for support staff members who were subject to minimum wage violations and of $177,680 back pay for teachers who were subject to equal pay violations. We also affirm the denial of prejudgment interest and injunctive relief.

AFFIRMED.

Glossary

Equal Pay Act of 1963 – federal statute requiring workers of opposite sexes performing equal work for the same employer to be paid equal wages

equal work – tasks requiring similar abilities and duties

Fair Labor Standards Act (FLSA) of 1938 – federal statute guaranteeing a minimum wage and maximum number of work hours

fully insured – meeting minimum 40-quarters requirement to qualify for Social Security

minimum wage – lowest legally permissible pay rate

pay rate – salary, benefits, and pension

red circle – temporary work assignment justifying a temporary pay change

same establishment – a facility owned by an employer, used to determine whether equal pay is paid to workers of different sexes performing the same work for the same employer

Social Security Act of 1935 – federal statute used to fund a retirement and disability account for U.S. workers

Social Security Administration – government agency formed to administer the Social Security Act

Social Security number – personal identifying number used, among other things, to determine Social Security benefits

Exercises

1. Argue for an employer that a paralegal should be exempt under the FLSA? How would you counter your own argument?

2. How can unequal pay for persons performing equal work for the same employer in the same establishment be justified under the Equal Pay Act?

3. The statement has been made that Social Security represents a benevolent paternalism. What is your opinion of this statement?

4. The common law supports the notion that employers and employees shall be free to contract for all the terms of employment, including pay. Do you think that any of the laws discussed in this chapter infringe on the freedom to contract? In which way? Do you think infringement with respect to pay is necessary? Why or why not?

Chapter Four

**DISCRIMINATION REGULATION:
THE CIVIL RIGHTS ACT & THE ADEA**

Chapter Overview

The third great social event that affected employment law was the civil rights movement of the 1960s. (The other two movements, the response to the Great Depression and the rise of trade unionism, were discussed in the preceding two chapters.) Although most lawyers date the beginnings of employment discrimination law from the Civil Rights Act of 1964, in fact, its origins go back almost a hundred years to the Reconstruction period following the Civil War.

In 1866, Congress enacted the first **Civil Rights Act** legislation, which was designed to grant newly freed slaves basic civil rights with respect to contract and property law. The Civil Rights Act stated, in part, that "all persons...shall have the same right...to make and enforce contracts as is enjoyed by white citizens...." This statute applied not only to federal and state action but also to municipal action. Although this law does not by name prohibit racial discrimination in employment (it refers to contract enjoyment and the right to hold and own property only), the statute was used as a basis to prevent employers from discriminating against employees because of race.

It was not until the widespread protests against racial discrimination in the 1960s that Congress actually enacted a statute directly addressing the problem of discrimination in the workplace. In 1964, the Civil Rights Act was passed, including **Title VII**, which prohibits discrimination on the basis of race, sex, color, religion, or national origin. It applies to employers, labor organizations, and employment agencies. Various laws have been enacted to deal with specific discrimination issues, but Title VII remains the cornerstone of this area of law.

One category that does not appear in Title VII is discrimination based on a person's age. The **Age Discrimination in Employment Act** (ADEA) was passed in 1967. Because the Civil Rights Act of 1964 and the ADEA concern basic categories that cover all employees, they will be discussed together.

History of the Civil Rights Act of 1964

Title VII of the Civil Rights Act of 1964[1] prohibits discrimination in employment based on a person's race, sex, color, religion, or national origin. The statute applies to employers, labor organizations, and employment agencies. The five categories specified in the act are called **protected categories.** This means that if an individual wishes to proceed with an action against an employer under Title VII, the basis of the complaint must be discriminatory practices against a person intended to be protected as a member of one of these categories.

---

[1] 42 U.S.C. § 2000(e), *et seq.*

> *Example: A paralegal wants to file an action against her corporate employer for discrimination under Title VII. The paralegal claims that she is being discriminated against in salary and promotion potential because she, a paraplegic, is physically challenged. The suit will fail because physical disabilities are not a protected category under Title VII. (See Chapter Six.)*

In 1972, Congress enacted the **Equal Employment Opportunity Commission** (EEOC) to oversee the implementation of the Civil Rights Act of 1964. Pursuant to **Executive Order 11246**, companies that supply goods and services to the federal government are required to plan and undertake affirmative action to rectify past discrimination in employment.

Affirmative action plans are designed to remedy racially discriminatory practices suffered in the past by members of certain minority groups. For a plan to be effective, it must be reasonable. This means that

- The objective of the plan must not exceed the percentage of qualified minorities available in the market.

> *Example: An employer, under its affirmative action plan, decides to have the percentage of its workforce that consists of minorities equal the percentage of minorities in the general population. The number of qualified minorities available, in percentage, is less than the percentage of minorities in the general population. In this instance, it would be unreasonable to set such a goal, because to do so the employer would have to hire unqualified individuals simply to meet a predetermined quota.*

- The plan must be temporary. Because the purpose of affirmative action is to rectify past injustices resulting from discriminatory employment practices, once the injustices have been corrected, there is no need to continue the corrective measures.

- The plan cannot "unduly trammel" the opportunities of the white male majority. This means that the plan cannot create a quota system that would prevent qualified white males from obtaining promotion because a certain number of jobs have been set aside for persons who fall into a protected category. This type of situation would create reverse discrimination, favoring a minority employee over an equally or better qualified white male employee.

> *Example: A school has an opening for a vice principal, and two candidates have applied. Both are teachers in the school; one is a black female and the other is a white male. The female has her master's degree and has taught for five years; the male has a doctorate in education, has taught for fifteen years, and has acted as a temporary vice principal in his former school. If the school decides to hire the black female because she is black and female, two protected categories under Title VII, instead of the better-qualified male, this would likely be reverse discrimination.*

Note that affirmative action plans have been specifically extended to give preferential treatment to Indians for businesses located near a reservation. (The statute[2] uses the term "Indian," not "Native American.") And note that opposition to affirmative action plans has risen in recent years. Various organizations argue that, after 30 years of affirmative action, the racial imbalance due to discriminatory employment practices have been eradicated, thereby making affirmative action obsolete.

Employers

Title VII does not apply to individuals but to "employers." This means that, in order for the provisions of the Act to apply, the entity being charged with a discriminatory practice must meet the statutory definition of "employer." These same requirements also apply to the Age Discrimination in Employment Act and the Americans with Disabilities Act, as will be discussed later.

To be classified as an **"employer"** under Title VII, the person must be in an industry that "affects Commerce [*sic*]" and has fifteen or more employees. Presumably, almost any business could be deemed to affect commerce, so the test really comes down to the number of employees. These employees must be employed "each working day for 20 or more calendar weeks in the current or previous year," and the 20 weeks do not have to be consecutive. All employees are considered in the calculation, not just permanent staff.

> *Example: An employer hires ten individuals on a full-time basis and supplements its work force by hiring temporary and part-time workers. At any given time, the total number of employees on hand is 14—the ten full-time employees and four part-time and temporary workers. This employer is not subject to Title VII because it does not have the requisite number of employees working each workday for the statutory period.*

> *Example: An employer hires 20 individuals on a full-time basis and complements its work force by hiring temporary and part-time workers. In this instance, the employer is subject to Title VII, and all of the employees—full-time, part-time, and temporary—are covered by the Act.*

Title VII covers all persons who meet the definition of employer with the minimum number of employees, including religious organizations and state and local governments. The federal government does not qualify as an employer under the Act, but other statutes prohibit the federal government from discriminating in employment, and federal workers are given special procedures and remedies to follow in case of discrimination.

Title VII does exclude certain organizations from its provisions:

- *Bona fide* membership clubs, other than labor organizations are exempt, if the avowed purpose of the organization is to "serve a social, recreational or charitable purpose" and is exempt from federal taxation.

---

[2] 433 U.S.C. § 2000(e)-2(I)

> **Example:** *A woman brings a charge for sexual discrimination against a hospital under Title VII. The hospital is considered an employer under the Act; it cannot claim exemption as a membership organization serving a charitable purpose. A hospital is not a "club."*

- The military is considered to be outside the provisions of the statute because the relationship between the military and the members of the armed forces is not considered "employment," but something special. Note, however, that nonmilitary personnel working for the military are covered under Title VII.

> **Example:** *A civilian paralegal is employed by the Judge Advocate General (JAG), the legal branch of the military. The employee charges several JAG officers with discrimination based on sex. In this instance, the employee is protected by Title VII.*

- Indian tribes are excluded from the Act because the tribes are legally considered separate nations.

The Protected Categories

To be protected by Title VII's prohibition against discrimination, an employee must fall within one of the protected categories specified in the statute. If the person does not come within the provisions of the "protected categories," he or she must seek redress based on some other legal right. Each of the protected categories will be discussed in turn.

Race and Color

Although race and color are separate categories in the statute, they are generally discussed together because it is usually difficult to separate one from the other. Under Title VII, all races are protected against discrimination, and the Act even extends to discrimination against persons of the same race whose shade of skin may be different from the majority of persons belonging to that racial category.

> **Example:** *A business is owned and operated by a black woman who is extremely active in the movement for racial equality. The majority of her employees are black. One of her employees wants to charge her with discrimination on grounds that all of the executives in the company have very dark complexions, but she, the employee challenging the employer, has a very light complexion. The employee is claiming that because of her light tint she has been denied promotion in favor of darker-skinned employees. If the employee can prove her allegations, this would be a case of discrimination based on race and color.*

Race has been defined by the courts as any identifiable class of persons, and have included, by judicial interpretation, Iraqis, Jews, Latinos, etc. In many instances, such racial classification may be discriminatory in and of itself by creating a stereotype of certain characteristics as belonging to a particular racial group.

> *Example: To remedy past discrimination, an employer decides to promote several Jews to executive positions. A Jewish employee is passed over because he has blond hair, blue eyes, and a Northern European surname. This employee charges the employer with racial discrimination, basing his claim on the fact that he was not promoted because he doesn't "look Jewish." This type of discrimination would be considered racial.*

Racial discrimination has also been held to apply to situations in which an employee is discriminated against not because of his or her race but because of the race of the employee's spouse.

> *Example: An employer decides to pass over a well-qualified employee for promotion because the employee's spouse belongs to a racial minority and the employer does not feel that this spouse would "fit in" with the other executives' spouses.*

The activities that are deemed discriminatory include:

- *Racial harassment*. Harassment refers to the continued and concerted action on the part of an employer, or tacitly condoned by an employer, that makes an employee feel uncomfortable in the workplace because of words or actions directed against the employee's race.

> *Example: A supervisor in a company calls his Hispanic employees "Spics" both to their faces and behind their backs. The employer is aware of the situation but does nothing. Even though this name-calling has not resulted in the Hispanic employees being discriminated against in hiring or promotion, it may still be considered racial discrimination under Title VII.*

- *Racially based compensation*. Paying the members of a particular race more than the members of another race who are performing equal work violates Title VII.

> *Example: Feeling guilty about past discrimination, an employer pays its black employees $1 per hour more that its other employees. Under Title VII, this is discriminatory to all the other employees.*

- *Racially motivated hiring, promoting, training, or firing*. Any time an employer makes an employment decision based on race, the action is automatically suspect as violating Title VII.

> *Example: An employer opens up a facility in what is considered a bad neighborhood. To run the facility, the employer promotes and transfers only his Hispanic employees. Even though the employees have been promoted, the action appears, if racially motivated, to be discriminatory.*

National Origin

National origin refers to the country or national group from which the employee or the employee's family came. An employer is generally prohibited from discriminating against a person because of his or her national origin, but there are several notable exceptions to the rule:

- If the employment position requires a federal security clearance and the person, because of his or her national origin, cannot obtain federal clearance, the employer may select a person who can obtain such clearance.

> **Example:** *An employer has contracted with the U.S. government to perform high-level research. All employees working on the project must get federal security clearance from the government. A particular job applicant, who is a native of a country that U.S. policy deems to be a security risk, cannot get clearance from the federal government. The employer is not required to hire this individual. Note, however, that if the same employer is engaged in work that is not involved with government security clearances, it cannot use the necessity of clearance for the other project as the basis for discriminating against the applicant because of his national origin.*

- If the job requires a fluency in English, the employer does not have to hire or employ a person whose English skills are inadequate. However, there must be a clear showing of the language necessity; discrimination based on accent alone is prohibited.

> **Example:** *A large law firm is looking for a paralegal. The work the paralegal will be required to perform requires a high level of skill in English. If an applicant has only recently immigrated to the U.S. and reads, writes, and speaks very little English, the firm's failure to hire that applicant is not based on national origin discrimination.*

- An employer may not hire an undocumented alien. This is expressly prohibited under the Immigration Reform and Control Act of 1986, and the failure to employ persons who are illegally in the country is not discrimination. Note that the employer cannot discriminate against aliens legally in the country.

- An employer may discriminate in favor of an alien over a U.S. citizen if the United States has a treaty with a foreign country specifying that preference will be given to that country's nationals for certain foreign employers operating in the United States. The United States has such a treaty with Japan. This is a very limited exception, and the treaty supersedes the provisions of Title VII.

An employer may not discriminate against persons by favoring one nationality over another, such as an employer who came from Argentina favoring other Argentineans as employees. Also, note the distinction between **national origin** and nationality. "**Nationality**" refers to the country to which the person owes allegiance, whereas national origin refers to the country of origin regardless of current allegiance. Although the concepts may overlap, they are distinct and separate. Questions of nationality are covered by the immigration and naturalization laws.

Sex

Under the Civil Rights Act, **sex** refers only to a person's gender, not his or her sexuality or sexual orientation. Therefore, this category is generally divided between male and female, and the law prohibits favoring one gender over the other in hiring, firing, promoting, or transferring. Discrimination in pay is covered under the provisions of the Equal Pay Act, discussed in Chapter Three.

> ***Example:*** *A restaurant typically only hires women as servers. A male applicant is turned away because the owner does not believe that his customers will be happy being served by a man. This is an example of sex discrimination and **sexual stereotyping**—assuming a particular characteristic to belong to a particular gender—and is illegal under Title VII.*

Title VII has been held to apply, under the category of sex discrimination, to pregnancy, childbirth, and related matters. Consequently, if an employer refuses to hire or promote a woman because she is pregnant, or may become pregnant, it is deemed sex discrimination.

> ***Example:*** *A law firm is looking for a new associate attorney. One of the applicants is a married woman in her late twenties. Although her credentials are impressive, the firm does not hire her because it believes that she will want to have children in the near future, and it does not want to deal with lawyers who cannot devote a substantial amount of time to their jobs. This is an example of sex discrimination.*

It is not considered sex discrimination if an employer hires only persons it considers physically "attractive," unless the employer specifically favors one gender over the other. Problems relating to physical characteristics may come within the purview of the Americans with Disabilities Act, discussed in Chapter Six.

> ***Example:*** *A law firm interviews two applicants for a paralegal position. Both applicants are women and are equally qualified. The paralegal coordinator of the firm hires the one who is perceived to be the more attractive so as to fit in with the firm's "image." This is not sex discrimination.*

> ***Example:*** *A law firm interviews two applicants for a paralegal position. Both applicants are women and are equally qualified. The paralegal coordinator of the firm hires the one who is perceived to be less attractive, because the coordinator feels that the attorneys and the clients cannot take an attractive woman seriously. This is sexual stereotyping and may be discriminatory.*

Hiring, firing, or promoting a person because of sexual favors the employee is willing, or not willing, to provide is sexual harassment. It is prohibited. The topic is discussed in detail in Chapter Eight.

Title VII's prohibition against sex discrimination has not been held to apply to discrimination based on sexual preference and, therefore, it is not a violation for an employer to discriminate against homosexuals, bisexuals, and transsexuals. Although several municipal governments and a few states have banned discrimination based on sexual orientation, these prohibitions are not part of Title VII, although the matter is currently being litigated.

> *Example: An employer refuses to hire lesbians because she finds their appearance and manners distasteful, but she has no problem hiring gay men. This may be a form of sex discrimination if it can be determined that the employer favors men over women; the sexual orientation of the employees is not a protected category under Title VII.*

Religion

Title VII does not specifically define "religion," although all of the major religions would definitely be included. Rather than a detailed list of religions, Title VII simply refers to "all aspects of religious observance and practice, as well as belief." This description has been judicially interpreted to encompass moral or ethical beliefs that are held in the same fashion as those beliefs held by traditional organized religions.

> *Example: A law firm represents, as one of its major clients, a synagogue. The firm gives preference in hiring to members of the Jewish religion to curry favor with the client. An applicant for a position as a paralegal is turned down because she is an atheist. This constitutes religious discrimination on the part of the law firm.*

The Act also prohibits discrimination based on the practices and observances of a religion as well as the religion itself. Consequently, it would be illegal for an employer to discriminate against employees who observed holy days or wore particular clothing as part of the religion's traditional practices.

> *Example: An employer refuses to promote an employee because she covers her hair with a partial veil in observance of her Islamic faith. If there is no bona fide reason why such a veil would be an impairment to her work (see below), such discrimination based on the religious dress of the member of a particular religion is prohibited under Title VII.*

Safeguards provided under Title VII do not apply if membership in a particular religion is a *bona fide* occupational qualification for the position.

> *Example: A religious seminary requires that its religious instructors all be members of its faith. This is a bona fide occupational requirement, and so the seminary may favor members of its own religion. Note, however, that secretarial or support staff employed by the seminary may not come under the same exception as the faculty, because the job requirements are different.*

The Act applies to all employers, labor organizations, and employment agencies. The persons subject to the Act are required to make reasonable accommodation for its employees so that they may practice their religion without negative employment consequences.

> *Example: A Jewish employee wants to observe the two High Holy Days of his religion. The employer must allow the employee to take this time off, by permitting the employee to use personal vacation time or providing the employee with unpaid leave. The employer may not retaliate against the employee.*

> *Example: A Muslim employee wishes to observe the 40 days of Ramadan at home and requests that the employer either let him work at night (when the business is closed but when the Ramadan restrictions do not apply) or to let him have leave. In this instance, because of the duration of the time and the fact that observance of Ramadan does not exclude working, this request on the part of the employee would be unreasonable and need not be met by the employer.*

If the employer could prove that letting the employee observe his or her religion would cause an undue hardship on the business, the employer is exempted from meeting the accommodation.

> *Example: An employee's weekly Sabbath day happens to be the busiest day at his employer's business. If the employee demands to be off on this day every week, the employer would be constantly shorthanded. This would cause an undue hardship for the employer.*

> *Example: An employer operates a business on a seven-day basis, and the employees are given days off on a rotation basis based on seniority. This system has been used by the employer since opening the business. An employee charges religious discrimination because she refuses to work on a particular day, which is her religion's weekly holy day. This causes disruption in the schedule and infuriates other employees. To accommodate this employee every week would create an undue hardship.*

A member of any of the above-enumerated categories may bring a charge of unlawful discrimination against an employer.

Employer Defenses to Title VII Charges

Not all charges of discriminatory practices under Title VII are well founded. The Act provides an employer with certain defenses if the employer can demonstrate that the discriminatory practice is a **bona fide occupational qualification** (BFOQ). To show that the practice is a BFOQ, the employer must prove the following:

- The excluded class cannot perform an essential task of the position. To maintain this defense, the employer must show that the task is essential to job performance and not based on stereotyping, custom, or any other condition that does not go to the essence of the job.

> ***Example:*** *An employer uses only women as receptionists for its business because it believes that customers and visitors prefer being greeted by a woman. Because the job of receptionist does not require any gender-specific talent, this practice is discriminatory based on gender stereotyping and not a BFOQ.*
>
> ***Example:*** *An airline hires only men as pilots because that has been the traditional practice in the industry. Because the job of piloting an airplane does not require any gender-based talent, this practice is discriminatory based on historical custom and not a BFOQ.*

> ***Example:*** *A law firm never hires attorneys of a particular national origin because the physical characteristics of that national group do not fit in with the "image" the firm wishes to present. This practice is discriminatory based on national origin, because an attorney's physical appearance based on national origin has nothing to do with the tasks required of the job.*

On the other hand, if it can be shown that the employer's customers actually prefer persons in a specific category that documented preference may be the basis of a *bona fide* occupational qualification.

> ***Example:*** *A health club provides massage services for its members. Studies show that both men and women feel more comfortable being massaged by members of the same sex, and when the club records show that only a few members would sign up for massage by therapists of the opposite sex, the club may discriminate in hiring therapists based on gender.*

- The employer must show that all, or substantially all, of the particular class cannot perform the essential tasks of the job. This qualification usually concerns only physical ability.

> ***Example:*** *A clothing manufacturer needs a model on whom to fit designs. The manufacturer can hire only female models for his women's line, because men do not have the necessary physical attributes.*

- The employer may discriminate if it can be shown that hiring a particular class would engender a substantial risk to third persons. The employer may discriminate even if such tasks would not apply to "all or substantially all" of the members of the class on the grounds that it would create a hardship for the employer to judge each and every applicant separately. A major case in this area concerned female guards at a male prison, in which the Supreme Court held (in *Dothard v. Rawlinson*[3]) that even though some women could perform the tasks requiring certain physical strengths, there had been an unusual number of problems in male prisons that were guarded by women, and that to hire women for such positions did involve a substantial risk.

- The employer may show a *bona fide* occupational qualification if the nature of the job makes it reasonably necessary to discriminate. In the example above concerning the religious seminary,

---

[3] 433 U.S. 321 (1977)

the seminary could discriminate in favor of its own religion in hiring instructors for religious instruction because of the nature of the task involved.

Race is never considered to be a business necessity or as the basis of a bona fide *occupational qualification.*

Age Discrimination

Shortly after the passage of Title VII, Congress enacted the **Age Discrimination in Employment Act of 1967** (ADEA) because age was not included as one of the protected categories under Title VII. The Act applies to all persons who are at least 40 years old and prohibits discrimination based on age with respect to hiring, firing, promoting and mandatory retirement plans. The ADEA applies only to those who employ a minimum of 20 employees.

Under the ADEA, an employer may discriminate by requiring a minimum age requirement for employees but is generally prohibited from imposing a maximum age limitation.

> *Example: An employer requires that its delivery van drivers be at least 25 years old because of reduced insurance premiums for person over 24. This age discrimination is perfectly permissible under the ADEA.*

A person who believes that he or she is the object of age discrimination in the workplace must prove his or her claim in the same manner as under Title VII, specifically:

- By a showing of express discrimination, such as announcing an employment policy based on age. If this can be shown, the burden shifts to the employer to demonstrate that this policy would qualify as a *bona fide* occupational qualification. The same BFOQ defenses that apply to Title VII apply to the ADEA as well.

> *Example: An employee who is 52 years old charges his employer with age discrimination because he was not promoted to a managerial position, although he was qualified. The employee can prove that he was told by the employer that he was not being promoted because he was "too old," that the position is usually filled by people in their thirties, and that, at his age, he could not continue to be promoted. This constitutes direct evidence of age discrimination.*

- An employee may be able to prove age discrimination by circumstantial evidence, such as preferential treatment given to persons in different age categories performing similar tasks. This different treatment based on unspoken age factors may constitute age discrimination.

> *Example: Two employees are performing the same job for the same employer. One is 30 years old; the other is 55. During a period of decreased sales, the employer fires the older employee while retaining the younger. This may be evidence of age discrimination, unless the employer can show a legitimate reason for the different treatment.*

- Statistical evidence can be introduced to show a consistent pattern of age discrimination. Of course, obtaining records from the employer would be a necessity in this case.

- The employee may be able to prove a discriminatory practice if he or she can show that the employer's policies have a negative impact on persons over the age of 40.

The Age Discrimination in Employment Act provides certain exemptions from the Act:

- Law enforcement officers and firefighters, for reasons of public safety.

- Executives, who may be retired at age 65, if the executive makes at least $44,000 per year and is entitled to an immediate retirement benefit.

- Elected officials and government appointees, because these persons are not considered "employees."

- *Bona fide* apprenticeship programs, because apprenticeships are considered to be educational rather than employment.

An employer charged with age discrimination under the ADEA can defend itself in the same manner as an employer can defend itself under Title VII by showing that:

- age represents a *bona fide* occupational qualification,
- a seniority system does not reduce benefits as a person ages, although it requires retirement at a specified age,
- the alleged discrimination was not based on age but on other factors, such as education or job experience.

Although an employer cannot mandate retirement for employees at a specific age, the employer may provide incentives to encourage older employees to voluntarily retire. The employer must show that the early retirement policy is voluntary and that the employee was not forced out because of age.

> **Example:** *To reduce expenses, an employer offers all employees who have attained the age of 60 increased benefits if they retire within three months. The purpose of this policy is to reduce the expense of these higher-paid employees' salaries, and the plan is totally voluntary. There is no retaliation against employees who do not avail themselves of this option. The plan is permissible under the ADEA.*

Chapter Summary

The Civil Rights Act of 1964 and the Age Discrimination in Employment Act of 1967 provide the basis of modern legislation concerning discrimination in the work place. Resulting from the civil rights movement of the early sixties, these two pieces of legislation have led the way in changing public policy and societal attitude towards employee rights, concepts that did not exist under the common law approach of employment at will. These two statutes, which protect workers from being discriminated against in hiring, firing, promoting, and benefits based on age, sex, race, color, religion, or national origin, may be viewed as the employee's Bill of Rights.

Bear in mind, however, that not all forms of discrimination are illegal. Under these statutes, employers may discriminate if they can show a *bona fide* occupational qualification for a particular position even though that would exclude workers in a protected class (except race). As will be discussed later, an employee in a protected category is never shielded from the consequences of his or her own incompetence. These statutes established a statutory standard of acceptable employment policies.

Edited Judicial Decisions

Gregory v. Ashcroft discusses the concept of the constitutionality of mandatory retirement for judges in light of the Age Discrimination in Employment Act. *Walker v. Secretary of the Treasury, I.R.S.*, concerns alleged color discrimination by a black supervisor against a lighter-skinned black employee.

GREGORY v. ASHCROFT
501 U.S. 452, 111 S.Ct. 2395, 115 L.Ed. 2d 410(1991)

Justice O'Connor delivered the opinion of the Court.

Article V, § 26, of the Missouri Constitution provides that "all judges other than municipal judges shall retire at the age of seventy years." We consider whether this mandatory retirement provision violates the federal Age Discrimination in Employment Act of 1967 (ADEA or Act), 81 Stat. 602, as amended, 29 U.S.C. §§ 621-634, and whether it comports with the federal constitutional prescription of equal protection of the laws.

I.   Petitioners are Missouri state judges. Judge Ellis Gregory, Jr., is an associate circuit judge for the Twenty-first Judicial Circuit. Judge Anthony P. Nugent, Jr., is a judge of the Missouri Court of Appeals, Western District. Both are subject to the § 26 mandatory retirement provision. Petitioners were appointed to office by the Governor of Missouri, pursuant to the Missouri Non-Partisan Court Plan, Mo. Const., Art. V, §§ 25(a)-25(g). Each has, since his appointment, been retained in office by means of a retention election in which the judge ran unopposed, subject only to a "yes or no" vote. *See* Mo. Const., Art. V, § 25(c)(1).

Petitioners and two other state judges filed suit against John D. Ashcroft, the Governor of Missouri, in the United States District Court for the Eastern District of Missouri, challenging the validity of the mandatory retirement provision. The judges alleged that the provision violated both the ADEA and the Equal Protection Clause of the Fourteenth Amendment to the United States Constitution. The Governor filed a motion to dismiss.

The District Court granted the motion, holding that Missouri's appointed judges are not protected by the ADEA because they are "appointees...'on a policymaking level'" and therefore are excluded from the Act's definition of "employee." App. to Pet. for Cert. 22. The court held also that the mandatory retirement provision does not violate the Equal

Protection Clause because there is a rational basis for the distinction between judges and other state officials to whom no mandatory retirement age applies. *Id.*, at 23.

The United States Court of Appeals for the Eighth Circuit affirmed the dismissal. 898 F.2d 598 (1990). That court also held that appointed judges are "appointees on the policymaking level," and are therefore not covered under the ADEA. *Id.*, at 604. The Court of Appeals held as well that Missouri had a rational basis for distinguishing judges who had reached the age of 70 from those who had not. *Id.*, at 606.

We granted certiorari on both the ADEA and equal protection questions, 498 U.S. 979 (1990), and now affirm.

II. The ADEA makes it unlawful for an "employer" "to discharge any individual" who is at least 40 years old "because of such individual's age." 29 U.S.C. §§ 623(a), 631(a). The term "employer" is defined to include "a State or political subdivision of a State." § 630(B)(2). Petitioners work for the State of Missouri. They contend that the Missouri mandatory retirement requirement for judges violates the ADEA.

In 1974, Congress extended the substantive provisions of the ADEA to include the States as employers. Pub. L. 93-259, § 28(a), 88 Stat. 74, 29 U.S.C. § 630(b)(2). At the same time, Congress amended the definition of "employee" to exclude all elected and most high-ranking government officials. Under the Act, as amended:

"The term 'employee' means an individual employed by any employer except that the term 'employee' shall not include any person elected to public office in any State or political subdivision of any State by the qualified voters thereof, or any person chosen by such officer to be on such officer's personal staff, or an appointee on the policymaking level or an immediate adviser with respect to the exercise of the constitutional or legal powers of the office." 29 U.S.C. § 630(f).

Governor Ashcroft contends that the § 630(f) exclusion of certain public officials also excludes judges, like petitioners, who are appointed to office by the Governor and are then subject to retention election. The Governor points to two passages in § 630(F). First, he argues, these judges are selected by an elected official and, because they make policy, are "appointees on the policymaking level."

Petitioners counter that judges merely resolve factual disputes and decide questions of law; they do not make policy. Moreover, petitioners point out that the policymaking-level exception is part of a trilogy, tied closely to the elected official exception. Thus, the Act excepts elected officials and:

1. "any person chosen by such officer to be on such officer's personal staff,"
2. "an appointee on the policymaking level,"
3. "an immediate advisor with respect to the exercise of the constitutional or legal powers of the office."

Applying the maxim of statutory construction *noscitur a sociis*—that a word is known by the company it keeps—petitioners argue that since (1) and (3) refer only to those in close working relationships with elected officials, so too must (2). Even if it can be said that judges may make policy, petitioners contend, they do not do so at the behest of an elected official.

Governor Ashcroft relies on the plain language of the statute: It exempts persons appointed "at the policymaking level." The Governor argues that state judges, in fashioning and applying the common law, make policy. Missouri is a common law state. *See* Mo. Rev. Stat. §, 1.010 (1986) (adopting "the common law of England" consistent with federal and state law). The common law, unlike a constitution or statute, provides no definitive text; it is to be derived from the interstices of prior opinions and a well-considered judgment of what is best for the community.

The Governor stresses judges' policymaking responsibilities, but it is far from plain that the statutory exception requires that judges actually make policy. The statute refers to appointees "on the policymaking level," not to appointees "who make policy." It may be sufficient that the appointee is in a position requiring the exercise of discretion concerning issues of public importance. This certainly describes the bench, regardless of whether judges might be considered policymakers in the same sense as the executive or legislature.

Nonetheless, "appointee at the policymaking level," particularly in the context of the other exceptions that surround it, is an odd way for Congress to exclude judges; a plain statement that judges are not "employees" would seem the most efficient phrasing. But in this case, we are not looking for a plain statement that judges are excluded. We will not read the ADEA to cover state judges unless Congress has made it clear that judges are included. This does not mean that the Act must mention judges explicitly, though it does not. Cf. *Dellmuth v. Muth*, 491 U.S. 223, 233, 105 L.Ed. 2d 181, 109 S.Ct. 2397 (1989) (Scalia, J., concurring). Rather, it must be plain to anyone reading the Act that it covers judges. In the context of a statute that plainly excludes most important state public officials, "appointee on the policymaking level" is sufficiently broad that we cannot conclude that the statute plainly covers appointed state judges. Therefore, it does not.

The ADEA plainly covers all state employees except those excluded by one of the exceptions. Where it is unambiguous that an employee does not fall within one of the exceptions, the Act states plainly and unequivocally that the employee is included. It is at least ambiguous whether a state judge is an "appointee on the policymaking level."

Governor Ashcroft points also to the "person elected to public office" exception. He contends that because petitioners—although appointed to office initially—are subject to retention election, they are "elected to public office" under the ADEA. Because we conclude that petitioners fall presumptively under the policymaking-level exception, we need not answer this question.

The extension of the ADEA to employment by state and local governments was a valid exercise of Congress' powers under the Commerce Clause. *EEOC v. Wyoming*, 460 U.S. 226, 75 L.Ed. 2d 18, 103 S.Ct. 1054 (1983). In *Wyoming*, we reserved the questions whether Congress might also have passed the ADEA extension pursuant to its powers under § 5 of the Fourteenth Amendment, and whether the extension would have been a valid exercise of that power. *Id.*, at 243, and n. 18. We noted, however, that the principles of federalism that constrain Congress' exercise of its Commerce Clause powers are attenuated when Congress acts pursuant to its powers to enforce the Civil War Amendments. *Id.*, at 243, and n. 18, citing *City of Rome v. United States*, 446 U.S. 156, 179, 64 L.Ed. 2d 119, 100 S.Ct. 1548 (1980). This is because those "Amendments were specifically designed as an expansion of federal power and an intrusion on state sovereignty." *Id.*, at 179. One might argue, therefore, that if Congress passed the ADEA extension under its § 5 powers, the concerns about federal intrusion into state government that compel the result in this case might carry less weight.

By its terms, the Fourteenth Amendment contemplates interference with state authority: "No State shall...deny to any person within its jurisdiction the equal protection of the laws." U.S. Const., Amdt. 14. But this Court has never held that the Amendment may be applied in complete disregard for a State's constitutional powers. Rather, the Court has recognized that the States' power to define the qualifications of their officeholders has force even as against the proscriptions of the Fourteenth Amendment.

We return to the political-function cases. In *Sugarman*, the Court noted that "aliens as a class are a prime example of a 'discrete and insular' minority (*see United States v. Carolene Products Co.*, 304 U.S. 144, 152-153, n. 4, 82 L.Ed. 1234, 58 S.Ct. 778 (1938)), and that classifications based on alienage are subject to close judicial scrutiny." 413 U.S. at 642, quoting *Graham v. Richardson*, 403 U.S. 365, 372, 29 L.Ed. 2d 534, 91 S.Ct. 1848 (1971). The *Sugarman* Court held that New York City had insufficient interest in preventing aliens from holding a broad category of public jobs to justify the blanket prohibition. 413 U.S. at 647. At the same time, the Court established the rule that scrutiny under the Equal Protection Clause "will not be so demanding where we deal with matters resting firmly within a State's constitutional prerogatives." *Id.*, at 648. Later cases have reaffirmed this practice. *See Foley v. Connelie*, 435 U.S. 291, 55 L.Ed. 2d 287, 98 S.Ct. 1067 (1978); *Ambach v. Norwick*, 441 U.S. 68, 60 L.Ed. 2d 49, 99 S.Ct. 1589 (1979); *Cabell v. Chavez-Salido*, 454 U.S. 432, 70 L.Ed. 2d 677, 102 S.Ct. 735 (1982). These cases demonstrate that the Fourteenth Amendment does not override all principles of federalism.

Of particular relevance here is *Pennhurst State School and Hospital v. Halderman*, 451 U.S. 1, 67 L.Ed. 2d 694, 101 S.Ct. 1531 (1981). The question in that case was whether Congress, in passing a section of the Developmentally Disabled Assistance and Bill of Rights Act, 42 U.S.C. § 6010 (1982 ed.), intended to place an obligation on the States to provide certain kinds of treatment to the disabled. Respondent Halderman argued that Congress passed § 6010 pursuant to § 5 of the Fourteenth Amendment, and therefore, that it was mandatory on the States, regardless of whether they received federal funds. Petitioner and the United States, as respondent, argued that, in passing § 6010, Congress acted pursuant to its spending power alone. Consequently, § 6010 applied only to States accepting federal funds under the Act.

The Court was required to consider the "appropriate test for determining when Congress intends to enforce" the guarantees of the Fourteenth Amendment. 451 U.S. at 16. We adopted a rule fully cognizant of the traditional power of the States: "Because such legislation imposes congressional policy on a State involuntarily, and because it often intrudes on traditional state authority, we should not quickly attribute to Congress an unstated intent to act under its authority to enforce the Fourteenth Amendment." *Ibid.* Because Congress nowhere stated its intent to impose mandatory obligations on the States under its § 5 powers, we concluded that Congress did not do so. *Ibid.*

The Pennhurst rule looks much like the plain statement rule we apply today. In *EEOC v. Wyoming,* the Court explained that Pennhurst established a rule of statutory construction to be applied where statutory intent is ambiguous. 460 U.S. at 244, n. 18. In light of the ADEA's clear exclusion of most important public officials, it is at least ambiguous whether Congress intended that appointed judges nonetheless be included. In the face of such ambiguity, we will not attribute to Congress an intent to intrude on state governmental functions regardless of whether Congress acted pursuant to its Commerce Clause powers or § 5 of the Fourteenth Amendment.

[The Equal Protection argument omitted.]

IV. The people of Missouri have established a qualification for those who would be their judges. It is their prerogative as citizens of a sovereign State to do so. Neither the ADEA nor the Equal Protection Clause prohibits the choice they have made. Accordingly, the judgment of the Court of Appeals is affirmed.

WALKER v. SECRETARY OF THE TREASURY
713 F.Supp. 403 (N.D. Ga. 1989)

FACTS

The plaintiff, Ms. Walker, was a permanent clerk typist in the Internal Revenue Service's Atlanta office. Ms. Walker is a light-skinned black person. Her supervisor was Ruby Lewis. Ms. Lewis is a dark-skinned black person. The employees in the office in which Ms. Walker and Ms. Lewis worked were predominantly black. In fact, following her termination, Ms. Walker was replaced by a black person. According to the record, the working relationship between Ms. Walker and Ms. Lewis was strained from the very beginning—that is, since approximately November 1985, Ms. Walker contends that Ms. Lewis singled her out for close scrutiny and reprimanded her for many things that were false or insubstantial. Ms. Walker's relationship with her former supervisor, Virginia Fite, was a cordial one. In fact, Ms. Walker received a favorable recommendation from Ms. Fite.

Ms. Walker met with Sidney Douglas, the EEO program manager for the Internal Revenue Service's Atlanta district, about the problems she was having with Ms. Lewis. Two weeks later, pursuant to Ms. Lewis's recommendation, Ms. Walker was terminated. The reasons given for her termination were: 1) tardiness to work; 2) laziness; 3) incompetence; and 4) attitude problems. It is Ms. Walker's belief that the reasons were fabricated and were the result of Ms. Lewis's personal hostility towards Ms. Walker because of Ms. Walker's light skin.

Ms. Walker has not presented any direct evidence that Ms. Lewis was prejudiced against light-colored blacks. There is evidence that Ms. Lewis might have harbored resentful feelings towards white people, and therefore by inference, possibly towards light-skinned black people. Ms. Walker maintains that she was treated unfairly before her termination for no apparent reason. She would have the court infer that the unfair treatment was due to Ms. Lewis's prejudice of her light skin color.

Following her termination, Ms. Walker filed this lawsuit *pro se* pursuant to Title VII of the Civil Rights Act of 1964, 42 U.S.C. § 2000e, *et seq.*; the Administrative Procedure Act (APA), 5 U.S.C. § 701, *et seq.;* and 42 U.S.C. § 1981 and § 1983. Walker alleges she was terminated because of invidious discrimination on the part of her supervisor Lewis, and that her termination constituted retaliation due to her complaining to the EEO. Due to the fact this is a Title VII action, the case was initially heard before a magistrate. The magistrate below recommended granting the defendant's summary judgment motion with respect to the claims under § 1981, § 1982, and the Administrative Procedure Act. The magistrate recommended granting the portion of the defendant's summary judgment motion that dealt with the Title VII invidious discrimination claim. The magistrate recommended denying the defendant's summary judgment motion with respect to the retaliation claim.

LEGAL DISCUSSION

A. The Title VII Discrimination Claim.

The principal issue in this case is a somewhat novel one: does a light-skinned black person have a cause of action pursuant to Title VII against a dark-skinned black person for an alleged discriminatory termination of employment? The defendant offers two reasons that there should be no such cause of action. First, the defendant contends that "although Title VII includes 'color' as one of the bases for prohibited discrimination, that term has generally been interpreted to mean the same thing as race" (Defendant's Memorandum in Support of Motion for Summary Judgment, p. 8). Second, the defendant contends that there simply is no cause of action pursuant to Title VII available to a light-skinned black person against a dark-skinned black person.

1) Discrimination on the basis of color.

Title VII is the exclusive remedy for federal employment discrimination lawsuits. *Brown v. GSA*, 425 U.S. 820, 96 S.Ct. 1961, 48 L. Ed. 2d 402 (1976); *Newbold v. United States Postal Service*, 614 F.2d 46 (5th Cir. 1980). The historical predecessor to Title VII is the Civil Rights Act of 1866 and, therefore, 42 U.S.C. § 1981. In fact, in a suit such as this one, the legal elements and facts necessary to support a claim for relief under Title VII are identical to the facts that support a claim under § 1981. *Lincoln v. Board of Regents*, 697 F.2d 28 (11th Cir. 1983); *Caldwell v. Martin Marietta Corporation*, 632 F.2d 1184, 1186 (5th Cir. 1980).

The stated purpose of § 1981 is the "protection of citizens of the United States in their enjoyment of certain rights without discrimination on account of race, color, or previous condition of servitude." *United States v. Cruikshank*, 92 U.S. 542, 555, 23 L.Ed. 588 (1875) (emphasis added). In *McDonald v. Santa Fe Trail Transportation Company*, 427 U.S. 273, 96 S.Ct. 2574, 49 L.Ed. 2d 493 (1976), the Supreme Court, in an exhaustive study of the legislative history of § 1981, makes repeated references to the fact that the statute was originally enacted to apply to citizens of "every race and color." 427 U.S. at 287 (emphasis added). In what is perhaps the most relevant case to this law suit, *Saint Francis College v. Al-Khazraji*, 481 U.S. 604, 107 S.Ct. 2022, 95 L.Ed. 2d 582 (1987), the Supreme Court stated in no uncertain terms that § 1981 "at a minimum reaches discrimination against an individual because he or she is genetically part of an ethnically and physiognomically distinctive subgrouping of Homo Sapiens." 107 S.Ct. at 2028 (emphasis added). In fact, the Supreme Court even goes further by stating that it is not even essential to be physiognomically distinctive. *See* 107 S.Ct. at 2028. *Webster's Seventh New Collegiate Dictionary* defines "physiognomic" as relating to physiognomy or "external aspect."

Title VII was amended in 1972 to provide generally that "all personnel actions affecting employees...shall be made free from any discrimination based on race, color, religion, sex or national origin." 42 U.S.C. § 2000e-16(a) (emphasis added). The Supreme Court has on at least two occasions stated that the purpose of Title VII is "to assure equality of employment opportunities by eliminating those practices and devices that discriminate on the basis of race, color, religion, sex, or national origin." *Alexander v. Gardner-Denver Company*, 415 U.S. 36, 44, 94 S.Ct. 1011, 1017, 39 L.Ed. 2d 147 (1974) (emphasis added); *McDonnell Douglas Corporation v. Green*, 411 U.S. 792, 93 S.Ct. 1817, 36 L.Ed. 2d 668 (1973).

It has always been the policy of the Supreme Court that the plain meaning of legislation should be conclusive, except in the rare cases in which literal application of a statute will produce results demonstrably at odds with the intention of its drafters. *U.S. v. Ron Pair Enterprises*, 489 U.S. 235, 109 S.Ct. 1026, 103 L.Ed. 2d 290 (1989). Yet the defendant in the instant case contends in its brief that in Title VII cases the word "color" has "generally been interpreted to mean the same thing as race." (Defendant's Memorandum in Support of Motion for Summary Judgment, p. 8). But the statutes and case law repeatedly and distinctly refer to race and color. This court is left with no choice but to conclude, when Congress and the Supreme Court refer to race and color in the same phrase that "race" is to mean "race," and "color" is to mean "color." To hold otherwise would mean that Congress and the Supreme Court have either mistakenly or purposefully overlooked an obvious redundancy. The Saint Francis case has definitively spoken on the subject: "we have little trouble in concluding that Congress intended to protect from discrimination identifiable classes of persons who are subjected to intentional discrimination solely because of their ancestry or ethnic characteristics. Such discrimination is racial discrimination that Congress intended § 1981 to forbid, whether or not it would be classified as racial in terms of modern scientific theory. The Court of Appeals was thus quite right in holding that § 1981 'at a minimum,' reaches discrimination against an individual 'because he or she is genetically part of an ethnically and physiognomically distinctive subgrouping of homo sapiens.' It is clear from our holding, however, that a distinctive physiognomy is not essential to qualify for § 1981 protection." 107 S.Ct. at 2028 (emphasis added) (citations omitted).

A person's color is closely tied to his ancestry and could result in his being perceived as a "physiognomically distinctive subgrouping of homo sapiens," which in turn could be the subject of discrimination. Notwithstanding that proposition, it is not even required that a victim of discrimination be of a distinctive physiognomical subgrouping, a particularly relevant fact to the case at hand.

The one case that defendant cites as authority for the proposition that the term "color" in Title VII generally means "race" is *Felix v. Marquez*, 24 Empl. Prac. Dec. (CCH) para. 31,279 (D.D.C. 1980), but that case lends itself to the opposite conclusion. As the court in *Felix* states: "color may be a rare claim, because color is usually mixed with or subordinated to claims of race discrimination, but considering the mixture of races and ancestral national origins in Puerto Rico, color may be the most practical claim to present." 24 Empl. Prac. Dec. (CCH) para. 31,279 (emphasis added). Discrimination against an individual because such individual comes from a racially mixed heritage possibly is of particular relevance to the instant case.

Another case that states specifically that discrimination as to color as opposed to race can be the gravamen of a civil rights lawsuit is *Vigil v. City & County of Denver*, 15 EPD para. 6937 (D.Co. 1977). As the court states in *Vigil:*

> The key factor in determining whether § 1981 should apply is whether a motivation for the discrimination was the victim's color. Plaintiff is a Mexican-American. Although skin color may vary significantly among those individuals who are considered Mexican-Americans, skin color may be a basis for discrimination against them. We note that skin color may vary significantly among individuals who are considered "blacks" or "whites"; both these groups are protected by § 1981, and § 1981 is properly asserted when discrimination on the basis of color is alleged...A particular act of discrimination against a Mexican-American may be motivated exclusively on the basis of the victim's national

origin, rather than the victim's color. It may also be true that in certain areas of the United States, Mexican-Americans are subject to discrimination on the basis of national origin, and not on the basis of color. However, we find that, at least in this area, Mexican-Americans are subject to color-based discrimination, and are within the coverage of § 1981. 15 Empl. Prac. Dec. (CCH) para. 8000 (emphasis added). *But see Waller v. International Harvester*, 578 F.Supp. 309 (D.C. Ill. 1984); *Brown v. EEOC*, Slip Op. No. 83 Civ. 2531 (S.D.N.Y. Oct. 11, 1984).

The few cases that might support the defendant's proposition are now obsolete in light of *Saint Francis College v. Al-Khazraji, supra*. In fact, at least one court has granted a rehearing because of *Saint Francis* and reversed its earlier decision. *Jatoi v. Hurst-Euless-Bedford Hospital Authority*, 819 F.2d 545 (5th Cir. 1987), cert. denied, 484 U.S. 1010, 108 S.Ct. 709, 98 L.Ed. 2d 660 (1988). Finally, in a case that predates *St. Francis*, the Supreme Court states that Title VII "was specifically designed to remove artificial, arbitrary, and unnecessary barriers to employment when the barriers operate invidiously to discriminate on the basis or racial or other impermissible classification." *Griggs v. Duke Power Co.*, 401 U.S. 424, 431, 91 S.Ct. 849, 28 L.Ed. 2d 158 (1971).

2)   A suit by a light-colored black person against a dark-colored black person.

The defendant also contends that it is simply not feasible or within the confines of § 1981 or Title VII to allow a lawsuit by a light-colored black person against a dark-colored black person. The court has already set out in detail above that in some situations the most practicable way to bring one's Title VII or § 1981 suit may be on the basis of color discrimination as opposed to race discrimination. To further illustrate why the instant action is appropriate under Title VII, it is once again necessary to refer to the *Saint Francis* case.

In *Saint Francis*, a United States citizen born in Iraq filed suit in federal district court against his former employer, alleging that the employer had discriminated against him on the basis of his Arabian ancestry. The district court granted summary judgment for the defendant on the ground that Arabs are Caucasians and that a suit could not be brought under § 1981 by a Caucasian against a Caucasian. The case eventually found its way to the Supreme Court. In its analysis, the Supreme Court carefully considered the legislative history of § 1981. The Court noted that Congress intended § 1981 to apply to all forms of discrimination, including acts of discrimination against groups including Finns, gypsies, Basques, Hebrews, Swedes, Norwegians, Germans, Greeks, Finns, Italians, Spanish, Mongolians, Russians, Hungarians, Chinese, Irish and French. *id.*, 107 S.Ct. at 2026-2028. It would take an ethnocentric and naive worldview to suggest that we can divide Caucasians into many subgroups but somehow all blacks are part of the same subgroup. There are sharp and distinctive contrasts amongst native black African peoples (sub-Saharan), both in color and in physical characteristics.

As mentioned above, the Supreme Court has said that "a distinctive physiognomy is not essential to qualify for § 1981 protection." *Saint Francis College, et al. v. Al-Khazraji*, 481 U.S. 604, 107 S.Ct. 2022, 2026, 95 L.Ed. 2d 582 (1987); *see also Jatoi v. Hurst-Euless-Bedford Hospital Authority*, 819 F.2d 545 (5th Cir. 1987). It therefore is not controlling that in the instant case a black person is suing a black person. In *Sere v. Board of Trustees University of Illinois, supra*, the Court noted that courts should not be placed in the "unsavory business of measuring skin color and determining whether the skin pigmentation of the parties is sufficiently different to form the basis of a lawsuit." 628 F.Supp. at 1546. This court recognizes full well that such difficulties are genuine and substantial. Nevertheless, the court must find that the issue is a question of fact that must be determined by the fact finder. This court holds, therefore, that the plaintiff in the instant case has stated a claim for relief that cannot be reached by summary judgment.

Thus, the court sets aside that portion of the magistrate's recommendation that grants defendant's motion for summary judgment as to plaintiff's Title VII discrimination claim.

This court sets aside that portion of the magistrate's recommendation that granted defendant's summary judgment motion with respect to plaintiff's Title VII discrimination claim.

SO ORDERED.

Glossary

affirmative action – policy prescribed by Title VII to remedy past discrimination

Age Discrimination in Employment Act (ADEA) of 1967 – federal statute prohibiting discrimination in the workplace based on age; covers people over the age of 40

***bona fide* occupational qualification (BFOQ)** – permissible employer defense to charges of discrimination under Title VII and the ADEA

Civil Rights Act of 1866 – federal statute providing equality in contract and property rights to persons of all races

Civil Rights Act of 1964 – federal statute prohibiting employment discrimination against employees in protected categories

employer – person who regularly employs a statutory minimum number of employees for a statutory minimum number of weeks in a given year

Equal Employment Opportunity Commission (EEOC) – federal agency empowered to implement Title VII

Executive Order 11246 – applies Title VII standards to persons with government contracts

national origin – country of a person's birthplace or ancestry

nationality – country to which a person owes allegiance

protected categories under Title VII: race, religion, color, national origin, and sex

protected categories under ADEA: age

religion – moral or ethical belief

sexual stereotyping – assuming particular characteristics to a particular gender

Title VII – federal statute prohibiting discrimination against protected categories; part of the Civil Rights Act

Exercises

1. Discuss why race is specified as the only category that can never be the basis of a *bona fide* occupational qualification.

2. Indicate five occupations not mentioned in this chapter in which it would be possible to argue for a BFOQ.

3. Discuss the factors that you would use to prove that a particular belief qualifies as a religion under Title VII.

4. Do you think that discrimination based on sexual orientation should be considered sex discrimination under Title VII? Why or why not?

5. Discuss the various methods of proving a claim of discrimination under Title VII or the ADEA.

Chapter Five

EMPLOYMENT LAW AND THE FAMILY

Chapter Overview

One of the most important consequences of the Social Security Act of 1935 and the Civil Rights Act of 1964 is the increasing awareness of the public and the government that there is a need for laws that protect the rights of employees with respect to family matters. In this regard, four important pieces of legislation have been enacted.

In 1974, Congress enacted the **Employee Retirement Income Security Act (ERISA)**[1]. ERISA is designed to protect the pension and benefit funds that employers maintain on behalf of their employees (and to which workers contribute) from being dissipated or reduced by the employers to the detriment of the employees.

ERISA establishes standards of care for pension fund managers and creates reporting requirements so that the employee and the employee's family will be afforded some financial protection for the worker's retirement years. ERISA also requires that all employees who work the statutory minimum number of hours must be included in the plan. This provision prohibits discrimination in favor of owners, managers, and other highly compensated employees.

The **Pregnancy Discrimination Act of 1978** expands on Title VII in granting specific rights to pregnant workers and expectant fathers, protecting them against job discrimination based on pregnancy. These rights were further expanded in 1993 in the **Family and Medical Leave Act (FMLA)**,[2] which provides workers with the right to nonpaid leave to handle family medical problems, including the birth and adoption of children. The employee who takes a leave is protected against job and benefit loss stemming from the leave.

Finally, although not federally recognized, many private employers and several municipalities have recognized what is known as "domestic partnership," whereby benefits that generally extend to employees' family members can be extended to members of an employee's nontraditional family.

This chapter will explore these legislative enactments and their impact on employees and their families.

The Employee Retirement Income Security Act of 1974

In response to growing concern over the dissipation of private pension funds, in 1974, Congress enacted the Employee Retirement Income Security Act, usually referred to as ERISA. This Act protects private pension funds in the same way that Social Security benefits are protected. ERISA

---

[1] 29 U.S.C. § 1001, *et seq.*
[2] 29 U.S.C. § 2601, *et seq.*

imposes certain fiduciary, reporting, and disclosure requirements on the managers of private pension funds. ERISA is enforced by both the Internal Revenue Service and the Department of Labor.

A **fiduciary** obligation means that a standard of care higher than that of ordinary care is imposed on the fund manager. Borrowing heavily from the Internal Revenue Code and the **Investment Advisors Act**, ERISA requires fund managers to exercise the care and diligence of a **reasonably prudent** investor. This standard means that the manager must maintain constant surveillance over the fund's investments and make sure that the investments are **diversified** (spread among various securities) to limit the potential risk of loss.

Before ERISA, fund managers were, more or less, left to their own discretion and expertise with respect to maintaining funds in appropriate securities. Now pension fund managers are federally accountable to employees for the results of their investment decisions.

> *Example: A pension fund manager believes that the stock of a particular corporation is greatly undervalued, and she invests 35 percent of the fund in that stock. Several months later, the stock price falls dramatically. Before ERISA, the pensioners lost out; after ERISA, the fund manager may now be personally liable for failing to meet the fiduciary standard by placing too large a percentage of the fund's money into one risky investment.*

ERISA also imposes reporting and disclosure requirements on the plan manager. The manager must make annual reports with respect to the status of the fund's investments and disbursements. In this manner, the government and the employees are able to keep an eye on the status of the fund assets. The reports also contain information regarding the number of participants as compared to the entire work force. This information enables the government to ensure that the plan does not discriminate by favoring higher paid employees.

> *Example: Some employees are questioning why the total value of their pension fund, which had been increasing at a steady rate, has now decreased. When the manager files his report, the report explains that a greater number of employees have retired than in the past; thus, the fund is now disbursing monies that had previously been used for reinvestment.*

To be covered by the provisions of ERISA, a retirement plan must meet the following requirements:

- The plan must be an **employee benefit plan**. An "employee benefit plan" is defined as one that provides welfare benefits, pension benefits, or a combination of both.

> *Example: An employer maintains a special fund to cover premiums for health and accident insurance for its employees, as well as for additional payments for sick leave and medical costs over those covered by the insurance. This plan is considered an employee benefit plan under ERISA because it provides employee welfare benefits.*

- The plan must be established or maintained by an employer or employee organization that represents employees. This requirement defines "employer" in the same fashion as Title VII and covers labor unions as well.

> **Example:** *A labor union desires to establish a fund to cover loss of wages and benefits its members may suffer if called upon to go on strike. This fund qualifies as an employee benefit fund under ERISA.*

- The employer who establishes and maintains the plan is engaged in commerce or any industry or activity that affects commerce. This requirement parrots the requirement found in Title VII (*see* Chapter Four).

Certain types of benefit plans are specifically exempted from ERISA's provisions. These exempt plans are:

- *Government plans*. Government plans, such as Social Security, are regulated by the statutes that create them, and therefore, Congress decided that additional safeguards were necessary to ensure their proper management.

- *Church plans*. Church plans were exempt because of the division between church and state inherent in the American constitutional system and the fact that religious organizations (because of their tax-exempt status) are subject to reporting and disclosure requirements under the Internal Revenue Code.

- *Plans established solely for workers' compensation*. Workers' compensation is governed by legislation that predates ERISA (*see* Chapter One).

- *Plans maintained outside the United States*. If the plan is maintained offshore, the United States government has little or no legal control over its operation.

- *Certain plans that are deemed to be exempt because they are established to provide benefits in excess of the limitations imposed by Section 415 of the Internal Revenue Code*. These are specific plans established and regulated by the Internal Revenue Service and are beyond the scope and purpose of this text.

Further, ERISA does not apply to plans maintained by **sole proprietorships** (businesses owned and managed by just one person) or **partnerships** (associations of two or more persons engaged in business for profit as co-owners). Additionally, ERISA does not apply to insured plans in which the policies are owned by the employer or the employer is the beneficiary.

> **Example:** *An employer maintains a fund to insure the lives of its employees. These insurance policies name the employer as the beneficiary. When an employee dies, the employer, not the employee's family, receives the insurance proceeds. Because the beneficiary of the plan is the employer, not the employee, the plan is not covered by ERISA.*

To meet ERISA requirements, an employee benefit plan must:

- be in writing and include a detailed statement of the procedures that are to be used to carry out its purposes, including who may participate in the plan;

- contain procedures to amend the plan if an amendment becomes necessary;

- state the basis on which payments are to be made, such as upon retirement, illness, injury, etc.;

- contain a *reasonable* procedure for presenting claims for benefits;

- state minimum age and service requirements necessary for an employee to be eligible for its benefits.

Note, however, that these plans have been held to be subject to the Age Discrimination in Employment Act discussed in the preceding chapter.

> **Example:** *A benefit plan states that to be eligible for retirement benefits the employee must be at least 55 and have been employed by the employer for at least 20 years. This provision is permissible under ERISA and the ADEA, and so the plan would be deemed valid.*

ERISA permits the plan to have **golden parachute** provisions. A golden parachute is an arrangement between an employer and an employee in which the employer agrees to provide certain benefits to an employee if there is a change in control of the company that forces out the employee. These provisions provide additional protection to employees and their families and are permitted under ERISA.

> **Example:** *Under a company's employee benefits plan, all senior managers (defined in the plan) who are forced out of the company because of a takeover are guaranteed a specified dollar amount for each year they have been employed by the company, plus a stated lump sum payment. This provision is a golden parachute and is permitted under ERISA.*

ERISA guarantees employees that the pension funds, to which they and their employers have contributed, will be well managed and preserved so that when needed, money will be available to provide the promised benefits to the employee and his or her family.

The Pregnancy Discrimination Act of 1978

The **Pregnancy Discrimination Act** of 1978 is a direct extension of Title VII's provisions prohibiting discrimination based on sex. This Act, which is also part of the Civil Rights Act,[3] provides that pregnant employees must be treated in the same manner as all other employees with

---

[3] 42 U.S.C. § 2000(e)(k)

respect to hiring, promotion, and firing. The Act also protects a man from being discriminated against because of his wife's pregnancy.

Pursuant to the statute, an employer who meets the definitional standards of Title VII must provide leave for the pregnancy-related needs of its employees and, if the employer maintains a health plan, the health plan must include coverage for pregnancy-related medical problems. The employer may require the employee to provide medical verification of the pregnancy and the medical reason for the necessity of the leave.

> *Example: Two employees become pregnant at the same time. At the beginning of her second trimester of pregnancy, one employee's physician mandates that the employee, to protect herself and her child, must stay in bed until delivery. She provides proof of the medical necessity of the bed rest, which entitles her to a pregnancy leave. The second employee, envious of the first employee's extended leave, requests leave for bed rest as well, but she cannot document any medical basis for the leave. In this instance, the employer does not have to grant the second employee extended leave.*

If an employee is discharged or denied promotion because she is either pregnant or requires a period of absence due to pregnancy, such discharge or denial of promotion is considered to be a violation of the Act. The employee may seek reinstatement, back pay, and repayment for lost benefits.

> *Example: An employee, who is due for promotion, learns that she is pregnant. She later requests leave under the Pregnancy Discrimination Act, which is granted. While she is away on maternity leave, she is passed over for promotion. If she can prove that the reason she was not promoted was that she took a pregnancy leave, she can present a claim against her employer.*

An employer may establish a **fetal protection policy** to prevent injury to fetuses, thereby avoiding the hiring or placing of pregnant or fertile women in areas of risk, but it is unlawful to use such a policy as a cover for discrimination against women. To be valid, these policies must be supported by medical evidence as to the risks to fetus, and it must be shown that such risks do not apply to men.

> *Example: A factory employer establishes a fetal protection policy for the assembly line, claiming that there is a risk of injury to pregnant woman, due to their extended bellies, which presents a danger to the fetus. This policy would not stand up to scrutiny under the Act because the same risks apply to overweight men and the alleged risk is occasioned by accident, not by the regular operation of the line.*

The Pregnancy Discrimination Act offers pregnant couples specific protections against discrimination beyond the protections of Title VII.

The Family and Medical Leave Act of 1993

The **Family and Medical Leave Act** of 1993 (FMLA) requires employers of 50 or more employees, as well as schools and government agencies, to provide employees up to 12 weeks of unpaid leave for birth, adoption, or the care of a severely ill family member. The Act helps employees meet the challenges of work and family in a society where almost all adult family members work. Also, be aware that many state statutes provide for leave under similar situations for employers with fewer than 50 employees.

During the period of the leave, the employee must be entitled to receive any health care benefits to which he or she would be entitled if actually at work, and the employee cannot be discriminated against in hiring, promotion, benefits, or firing because of taking the leave permitted under the statute. This Act is an extension of the rights currently granted under the Pregnancy Discrimination Act to cover other types of medical needs, including those of family members.

> *Example: An employee's father requires heart surgery and will need assistance for several months afterwards. Under the FMLA, if the worker is employed by a company with more than 50 employees, he is entitled to take up to 12 weeks of unpaid leave to assist his father during the period of his father's medical emergency. When the employee returns to work, he must be reinstated at his job and cannot be denied any benefits because of his extended period of absence.*

Domestic Partnership

Domestic partnership is defined as a relationship between two or more persons who live together in a manner similar to marriage but who are not married. To be considered domestic partners, the people must be able to demonstrate a close, committed personal relationship. The concept of domestic partnership covers both heterosexual and homosexual couples living together, without the benefit of marriage, and their children and other dependents.

Although there is no federal legislation covering the issue, several states, municipalities, and the District of Columbia have enacted domestic partnership legislation that extends employee benefits, normally available only to the employee's spouse and children, to employees' domestic partners. Additionally, some private employers have voluntarily extended domestic partnership benefits to their employees. This area of employment law and civil rights will continue to be the subject of much attention in the near future by legislatures, the media, the courts, and the public.

> *Example: For more than 10 years, a paralegal in a 200-person law firm in the District of Columbia has been living with a partner in a committed relationship. When his partner loses his job and, consequently, his health benefits, the paralegal names his partner as his formal "domestic partner" under the firm's policy so his partner can qualify for health benefits under his employer's domestic partnership policy. The partner will now receive the same health care benefits as those of any other dependant claimed by an employee of the firm.*

Chapter Summary

This chapter has briefly explored some of the laws enacted in the wake of the Social Security and Civil Rights Acts to protect employees and their families or domestic partners from discrimination. These laws guarantee the security of the employee's privately funded benefit plan and allow the employee leave from work to take care of family medical problems without fear of reprisal. By enacting these laws, Congress has acknowledged society's changing attitudes toward the needs of an employee with respect to the employee's familial concerns.

Edited Judicial Decisions

The two decisions presented below are intended to underscore some of the issues discussed in the body of this chapter. *Nicol v. Imagetrix, Inc.* concerns a husband's claim that he was discriminated against by his employer because of his wife's pregnancy. *Rovira v. AT&T* discusses discrimination based on sexual orientation and marital status under ERISA.

NICOL v. IMAGETRIX, INC.
773 F.Supp. 802 (E.D. Va. 1991)

This case presents the question whether a husband, who claims his employer discharged him because of his wife's pregnancy, has standing to sue under Title VII, 42 U.S.C. § 2000e et seq., as amended by the Pregnancy Discrimination Act (the "Act").

I.   Background

Mr. and Mrs. Nicol worked for Imagetrix, Inc., as vice presidents from approximately April 1988 until their termination in November 1989. On October 3, 1989, the results of a blood test confirmed Mrs. Nicol's suspicion that she was pregnant. She promptly advised Mr. Eggleston, the president of Imagetrix, of this fact. Six weeks later, on November 15,1989, Mr. Eggleston terminated Mrs. Nicol, citing declining sales in her department and a company cash flow problem. Later that same day, Mr. Eggleston discharged Mr. Nicol, citing the same cash flow problem. Mr. and Mrs. Nicol claim that Imagetrix, Inc. discharged them solely because of Mrs. Nicol's pregnancy.

On March 5, 1990, Mr. and Mrs. Nicol filed a discrimination complaint with the Equal Employment Opportunity Commission ("EEOC"). The EEOC issued a right to sue letter to Mr. and Mrs. Nicol with respect to Mr. Nicol's claim, in addition to other claims, on December 14, 1991. Mr. Nicol claims that he has standing to sue under Title VII, as amended by the Pregnancy Discrimination Act, because he was discriminated against based on his sex due to his wife's pregnancy. This matter is now before the Court on defendants' motion for partial summary judgment on the issue of Mr. Nicol's standing to sue.

II. Analysis

Analysis of the standing issue properly begins with the words of Title VII that define who can sue for discriminatory discharge. Section 2000e-2(a)(1) states:

It shall be an unlawful employment practice for an employer to fail or refuse to hire or to discharge any individual, or otherwise to discriminate against any individual with respect to his compensation, terms, conditions, or privileges of employment, because of such individual's race, color, religion, sex, or national origin. 42 U.S.C. § 2000e-2(a)(1).

Thus, Title VII, by its terms, confers standing to sue on persons who claim they were discharged because of their gender. Mr. Nicol fits this category. He claims his discharge was the result of discrimination because of his sex. More specifically, he argues that defendants terminated him for a reason that a female employee could never be terminated. A woman could never be terminated due to her employer's animus against a pregnant spouse because her spouse could not be pregnant. Therefore, defendants allegedly treated Mr. Nicol, a male employee, "in a manner which but for (his) sex would be different," *Los Angeles Dept. of Water & Power v. Manhart*, 435 U.S. 702, 55 L.Ed. 2d 657, 98 S.Ct. 1370 (1978). This alleged difference in treatment affords Mr. Nicol standing under Title VII. Whether Mr. Nicol can prove at trial that defendants were prejudiced against pregnant women and fired him because he was married to a pregnant woman is another matter.

Defendants' argument focuses not on Title VII's basic language, but on the expansion of that language as a result of the Pregnancy Discrimination Act. In that Act, Congress expanded the meaning of the term "sex" to include pregnancy. The Act states in pertinent part "The terms 'because of sex' or 'on the basis of sex' include, but are not limited to, because of or on the basis of pregnancy, childbirth, or related medical conditions." 42 U.S.C. § 2000e(k). Distilled to its essence, defendants' argument is that Mr. Nicol has no standing to sue for discriminatory discharge because he is not the pregnant employee. Put another way, defendants claim that the Act limits standing to a person discriminated against on the basis of such person's pregnancy, childbirth, or related medical conditions. This argument founders on the statutory language itself. The first clause of the Act plainly states: "The terms 'because of sex' or 'on the basis of sex' include, but are not limited to on the basis of pregnancy, childbirth, or related medical conditions" (§ 2000e(k)). Although this Act expands Title VII's scope of prohibited discriminatory conduct to include an employee's pregnancy, the words "but are not limited to" in the Act indicate that the original prohibition in Title VII against discrimination on the basis of an employee's own sex still exists. *See Newport News Shipbuilding and Dry Dock Co. v. EEOC*, 462 U.S. 669, 684 L.Ed. 2d 89, 103 S.Ct. 2622 (1983) ("By making clear that an employer could not discriminate on the basis of an employee's pregnancy, Congress did not erase the original prohibition against discrimination on the basis of an employee's sex."). Therefore, under the terms of the Act itself, Mr. Nicol need not be the pregnant employee to have standing.

Defendants also point to the legislative history of the Pregnancy Discrimination Act, much of which indicates that the main purpose of the Act was to protect working women against all forms of employment discrimination based on sex. This alone, however, is not a basis on which defendants can argue that only pregnant, female employees have standing to sue under the Act. Congress may have focused on female employees when passing the Pregnancy Discrimination Act, but this emphasis "does not create a 'negative inference' limiting the scope of the (Pregnancy Discrimination) Act to the specific problem that motivate its enactment." *Id.* at 679. Furthermore, "proponents of the (Pregnancy Discrimination Act) stressed throughout the debates that Congress had always intended to protect all individuals from sex discrimination in employment—including, but not limited to, pregnant women workers." *Id.* at 680. Therefore, the legislative history points to no limitation in the Act that would preclude Mr. Nicol's standing.

Though not directly on point, *Newport News* squarely supports the result reached here. There, the Supreme Court held that an employer's health insurance plan providing female employees with pregnancy related benefits, but not providing the same benefits to the spouses of male employees, discriminated against the male employees in violation of Title VII, § 2000e(k), 462 U.S. at 684. In reaching this result, the Court explicitly recognized that male employees could recover under § 2000e(k) even though they could not become pregnant themselves. *Id.* at 682–685. The Court reasoned that "the meaning of the first clause (of the Pregnancy Discrimination Act) is not limited by the specific language in the second clause, which explains the application of the general principle to women employees." *Id.* at 679.

Newport News, therefore, establishes that Title VII's prohibitions cover discrimination against pregnant spouses. As Justice Stevens explained, discrimination against pregnant spouses is in essence discrimination against male employees because the sex of the spouse and the sex of the employee are always opposite. *Id.* at 684. Thus, even though Mr. Nicol is not a pregnant employee, he has standing to sue under Title VII because he was allegedly discharged and discriminated against on the basis of his own sex.

Also instructive here are the Title VII interracial relationship cases; Mr. Nicol's claim is analogous to claims of discrimination based on interracial relationships and courts have consistently and sensibly recognized that discrimination on the basis of interracial marriage or association and discrimination on the basis of race are one and the same. *See Parr v. Woodmen of the World Life Ins. Co.*, 791 F.2d 888, 892 (11th Cir. 1986) ("Where a plaintiff claims discrimination based upon an interracial marriage or association, he alleges, by definition, that he has been discriminated against because of his race."); *Reiter v. Center Consol. School Dist. No. 26-JT*, 618 F.Supp. 1458, 1460 (D. Colo. 1985) (same); *Greshem v. Waffle House, Inc.*, 586 F.Supp. 1442, 1445 (N.D. Ga. 1984) (same); *Whitney v. Greater New York Corp. of Seventh Day Adventists*, 401 F.Supp. 1363, 1366 (S.D.N.Y. 1975) (same). In other words, a white employee who is discharged because his spouse is black is discriminated against on the basis of his race, even though the root animus for the discrimination is an anti-black prejudice. Similarly, the root animus here may be an anti-pregnancy prejudice, but the resulting discrimination is against Mr. Nicol's gender, for only males can have pregnant spouses.

Parr illustrates well the relevance of the interracial relationship cases. There, a white male job applicant alleged that he had been denied employment by the defendants because of his marriage to a black woman. The Eleventh Circuit held that the plaintiff had been discriminated against because of his race. The Court found that the plaintiff had stated a claim as a white man who had been discriminated against because of his own race and the racial prejudice against white men who are married to black women. The root animus is, of course, an anti-black prejudice. This analogous to Mr. Nicol's situation. Mr. Nicol has stated a claim as a married man who has allegedly been discriminated against because of his own sex and the prejudices of the defendants against men who are married to pregnant women. Thus, just as the plaintiff in *Parr* was discriminated against because of his race, Mr. Nicol had been discriminated against because of his sex.

Defendants contend that Mr. Nicol is asserting third-party standing on the basis of his wife's pregnancy and that such derivative standing is not contemplated under Title VII. This Court agrees; third party standing is not adequate for a prima facie Title VII claim. But this argument misses the point, for Mr. Nicol is asserting standing on the basis of his own sex. Thus, in recognizing Mr. Nicol's standing, this Court has not opened the door to other derivative suits under the Pregnancy Discrimination Act. For example, a discharged employee who is also a parent could not state a prima facie Title VII claim under the Act based on his or her daughter's pregnancy, because the status of a parent is not gender-based. Parents are both male and female. Thus, discharge because of a daughter's pregnancy would not be discrimination against the employee based on his or her sex. The result would be the same for a sibling or a neighbor. The status of husband, however, is distinctly gender-based. Therefore, Mr. Nicol was discriminated against on the basis of his sex if defendants indeed discharged him due to his wife's pregnancy.

For the reasons stated above, Mr. Nicol has standing to sue under Title VII, as amended by the Pregnancy Discrimination Act. Thus, the Court DENIES defendants' motion for a partial summary judgment on the issue of Mr. Nicol's standing.

An appropriate order will be entered.

ROVIRA v. AT&T
760 F.Supp. 376 (S.D.N.Y. 1991)

BACKGROUND

Plaintiff Sandra Rovira ("Rovira") was the gay life partner of Marjorie Ferlini, who died of cancer in 1988. Plaintiffs Frank and Alfred Morales are Rovira's children from a prior marriage and are alleged to have lived with Rovira and Ferlini for 10 of the 12 years the two women lived together. At the time of Ferlini's death, they were, respectively, 22 and 19 years of age. Ferlini was an AT&T sales manager, covered under AT&T's Management Pension Plan, which provides for a sickness death benefit to the qualified beneficiaries of eligible employees. The complaint states that each of the plaintiffs was "one of Ferlini's beneficiaries under the AT&T Management Pension Plan," and seeks sickness death benefits on that basis. Complaint, paras. 4–6.

After Ferlini's death on September 19, 1988, Rovira inquired about and applied for benefits, alleging that she and her children stood in the position of spouse and dependent children of Ferlini. AT&T's benefits department denied the claim orally, and plaintiffs appealed the denial to the AT&T benefit committee. The benefit committee affirmed the denial of plaintiffs' claim by letter of July 26, 1989. Rovira further appealed the denial of benefits to the AT&T employees' benefits committee, which by letter of January 17, 1990, denied the claim, allegedly stating that Rovira did not qualify as a plan beneficiary because her relationship with Ferlini did not constitute a valid marriage under New York law, and Frank and Alfred Morales did not qualify because they were not the natural or adopted children of Ferlini or her legal spouse. Plaintiffs also allege that the same letter stated that AT&T benefits were "administered uniformly to all employees without discrimination on the basis of age, race, color, religion, mental or physical handicap, national origin, sex, sexual preference, or orientation." Complaint, para. 36. The complaint includes allegations of hostile, offensive, and degrading treatment Rovira received at the hands of AT&T's benefits department employees when she inquired about any benefits for herself and her children as Ferlini's family, and the refusal of the benefits department employees to respond to her requests for information, in spite of her telling them she was also the executor of Ferlini's estate.

DISCUSSION

On a Rule 12 motion, the pleadings must be read liberally, and the court "must accept all of the plaintiffs' allegations as true and draw all inferences in their favor." *In re United States Catholic Conference*, 885 F 2d 1020 (2d Cir. 1989), cert. denied, 495 U.S. 918, 109

L.Ed. 2d 309, 110 S.Ct. 1946 (1990). *See also, Lujan v. National Wildlife Federation*, 497 U.S. 871, 111 L.Ed. 2d 695, 110 S.Ct. 3177, 3188–89 (1990). In deciding whether a plaintiff has standing to sue, a court must determine whether the pleadings sufficiently allege that the plaintiff has suffered or will suffer the type of actual injury which can be fairly traced to the challenged action and may be redressed by a court decision, and that the plaintiff's claims "fall within 'the zone of interests to be protected or regulated by the statute or constitutional guarantee in question.'" *Valley Forge Christian College v. Americans United for Separation of Church and State*, 454 U.S. 464, 70 L.Ed. 2d 700, 102 S.Ct. 752 (1982) (quoting *Ass'n of Data Processing Service Organizations v. Camp*, 397 U.S. 150, 25 L.Ed. 2d 184, 90 S.Ct. 827 (1970).

Count IV claims a violation of the New York City Human Rights Law, in that AT&T is alleged to have discriminated against Rovira on the basis of sexual orientation, in its employees' treatment of her when she, as executor of Ferlini's estate, made application on behalf of the beneficiaries. New York City Administrative Code, Chap. 1, § 108.1 (1986) ("New York City Human Rights Law"). Count V claims a violation of the New York State Executive Law because in that same context it is alleged that AT&T employees discriminated against Rovira on the basis of marital status. N.Y. Exec. L. § 296(1)(a)("New York State Human Rights Law"). Count VI claims breach of contract based on AT&T's contractual promise to apply AT&T's overall equal opportunity policy when providing sickness death benefits to all eligible employees, without discrimination as to marital status or sexual orientation. AT&T claims that Counts IV, V, and VI arise from the administration and denial of employee benefits and so are preempted by ERISA, and that plaintiffs lack standing under the above statutes and under the common law for breach of contract. At the outset, the Court notes that Counts IV, V, and VI are asserted only on behalf of plaintiff Rovira and so it is as to her alone that the questions of standing and preemption are at issue here. Complaint, paras. 77–79, paras. 81–83, paras. 86–87.

I.   ERISA Preemption

Plaintiffs assert their claims under Counts IV, V, and VI are distinguished from their ERISA claims in accordance with the holding in *Aetna Life Insurance Co. v. Borges*, 869 F.2d 142 (2d Cir. 1989), cert. denied, 493 U.S. 811, 110 S.Ct. 57, 107 L.Ed. 2d 25 (1989). *Aetna v. Borges* involved a claim of preemption of Connecticut's escheat laws by ERISA, in a proceeding by the state to take control over uncollected drafts for ERISA benefits held by *Aetna*. The Second Circuit held that while ERISA's preemption provision is deliberately very broad, it was not meant to preempt every state law having any impact on employee benefit plans and will not be held to preempt statutes whose effect on pension plans is "tangential and remote." 869 F.2d at 145. The Second Circuit held, in general, that laws that have been ruled preempted by ERISA are those that "provide an alternative cause of action to employees to collect benefits protected by ERISA, refer specifically to ERISA plans, and apply solely to them, or interfere with the calculation of benefits owed to an employee." 869 F.2d at 146. While anti-discrimination statutes are "laws of general application" and constitute "traditional exercises of state power or regulatory authority," *Id.*, their effect on ERISA plans is not incidental if they are asserted to determine whether benefits are paid or who is a beneficiary. 869 F.2d at 147. *See also, Shaw v. Delta Air Lines, Inc.*, 463 U.S. 85, 77 L.Ed. 2d 490, 103 S.Ct. 2890 (1983).

Plaintiffs acknowledge that their claims under Counts IV, V, and VI for benefits under an ERISA plan would be preempted by ERISA and state these counts are claims for emotional distress caused by the hostile and degrading treatment of Rovira by AT&T employees due to her sexual orientation or marital status. Accordingly, the remainder of the opinion will address those claims as so delineated.

AT&T argues that ERISA preempts Rovira's claims for emotional distress because the acts giving rise to the claims occurred during the processing or administration of benefits. Such a wide-ranging interpretation of ERISA preemption is not totally persuasive. While the Fourth Circuit has held that "state laws, insofar as they are invoked by beneficiaries claiming relief for injuries arising out of the administration of employee benefit plans, 'relate to' such plans and, absent an applicable exemption, are preempted by ERISA," *Powell v. Chesapeake and Potomac Telephone Co.*, 780 F.2d 417, 421 (4th Cir. 1985), cert denied, 476 U.S. 1170, 90 L.Ed. 2d 980, 106 S.Ct. 2892 (1986), finding a preemption in the present case would constitute a broader ruling. The plaintiff in *Powell* claimed intentional infliction for emotional distress in the mishandling of an ongoing, established beneficiary relationship with her employer's benefits department, in connection with her disability and claims thereunder. In *Pilto Life Insurance v. Dedeaux*, 481 U.S. 41, 95 L.Ed. 2d 39, 107 S.Ct. 1549 (1987), the Supreme Court held that state common law causes of action by an employee asserting improper processing of a claim for benefits under an employee benefit plan were preempted by ERISA. Similarly, in *Metropolitan Life Insurance Co. v. Taylor*, 481 U.S. 58, 95 L.Ed. 2d 55, 107 S.Ct. 1542 (1987), the Supreme Court held that a former employee's state law breach of contract and tort claims for intentional infliction of mental anguish and for wrongful termination of disability benefits were preempted by ERISA and thus removable to federal court.

Here, plaintiff claims she was treated impermissibly before she had any established beneficiary relationship with AT&T or its benefits department. AT&T is alleged to have ignored Ferlini's survivors and refused to give Rovira the attention, help, or information she needed even to request such a relationship, contrary to its usual practice when an employee dies. This conduct may not constitute administration of an employee benefit plan such that it is covered by ERISA. The Supreme Court noted in *Shaw*, *supra*, with specific reference to the New York State Human Rights Law, that "§ 514(a) preempts state laws only insofar as they relate to plans covered by ERISA. The Human Rights Law, for example, would be unaffected insofar as it prohibits employment discrimination in hiring, promotion, salary, and the like." 463 U.S. at 99. The Ninth Circuit held in *Lane v. Goren*, 743 F.2d 1337 (9th Cir. 1984), that a state anti-discrimination charge was not preempted by ERISA when the defendant was sued in its sole role as an employer and not in its role as an ERISA trustee. 743 F.2d at 1340. In the present case, the claims for emotional distress are alleged against AT&T and its benefits department not in its role as an ERISA administrator, but as an employer dealing with an employee's survivor or as a corporation interacting with the public. Accordingly, these claims, as limited by plaintiff's own characterization, may not be preempted by ERISA. Therefore, without determining the ERISA preemption issue, the Court will examine whether it would be appropriate to exercise pendent jurisdiction.

[Pendent jurisdiction argument omitted.]

The Breach of Contract Claim (Count VI).

Count VI claims that Rovira is a third-party beneficiary of the employment contract between AT&T and Ferlini and that part of the contract was a promise not to discriminate on the basis of marital status or sexual orientation, under the AT&T equal employment opportunity policy. The conduct alleged to have violated that promise is not the denial of benefits itself but by the treatment given by the benefits department employees to Rovira when she made inquiries. In essence, plaintiffs argue that due to the equal employment opportunity policy, an employee has an agreement with AT&T for non-discrimination treatment of her family or "significant others." Nothing cited by plaintiffs in their pleadings as constituting AT&T's equal opportunity policy indicates that the policy is intended to apply to any person other than the employee herself. *See, e.g.*, Complaint, para. 22. No state law precedent clearly supports such a claim.

Because Counts IV, V, and VI, as restricted by plaintiffs, may not be preempted by ERISA, and because retaining these counts would put this Court in the position of interpreting an uncharted area of state and local law as well as state common law, the Court declines to exercise pendent jurisdiction over Counts IV, V, and VI. "Needless decisions of state law should be avoided both as a matter of comity and to promote justice between the parties, by procuring for them a surer footed reading of applicable law." *United Mine Workers of America v. Gibbs*, 383 U.S. 715, 726, 16 L.Ed. 2d 218, 86 S.Ct. 1130 (1966).

CONCLUSION

Accordingly, Counts IV, V, and VI are dismissed without prejudice to their being brought in state court. Counsel are directed to appear for a conference on April 16, 1991, at 9 a.m. in Courtroom 302 at the United States Courthouse, Foley Square, New York, New York.

IT IS SO ORDERED.

Glossary

diversified investments – assets placed in various securities to minimize the risk of loss

domestic partnership – people living in a close committed relationship without the benefit of marriage

employee benefit plan – qualifying plan under ERISA

Employee Retirement Income Security Act of 1974 (ERISA) – federal statute designed to provide protection for employee benefit funds

Family and Medical Leave Act of 1993 (FMLA) – federal statute providing leave for employees to take care of family medical emergencies

fetal protection policy – employer policy designed to protect fetuses from harm, allowing them to avoid hiring or placing pregnant women in areas where there may be danger for fetuses

fiduciary – person held to a standard of care higher than ordinary care

golden parachute – special provision to protect an employee who may be terminated because of a change in the company's control or ownership

partnership – an association of two or more persons engaged in business for profit as co-owners

Pregnancy Discrimination Act of 1978 – federal statute extending protection of Title VII to pregnant women and their husbands

sole proprietorship – business owned and managed by just one person

Exercises

1. Check your state's statutes for any provisions covering domestic partnerships.

2. Discuss the reasons why ERISA's provisions are beneficial for employers as well as employees.

3. Golden parachute provisions are usually reserved only for upper-echelon employees. Discuss why you feel this is fair or unfair to other employees.

4. Some family medical emergencies require more time than that allowed under the FMLA. To what extent do you feel the FMLA should be amended to take into consideration extreme medical situations? Also, should persons not considered part of the "traditional family" be covered by the FMLA? Why or why not?

Chapter Six

**PROTECTING WORKERS WITH DISABILITIES:
THE AMERICANS WITH DISABILITIES ACT**

Chapter Overview

Historically, one of the primary functions of a government has been to protect the health and welfare of its citizens. The **Occupational Safety and Health Act (OSHA)** was enacted by Congress to protect employees from hazardous conditions in the workplace. Under OSHA, the government inspects workplaces and investigates complaints of physical problems, including noxious fumes, hazardous facilities, faulty machinery, etc., that could injure employees.

A natural outgrowth of the government's concern for the welfare of its citizens is the protection of disabled workers from discrimination in employment. In 1973, the **Rehabilitation Act**[1] was passed to protect persons who suffer from certain handicaps from being fired or discriminated against in the workplace. However, the Rehabilitation Act covered only government employees, recipients of federal financial incentives, and employers who had federal government contracts. These protections were finally extended to cover the broad spectrum of employees in 1990 with the passage of the **Americans with Disabilities Act (ADA)**,[2] which grants physically and mentally disabled workers the same protection against job discrimination given to the protected categories under Title VII.

The ADA prohibits an employer from discriminating against persons with disabilities with respect to "job application procedures, hiring, advancement or discharge of employees, employee compensations, and other terms and conditions and privileges of employment." However, several problems have arisen with respect to the interpretation and implementation of the ADA.

The ADA does not provide a specific definition of the term "disability" because it is intended to encompass a wide variety of physical and mental problems. This broad approach has resulted in various questions about whether or not a particular problem is a "disability" under the Act. While a broad definition may afford the employee with a problem some protection against discrimination, in many instances it also raises the question whether the problem is beyond the intended scope of the statute.

The Americans with Disabilities Act requires employers to make "reasonable accommodation" for employees who are covered by the ADA. However, what is "reasonable" is not specifically defined by the statute, and many lawsuits have resulted from a difference of opinion as to the extent of accommodation the employer must make.

An employer may limit the amount of its "accommodation" if it can demonstrate that the accommodation would create an undue hardship on the business. To prove undue hardship,

---

[1] 29 U.S.C. § 791
[2] 42 U.S.C. § 12100, *et seq.*

employers are required to provide detailed financial records to substantiate the degree of economic hardship the accommodation would cause.

In addition to the foregoing, many workers have instituted frivolous lawsuits against their employers under the color of the ADA merely to force some financial settlement. In many instances, it is less expensive for an employer to settle than to litigate the matter.

This chapter will focus on the ADA and the government's attempt to balance the legitimate needs of disabled workers against the financial resources of employers.

Background of the Americans with Disabilities Act

The ADA prohibits both public and private employers from discriminating against persons with physical or mental disabilities. Under the Act, an employer must make **reasonable accommodation** for its disabled workers to ensure that the worker can perform his or her job. The ADA applies to workers in the United States regardless of the employer's domicile. The ADA also applies to United States citizens who are working abroad for American employers.

The purpose behind the ADA is to provide disabled Americans with the dignity and economic benefit of gainful employment. Work fosters self-confidence in the worker and also increases tax revenue from income the worker would earn. At the same time, it reduces tax expenditures that provide financial assistance to persons who are capable of performing work but who need some additional assistance to function in the workplace.

> *Example: A paraplegic worker was unable to get a job because she could not travel on public transportation with her wheelchair, nor could she enter buildings because of stairs and narrow doorways. To survive, the woman was on public assistance. After the passage of the ADA, public transportation became available to her, because the public transportation vehicles were redesigned to accommodate wheelchairs, and employers were required to provide ramps and broaden doorways. The woman was now able to get a job, went off public assistance, and became a taxpayer with her earned income.*

The ADA prohibits discrimination in four main areas:

- employment
- public services and transportation
- public accommodations
- telecommunication services.

The ADA also applies to job application procedures, the hiring process, job training, compensation, benefits, and all other conditions and privileges of employment.

> *Example: An employer agrees to hire a worker who does not have the use of his hands. To accommodate the employee, the employer agrees to purchase and modify equipment, such as computer terminals, telephones, file cabinets, and so forth. However, because of the cost factor in making these changes, the employer only agrees to pay the worker a salary equal to 80% of the salary nondisabled workers receive for performing the same functions. This is prohibited under the ADA. The worker must be paid the same salary as all other workers performing identical work for the same employer.*

The Act also protects employees from being discriminated against because of their relationship with a disabled person.

> *Example: An employee has a disabled child and must prepare that child every weekday to be picked up by the bus to a special school. The bus does not arrive until 9:30 a.m., so the employee cannot arrive at work until ten a.m. The employee is willing to work after five p.m. and to take shorter lunch breaks to make up the time, but the employer refuses, even though the office is usually open until seven p.m., and there is no particular work necessity that the employee be at work by nine a.m. This is prohibited under the ADA. The employee is being discriminated against because of the care required by the disabled child.*

Similarly to Title VII, the ADA applies to any employer in any industry affecting commerce who has 15 or more employees, as well as labor organizations, employment agencies and joint labor-management committees. The determination as to whether the employer has the requisite number of employees is made in the same manner as under Title VII, meaning that the employer has the minimum number of employees in each of 20 or more calendar weeks in the current or preceding calendar year. A workweek is any five out of seven consecutive days.

> *Example: An employer is involved in an industry that has seasonal work. Three times a year it is very busy, and the rest of the year, work is very slow. During the busy season, which amounts to periods of eight weeks each, the employer hires an additional 20 workers on a temporary basis to complement its regular staff of 12. This employer comes within the ADA, because for 24 weeks each year it employs more than 15 workers.*

Person with a Disability

To qualify for protection against employment discrimination under the ADA, an employee must meet two standards:

1. **Qualified**. The person must be able to perform the essential functions of the job. If the person, because of the disability, education, background, experience, or general ability, is incapable of performing the basic job functions, he or she is not protected under the Act.

> *Example:* A disabled person applies for a job as a paralegal at a law firm. The law firm requires its legal assistants to have at least two years of college education and a certificate from an accredited paralegal institution. The applicant has only a high school diploma and work experience as a receptionist. This person is not protected by the ADA for this particular job, because she lacks the requisite background for the position.

2. **Disabled**. The person must have a "physical or mental impairment that substantially limits one or more major life activities." This language is the ADA's definition of **disability**. Additionally, the person must have a substantiated record of the impairment and generally be regarded as having the impairment. This is a three-pronged test, and all three elements must be satisfied for the individual to be considered disabled.

> *Example:* A job applicant is legally blind and has been so since birth. The blindness is well documented by medical and school records. The applicant has graduated from college with a degree in the area of the job opening and can perform all of the job tasks if he has a reader or documents are written in Braille. This person would be considered disabled under the ADA.

> *Example:* An employee claims that he is being fired from his job because he suffers from a disability. He claims to have Chronic Fatigue Syndrome, which makes him unusually tired and reduces his physical abilities by more than 10 percent. He has never been diagnosed, nor is he willing to see a physician. His work performance has been far below that of other employees performing similar functions. In this instance the employee would not be considered disabled or entitled to protection under the ADA.

Physical impairment is defined by the ADA as a physical disease or condition, cosmetic disfigurement, or anatomical loss.

> *Example:* An employee is diagnosed as having diabetes requiring regular insulin injections and a special diet. This person is considered to have a physical impairment under the ADA.

Mental impairment is defined by the ADA as any mental or psychological disorder, including various learning disabilities such as dyslexia.

> *Example:* A person is diagnosed as a manic-depressive, which makes it difficult for him to accept constructive criticism or comments. This person would be considered mentally impaired under the ADA.

These impairments, either physical or mental, must limit one or more *significant* life activities, but do not include impairments that are temporary in nature; the disability must be permanent. Significant life activities include

- caring for oneself
- performing manual skills

- walking
- seeing
- breathing
- learning.

> *Example: An employee suffers from an unusually quick temper and constantly lashes out at fellow workers. Because of the disruption the employee's temper causes, the employer wishes to fire him, but the employee claims to be impaired under the ADA. A personal characteristic or common personality trait such as a quick temper is not considered to be a disability under the ADA.*

> *Example: An employee injures herself in a skiing accident, breaking both her legs. She is demanding that her employer reorganize the office to accommodate her disability. The employee does not come within the purview of the ADA; her disability is temporary and her employer is not required to accommodate her.*

One of the most important implications of the ADA is that it covers not only people who are in fact disabled, but also extends its protection to persons who are *regarded* **as disabled** even though they suffer no disability.

> *Example: An employee is openly gay, and his fellow workers refuse to have any contact with him because they believe that he must be infected with the AIDS virus. The employer wants to fire him, but he is protected from discrimination under the ADA. Even though the employee is healthy, he is being discriminated against because he is regarded as having a physical impairment.*

Always remember that the primary requirement for protection under the ADA is that the employee be qualified for the job. Even disabled workers may be fired for incompetence.

> *Example: An accounting firm hires a paraplegic accountant and acquires all of the special equipment he needs to perform his job. Despite these accommodations, the accountant is sloppy and inaccurate, and his work constantly has to be redone. The accounting firm would be justified in firing this employee. His inability to perform the job has nothing to do with his disabilities; he is incompetent.*

Reasonable Accommodation

If an employee qualifies as disabled under the ADA, the employer is required to make **reasonable accommodation** to assist the employee in performing his or her job function. Section 12111(a)(b) of the ADA provides certain examples of reasonable accommodation:

- making employment facilities readily accessible to disabled workers
- restructuring a job

- providing part-time or modified work schedules
- providing modified equipment or devices
- reassigning an employee
- providing qualified readers or interpreters
- other similar accommodations.

In this context, an employer is prohibited from using bogus qualification standards, employment tests, or other selection criteria designed to eliminate disabled job applicants.

Example: *A law firm tells an applicant for a paralegal position that to qualify for the job the applicant must be able to cover 50 yards carrying ten law books in under one minute, because the firm's lawyers require speedy retrieval of materials from their assistants. The applicant has two amputated legs and cannot possibly perform the task. The task is not really job-related but is being used to discourage disabled persons from applying for the job. This job function standard is prohibited under the ADA.*

Example: *A law firm requires that its new associates pass the bar exam within 15 months of being hired, or they will be discharged. An associate is clinically deaf and has been unable to pass the bar exam within the 15-month period. When the firm fires the associate, he has no recourse under the ADA, because the job requirement is legitimately related to the job function, not to any disability.*

To determine whether a person is considered qualified for the position, the employer may use standards such as education, background, or experience, as well as tests to determine that the person can perform the essential functions of the job. These are known as **job-related qualification standards** and are permissible under the ADA.

Example: *An employer is looking for a computer operator. The employer has a job requirement that the operator be able to input 120 words per minute. A person who has lost the use of his hand applies for the job but is unable to input more than 25 words per minute. To input at even the 25-word-per-minute rate, he must use specially designed equipment. Although this man is disabled under the Act, establishing a minimum speed for inputting data is a legitimate, job-related qualification standard, and the employer is not required to hire this applicant.*

Once the employee has been deemed qualified to perform the essential job function, the ADA requires that the employer make reasonable accommodation to assist the disabled worker to perform the job functions. These accommodations *must* be made if they do not create an undue hardship on the employer. These accommodations can include:

- Changing the physical facilities to accommodate the needs of the worker.

> **Example:** *An employee who must use a wheelchair cannot fit through many of the employer's doorways. A reasonable accommodation would be to enlarge the doorways that currently create a barrier for the employee.*

- Restructuring the job to accommodate the worker's disability.

> **Example:** *One of the functions of a disabled employee is to deliver documents at various times throughout the workplace. This is an incidental job function. The employee has phlebitis in her legs and cannot walk great distances without rest periods. The employer could have another worker make the deliveries.*

- Providing qualified readers and interpreters for persons whose disabilities limit their reading abilities, such as blind or dyslexic employees.

- Modifying a work schedule to accommodate the employee's disability.

> **Example:** *In the example discussed earlier concerning the employee with a disabled child who could not arrive at work until ten a.m., a reasonable accommodation might be to restructure the employee's work schedule to different hours to accommodate the needs of the disabled child.*

- Modifying equipment to assist the disabled employee.

> **Example:** *An employee is in a wheelchair and cannot reach the upper shelves of bookcases or file cabinets. The employer could modify the storage system to low-rise shelves and cabinets for the materials the employee needs.*

- Modifying training materials to accommodate the employee's disability.

> **Example:** *An employer provides training tapes to its employees. One of its employees is deaf and cannot hear the tapes. The employer can have the tapes reduced to writing so that the deaf employee can read the materials and thereby not be hindered in job performance or potential promotion.*

- Making any other reasonable and similar adjustments to meet the needs of the disabled employee. These types of accommodations must be determined on a case-by-case basis.

Before an employer is required to make these accommodations, however, the employee must make the employer aware of the disability. Consequently, if the disability is not visually apparent, and the employee fails to inform the employer of the problem, the employer has not failed to make a reasonable accommodation.

> *Example:* *Although she is not clinically deaf, an employee does have some hearing problems. She refuses to wear a hearing device and is ashamed of her disability, so only her family and close friends know of her condition. At work she does not perform her job well, because she only hears a portion of what she is told, especially if people talk to her outside her line of vision. Since she failed to make the employer aware of her disability, she cannot charge the employer with unlawful discrimination under the ADA when her employer fires her for poor job performance.*

Undue Hardship

Even if an employee is deemed disabled under the ADA, an employer may not be required to make accommodation to assist the employee in performing his or her job if the accommodation would result in an **undue hardship** for the employer. In determining whether the accommodation would result in an undue hardship, the ADA provides certain criteria.

- The nature and cost of the accommodation. If the cost of the modification is so exorbitant that it goes beyond the concept of "reasonable," the employer will not have to make the accommodation.

> *Example:* *An employee who is diagnosed as being severely environmentally allergic complains that all of the papers, paint, and construction materials at work make him ill. He wants the employer to rebuild the factory with hypoallergenic materials. Because these modifications would require enormous costs, such an accommodation would be considered unreasonable.*

- The financial resources of the employer. If the requested accommodation would be beyond the financial resources of the employer, it would not have to make the accommodation, as in the above example.

- The number of employees working for the employer. If the employer had to provide special services for only one out of many employees, the expense may not justify the accommodation and would be an undue hardship. This criterion applies to large businesses.

> *Example:* *A nonprofit organization operates many social welfare programs. One of its employees is blind and requires the services of a reader and expensive equipment to perform his job. Because the organization has no profit margin, and a full-time reader would need to be employed and expensive equipment purchased to accommodate this one employee, providing the equipment and a reader may be considered an undue hardship—especially since the funds could be used to further the organization's charitable purposes.*

- The impact the accommodation would have on the operation of the facility. If the changes would require a complete restructuring of the facility, thus creating a hardship on all of the other employees, the employer would not have to make the modifications.

> *Example: An employee has an eye condition that makes her extremely sensitive to light, so sensitive that even using dark glasses does not help. To accommodate this employee, the workplace would have to be kept very dim, and special light fixtures would have to be installed. This accommodation would adversely affect the performance of all of the other workers; therefore, its implementation would be considered an undue hardship.*

- The overall size of the business. If the employer just meets the minimum number of employees to be defined as an "employer" under the ADA and is a small business, a major accommodation for just one employee may be considered an undue hardship. This criterion applies to small businesses, in contrast to the criterion discussed above that relates to the number of employees working for an employer.

> *Example: An employer has the minimum number of employees to come within the purview of the ADA. She has one blind employee who requires a reader. The additional expense of a reader may be considered minimal, even for a small business, and might not qualify as an undue hardship without a showing of some other factor.*

- The number and type of facilities owned by the employer. If the employer has multiple facilities, it may be able to make accommodation for a particular disability at one and transfer workers with that disability to that workplace, but making accommodations at all of the facilities might constitute an undue hardship if only a few employees are involved. Note, however, that an employer cannot create a separate facility for *all* of its disabled workers as a form of segregation; that act would be discriminatory itself.

- The structure of the workplace. If the particular needs of the business or the physical structure of the facility require or prohibit changes, making an accommodation for a disabled employee might constitute an undue hardship.

> *Example: A factory is set up with machinery in the most efficient and productive manner to manufacture the company's products. To accommodate a physically challenged worker, the entire operation would have to be reorganized, thereby making the factory less efficient and less profitable. In this instance restructuring for the disabled worker would probably be considered an undue hardship.*

Whether or not a particular accommodation would constitute an undue hardship for the employer is determined on a case-by-case basis.

Persons who are covered by the Americans with Disabilities Act are afforded all of the rights and remedies given by the Civil Rights Act. The Equal Employment Opportunity Commission is authorized to investigate cases arising under the ADA.

Chapter Summary

The Americans with Disabilities Act is intended to give job protection and security to vast numbers of American workers who are physically or mentally impaired. However, the ADA has also raised many problems of interpretation.

Because the ADA does not specifically define "disability," nor enumerate an inclusive list of physical and mental impairments, many lawsuits have been instituted claiming discrimination for all sorts of ailments that would not necessarily be considered disabilities. Examples include being a slow worker, being unable to get up early in the morning, and—as was cited in an above example—having so many allergies that the only way the employee could be accommodated would be to have an entirely new facility built to the employee's specifications.

Also, it is important to remember that being disabled does not by itself automatically afford an employee protection in the workplace. To maintain a claim for violations of the ADA, the employee must prove that he or she is qualified for the job in question and that the disability does not prevent him or her from performing an essential function of the job. Conversely, an employer must maintain detailed records of job performance to document a worker's ability, or lack thereof, to perform a particular job.

In this context, an employer is prohibited from applying non-job-related standards that are designed to discriminate against disabled workers. If a worker is deemed qualified but disabled, the employer is required to make reasonable accommodation to assist the employee in performing his or her job. Unless making the accommodation would impose an undue hardship on the employer, failure to make the accommodation violates the ADA.

The procedures for prosecuting and defending a claim under the ADA, as with other Civil Rights Act claims, will be discussed in detail in Chapter Ten, "Employment Law in a Regulated Society."

Edited Judicial Decisions

Carlson v. InaCom Corp. discusses migraine headaches as a disability under the ADA. *Muller v. Automobile Club of Southern California* concerns psychological disorders and the ADA.

CARLSON v. INACOM CORP
885 F.Supp. 1314 (D. Neb. 1995)

I.   FINDINGS OF FACT.

Debra Carlson is a United States citizen and a resident of the City of Lincoln, Lancaster County, Nebraska. InaCom Corporation ("InaCom") is a Delaware corporation qualified to do business in the State of Nebraska. InaCom sells computers and computer-related products and services. InaCom is an employer within the meaning of the ADA, as defined by 42 U.S.C. § 12111(5)(a).

On December 7, 1987, the plaintiff completed an employment application with the defendant and answered the question "do you have any physical or health limitations which affect your job performance?" in the negative. On December 29, 1987, Carlson commenced her employment with InaCom as a secretary in what was known as the Franchising Department, now known as the Corporate Development Department ("Corporate Development"). In her initial position as secretary, Carlson received an hourly wage of $7.69 plus $25.00 in commission income for each franchise and value-added reseller recruited by the department. On March 26, 1990, Carlson was promoted to executive secretary, a position she held until her termination on November 9, 1992. As an executive secretary, Carlson was paid an hourly rate of $8.58 plus a commission income of $50.00 for each new client recruited.

The plaintiff's duties included performing such clerical tasks as answering the phone, typing, handling mail, making travel arrangements, processing paperwork, product applications, financial reports, updating addresses and authorization numbers, and monitoring the timely completion of franchise tax returns. Carlson testified that she reported to Michael Steffan, then Vice President for Corporate Development, and she estimated that approximately fifty percent of her workload comprised providing secretarial support to Steffan and fifty percent to the other employees in Corporate Development.

Between December 1987 and April 1992, Carlson was the only staff support person working in Corporate Development, a department which increased in size from approximately five employees in 1987 to twelve employees in 1992. Between 1989 and early 1992, Ms. Carlson was given the additional responsibility of being the phone administrator of the Audix phone system for the entire InaCom corporate office. Her duties as phone administrator included programming phones for employees for voice mail usage.

During her employment with InaCom, the plaintiff performed her secretarial duties efficiently and satisfactorily. At an awards banquet held in December 1988, the president of Valmont Industries presented the Corporate Development employees, including Carlson, with individual plaques commemorating the department's outstanding business development. Plt. Ex. 30. Penny Klug, who worked for Corporate Development and later became the Director of Human Resources, testified that when Carlson was at work, she worked hard and produced satisfactorily. Teresa Vance, who was formerly employed in the Franchising/Corporate Development Department at InaCom, testified that, at least initially, Carlson impressed her as being intelligent and a good worker. Steffan, Carlson's supervisor, testified that Carlson completed his work quickly.

Since 1980, Carlson has suffered from migraine headaches. She has reported her migraine headaches to attending physicians on several occasions. According to Carlson's testimony, she suffers from at least one severe migraine headache every month or two. When she feels an oncoming migraine headache, she takes 800 milligrams of Motrin. Physicians have prescribed other medications, but Carlson testified that Motrin seems to be the most effective medication. The Motrin does not prevent the migraine headaches and rarely relieves all the pain, but it does provide some pain relief.

Carlson testified that her migraine headaches remain, on average, from one to two days, and, on occasion, three to four days. Her migraine symptoms include blurred vision, nausea, vomiting, and severe head pain. During periods when Carlson experiences severe migraine headaches, light and noise are painful to her, and she must retreat to a dark, silent room. Gary Carlson, the plaintiff's husband, testified that, when his wife suffers from migraines, she cannot concentrate on household tasks, interact with others, care for her minor son, drive a motor vehicle, or work.

Carlson experienced migraine headaches during her employment with InaCom. The plaintiff estimated that she missed work unexpectedly due to illness on the average of nine times per year, with an average seven absences attributed to migraine headaches. Between December 1987 and September 1992, Carlson missed 44 days of work due to unexpected illness and missed four additional scheduled days for foot surgery.

As of December 1988, the plaintiff's first anniversary date, InaCom's employee benefits policy entitled her to ten days annual vacation, one free day, and an unspecified number of sick days per year. No absentee policy existed at InaCom. Each time Carlson was ill, either she or her husband phoned Corporate Development and notified either Mike Steffan or Chris Friewald, who served as Carlson's supervisor in Steffan's absence. Steffan testified that on occasions Carlson left voice messages informing him that she was ill and would not be in that day. Steffan testified that he did not recall Carlson giving reasons for her absences. Upon her return to work Carlson would complete a time-off form and submit it to Steffan, Friewald, or another supervisor for signature.

Beginning in 1991, several Corporate Development employees voiced complaints to Steffan about Carlson's absences causing a negative impact on the department. Teresa Vance testified that, for over a year, she "nagged" Steffan about Carlson's absences, telling him that Carlson was taking advantage of the company, and urging Steffan to do something about Carlson's unscheduled absences. In addition to Vance, Steffan testified that he received complaints about Carlson's absences from Chris Friewald, Marcia Karakas, Christie Pavel, and Penny Klug. Although Steffan made no written record of specific complaints lodged against Carlson, he testified that he told Carlson that her fellow employees had voiced complaints to him about her absenteeism.

In April 1992, Steffan told Bill Fairfield, President and Chief Executive Officer of InaCom, that he was dissatisfied with Carlson and needed to hire a more reliable employee, who could be trained to replace Carlson. Steffan reached an agreement with Fairfield that after a replacement was hired and trained, Carlson would be transferred to another part of the company. On April 27, 1992, Steffan hired Rita Rocker as a staff support person to assist with paperwork and other secretarial duties. When Carlson asked Steffan why Rocker had been hired, Steffan told Carlson that he had become dissatisfied with her performance and advised her to work on improving her attendance. On cross-examination Steffan also testified that he never documented his meetings with Carlson, never wrote a memorandum to the file, never refused to sign Carlson's PTO forms, never requested that Carlson provide him with a physician's note to verify an absence, and never performed a written evaluation of the plaintiff. Steffan also testified that he did not personally believe in writing up employees for disciplinary infractions.

Both on direct examination and rebuttal Carlson admitted that Steffan had spoken to her about her absenteeism. However, she testified that Steffan had casually raised the issue on only two occasions when she was passing through his office. Carlson further testified that Steffan never informed her that her employment with InaCom was in jeopardy due to her absences.

Steffan testified that shortly after Carlson's unscheduled absence from work on July 6, 1994, but prior to her ankle injury in September 1992, he was determined to get Carlson out of Corporate Development and thought termination was the best means. Steffan testified that he did not terminate Carlson immediately because he wanted Rita Rocker, a staff support person hired in April 1994, to finish training on Carlson's duties. Steffan also delayed terminating Carlson because it was necessary to reassign the Audix phone system duties to another employee.

On September 14, 1992, the plaintiff broke her ankle and was placed on short-term disability leave. When Carlson returned to work on November 9, 1992, Steffan terminated her. Penny Klug testified that she was present in the conference room when Steffan notified Carlson that she was being terminated for excessive absenteeism. Neither Steffan nor Klug discussed with Carlson the nature or causes of the her absences, the inappropriateness of any unscheduled absences, or the possibility of relocating Carlson to another department within the company. Carlson testified that she did not discuss the reasons for her unscheduled absences with Steffan and Klug, nor did she ask for an accommodation, or transfer to another department. Carlson did ask Klug if she could resign, and Klug advised Carlson that she would be permitted to resign if she tendered a letter to the Human Resources Department. Carlson never tendered a resignation letter.

On December 5, 1992, Carlson completed an employment application with Lincoln Aviation Insurance, Inc. ("Lincoln Aviation"). The employment application did not inquire whether the applicant suffered from any physical or mental disability. Def. Ex. 114. Carlson made no mention on her application of being disabled by migraine headaches. On December 28, 1992, Carlson began working for Lincoln Aviation. Beginning in June 1993, Carlson took unpaid sick leave because of pre-term labor problems related to her pregnancy. On July 2, 1993, Carlson's supervisor terminated her because her lengthy absence was too difficult on the company.

On June 29, 1994, Carlson completed an application for employment with the Lincoln Chamber of Commerce. The application did not inquire about, nor did Carlson voluntarily reveal, any information concerning a disability. On July 1, 1994, Carlson commenced employment with the Lincoln Chamber of Commerce, where she is currently employed.

II. CONCLUSIONS OF LAW.

The Americans with Disability Act ("ADA") prohibits employment discrimination "against a qualified individual with a disability because of the disability of such individual..." 42 U.S.C. § 12112(a). The ADA prohibits an employer from discriminating against such persons with regard to "job application procedures, the hiring, advancement, or discharge of employees, employee compensation, job training, and other terms, conditions, and privileges of employment." *Id.* The term "discriminate" is given various definitions in section 12112 of Title 42 of the United States Code. For the purposes of this lawsuit, the plaintiff has alleged that InaCom discriminated against her by "not making reasonable accommodations to the known physical...limitations of an otherwise qualified individual with a disability who is an...employee..." 42 U.S.C. § 12112(b)(5)A).

To establish a *prima facie* case of disability discrimination under the ADA, the plaintiff must prove that she is "disabled" and "qualified" to perform the essential functions of the job either with or without reasonable accommodation. *Dutton v. Johnson County Bd. of County Comm'rs*, 859 F.Supp. 498, 504 (D. Kan. 1994) (citing *Pushkin v. Regents of the University of Colorado*, 658 F.2d 1372, 1385 (10th Cir. 1983)). The burden of production then shifts to the defendant either to rebut those claims or establish that the reasonable accommodation required would create an undue hardship.

In this case, Carlson contends that she is disabled but would have been qualified to perform the essential functions of the executive secretary job at InaCom with a reasonable accommodation. The defendant argues that: 1) Carlson is not disabled within the meaning of the statute; 2) she is not a "qualified individual" because her record of absenteeism precludes her from performing essential functions; and 3) the defendant did not know the plaintiff was disabled and had no duty to provide a reasonable accommodation.

A.   Plaintiff's Disability.

Under the ADA a disability is defined as "(A) a physical or mental impairment that substantially limits one or more of the life activities of [an] individual; (B) a record of such an impairment; or (C) being regarded as having such an impairment." 42 U.S.C. § 12102(2). The plaintiff claims she is disabled by reason of a physical impairment— migraine headaches—which substantially limits her major life activities. The Code of Federal Regulations defines a "physical or mental impairment" as "any physiological disorder, or condition" which affects one or more of the various body systems, including the cardiovascular system. 29 C.F.R. § 1630.2(h)(1). Examples of "major life activities" include those activities which an average person can perform with little or no difficulty, such as "caring for oneself, performing manual tasks, walking, seeing, hearing, speaking, breathing, learning, and working." 29 C.F.R. § 1630.2(i). "Substantially limits" is defined as either the inability to perform a major life activity, or a serious restriction on the ability to perform a major life activity as compared to an average person in the general population. 29 C.F.R. § 1630.2(j)(1).

The preponderance of the evidence in this case easily establishes that the plaintiff's migraine headaches constitute a physiological disorder which affects both the Carlson's neurological and vascular systems. *Dutton, supra*, 859 F.Supp at 506. When Carlson gets a migraine, the headache is severe and debilitating. Both the plaintiff and her husband testified that when Carlson has a migraine headache, she is substantially limited in major life activities. She is unable to care for her infant son, drive a car, or concentrate on work. Carlson testified that the headaches last in duration from one to four days. Treatment consists of Carlson taking 800 milligram dosages of Motrin for pain relief and sleeping off the headache. Carlson also testified that she has suffered from migraine headaches since she was in high school, a period of nearly twenty years.

In closing argument, the defendant presented reasons why the court should not find a disability. First, the defendant argues that Carlson has presented no independent, empirical evidence to establish that she suffers from migraine headaches. The only documentary evidence of Carlson's migraine headaches are Dr. Domalake's medical notes, which are based upon one appointment with Carlson and whose contents are derived solely from information provided to him by Carlson. Nothing in the ADA mandates that the existence of a disability must be independently proven by a medical test. Dr. Domalakes testified by deposition that he was not aware of any test that could be performed on a patient to verify the presence of a migraine, "other than some rather exotic research type studies that would not be readily available to a practicing physician." Dep. Domalakes 38:2–5, Filing 32. Domalakes further testified that the diagnosis of a migraine headache is made only on patient history. *Id* 38:6–8.

The defendant also contends that the infrequency in which Carlson sought medical treatment for her migraine headaches—five treatments in twelve years—should preclude me from finding the presence of a disability. The defendant presents no legal authority to support its contention that the frequency in which a plaintiff seeks medical treatment is or should be a determinative factor in finding that she is substantially limited in a major life activity. Rather, the evidence in this case clearly establishes that the plaintiff's migraine headaches are debilitating and contributed significantly to her unscheduled absences for which she was ultimately terminated. Accordingly, I find that the plaintiff has successfully established the *prima facie* element of disability.

B. Qualified Individual.

Next, the plaintiff must establish that she is a qualified individual with a disability who can perform the essential functions of the job of executive secretary with or without reasonable accommodation. The plaintiff claims that the fact that she performed her job duties competently and efficiently when she was at work establishes that she is a qualified individual with a disability. The defendant contends that regular, predictable attendance is an essential requirement of the executive secretary position. Because Carlson's absences were substantial and unpredictable, the defendant argues that she could not perform the essential functions of the job.

Whether a plaintiff is "otherwise qualified" requires a highly fact-sensitive and individualized inquiry, resulting in a case-by-case determination. Generally and broadly speaking, an employee "cannot perform [her] job successfully without meeting some threshold of both attendance and regularity." *Walders v. Garrett*, 765 F.Supp. 303, 309 (E.D. Va 1991), aff'd, 956 F.2d 1163 (4th Cir. 1992). While legal authority supports this common-sense conclusion, no legal authority establishes any specific attendance requirements for government or private sector jobs. *Id.* at 310. Rather, the requisite levels of attendance and regularity depend upon the circumstances of each employment position. *Id.* (citing 29 C.F.R. § 1613.702(f) and *School Board of Nassau County, Fla. v. Arline*, 480 U.S. 273, 287–88, 94 L.Ed. 2d 307, 107 S.Ct. 1123 (1987)).

I have read the ADA cases supporting the defendant's argument that an essential part of any job is the requirement of regular and predictable attendance. *See Carr v. Reno*, 306 U.S. App. D.C. 217, 23 F.3d 525 (D.C.Cir 1994); *Walders v. Garrett*, 765 F.Supp. 303 (E.D. Va 1991), aff'd, 956 F.2d 1163 (4th Cir. 1992); *Santiago v. Temple Univ.*, 739 F.Supp. 974, 979 (E.D. Pa 1990) aff'd, 928 F.2d 396 (3d Cir. 1991); *Matzo v. Postmaster Gen.*, 685 F.Supp. 260, 263 (D.D.C. 1987), aff'd, 274 U.S. App. D.C. 95, 861 F.2d 1290 (D.C. Cir 1988); *Lemere v. Burnley*, 683 F.Supp. 275, 280 (D.D.C. 1988); *Wimbley v. Bolger*, 642 F.Supp 481, 485 (W.D. Tenn. 1986), aff'd, 831 F.2d 298 (6th Cir. 1987). However, my review of these cases reveals that the present case is distinguishable on several grounds.

First, I find that the evidence at trial establishes that Carlson was not excessively absent from her job. On an annual basis, Carlson averaged nine unscheduled absences due to illness, seven of which she testified were due to migraine headaches. While this number of unscheduled absences is not insubstantial, the number of unscheduled absences in no way compares to the weeks and months missed by employees in the above-cited cases.

Second, while the defense presented much testimony regarding the time-sensitive, time-critical nature of the corporate development business, no evidence was presented to establish that Carlson's absences resulted in essential business not being completed in a timely and efficient manner. The defense produced no evidence of either threatened or actual lost business or profits resulting from Carlson's unscheduled absences. Certainly, Carlson's coworkers were inconvenienced and annoyed by her absences, and customer correspondence may have been postponed for a day or two. Even so, the defense has presented no evidence that Carlson's unscheduled absences were unduly disruptive. *Cf. Dutton*, 859 F. Supp. at 508.

Last, I decline to find that attendance is an essential element in this case, because InaCom has no policy on unscheduled absenteeism. Testimony by multiple witnesses established that prior to the implementation of the PTO program, no limitation existed on the number of days an employee could acceptably be absent from work due to illness. Once the PTO program was implemented in January 1992, an employee's unscheduled absences became limited only by the number of paid-time-off days allocated to the employee based on his or her length of service.

The InaCom Corporation's Personnel Policies and Procedures Manual, Plt. Ex. 15 & Def. Ex. 110, is void of any absenteeism policy pertaining to unscheduled absences due to illness. The only reference to "illness" occurs in section 40 on page 40.2. The text states: "InaCom supports the philosophy that each individual should have a regular period of "paid time off" (PTO) from their work for rest and relaxation and for times when their own or a family member's illness should require their absence from the workplace." Def. Ex. 110, § 40 at p. 40.2.

The evidence at trial established that in 1992 Carlson missed between 17 and 17 3/8 days of work. Two of the days were unpaid time off work. Under the PTO plan Carlson was entitled to 16 paid-off days. The record establishes that she did not exceed this allotment of paid time off.

Given these facts, I decline to make a judicial determination that attendance is an essential element of employment at InaCom, especially when the defendant company has declined to formulate and publish a policy relating to unscheduled absences. Accordingly, I find that Carlson is an otherwise qualified individual with a disability as defined under the ADA.

C. Reasonable Accommodation

Having successfully established that she is disabled and qualified to perform the essential functions of the job, I must next decide whether InaCom's failure to accommodate the plaintiff's unscheduled absences constituted discrimination on the basis of disability. The term "discriminate" includes an employer's not making reasonable accommodations to a known physical limitation of an otherwise qualified individual with a disability who is an employee, unless the employer can demonstrate that the accommodation would impose an undue hard ship. 42 U.S.C. § 12112(b)(5)(A). The ADA does not define the term "reasonable accommodation," but the ADA does provide these examples: making employment facilities readily accessible to disabled employees, restructuring a job, providing part-time or modified work schedules, providing modified equipment or devices, reassigning an employee to a vacant position, providing qualified readers or interpreters, and other similar accommodations. 42 U.S.C. §12111(9)(B).

To be liable for failing to provide a reasonable accommodation, Carlson must establish that the defendant had knowledge of her disability. *See Landefeld v. Marion Gen. Hosp. Inc.*, 994 F.2d 1178, 1181 (6th Cir. 1993); *Grimes v. U.S. Postal Service*, 1994 WL 732557, (W.D. Mo. 1994); *Hedberg v. Indiana Bell Telephone Co.*, 1994 WL 228184, (S.D. Ind. 1994); and *O'Keefe v. Niagara Mohawk Power Corp.*, 714 F.Supp. 622 (N.D.N.Y 1989). The evidence at trial establishes, at best, that management personnel—consisting of Steffan, Friewald, and Klug—knew that Carlson suffered from an occasional headache. The greater weight of the evidence does not show that any of these three individuals knew or should have known that Carlson suffered from a severe, medically diagnosable condition. That a few of Carlson's coworkers may have known that she suffered from migraine headaches is not controlling, because her coworkers were not in a position to offer and provide Carlson with a reasonable accommodation.

Under the ADA, an employer is required to accommodate a known disability of a qualified applicant or employee. 42 U.S.C. § 12112(b)(5). The preponderance of evidence at trial established that Carlson never told Steffan or other members of InaCom's management that she had a disability which required an accommodation. During the application process, Carlson did not inform InaCom that she suffered from periodic migraine headaches. When Steffan reprimanded Carlson for her unscheduled absences, she did not explain to Steffan that she suffered from a disability and required an accommodation. When she was terminated for excessive absenteeism, she did not explain to Steffan or Klug that she suffered from a disability and needed an accommodation. Instead, the evidence presented reveals that Carlson did not view her migraine headaches as a disability and failed to request an appropriate accommodation from any employer, past or present.

I find that Carlson has not made a *prima facie* showing that the defendant failed to provide a reasonable accommodation. Because InaCom did not have sufficient knowledge of Carlson's migraine headaches, InaCom cannot be held liable for failing to attempt a reasonable accommodation.

D. Disparate Impact/Treatment.

In order to make out a *prima facie* case of disparate impact, the plaintiff must show that the defendant's PTO program, although facially neutral, "disparately disadvantages the protected group of which [she] is a member and that [she] is qualified for the position under all but the challenged criteria." *Wimbley v. Bolger,* 642 F.Supp 481, 483 (W.D. Tenn 1986), aff'd, 831 F.2d 298 (6th Cir. 1987) (quoting *Prewitt v. USPS*, 662 F.2d 292, 306 (5th Cir. 1981)). I find that the plaintiff has offered no evidence to show that the InaCom's PTO program had a disparate impact on disabled employees.

Similarly, to establish a *prima facie* case for disparate treatment, the plaintiff must show that she was treated differently from others because of her disability. *Wimbley,* 642 F.Supp. at 484 (citing *Prewitt v. USPS*, 662 F.2d at 305, n. 19). Although during trial Carlson hinted that other InaCom employees with comparable absenteeism records have not been terminated, she has presented no evidence to show that she was treated differently from any other InaCom employee under the PTO program. Therefore, she has failed to make out a showing of disparate treatment based on disability.

III. CONCLUSION.

For the foregoing reasons, I find that the plaintiff has failed to establish that the defendant discriminated against her on the basis of disability. Accordingly, judgment is to be entered for the defendant.

MULLER v. AUTOMOBILE CLUB OF SOUTHERN CALIFORNIA
897 F.Supp. 1289 (S. D. Cal. 1995)

I. Background.

Plaintiff started working for Defendant in October 1977. Over the course of fifteen years, Plaintiff received a number of commendations and promotions. (Pl.'s Decl. PP 3–14.)

On April 26, 1993, everything changed. Plaintiff received a call from the son of an insured. The son, irate over Plaintiff's conclusion that his father would have to pay more than one deductible for damage arising from more than one accident, threatened Plaintiff. Plaintiff hung up on the caller, a Mr. Williams, but Williams called back a number of times on the afternoon of April 23. Among his threats, Williams told Plaintiff that he would meet her in the parking lot. An Escondido police officer escorted Plaintiff to her car at the end of the day. (Pl.'s Decl. PP 16–21.)

During the week following the threats, Plaintiff encountered what she considered to be insensitive conduct on the part of some of her coworkers. One, Escondido District Office Supervisor Jack Lape, asked Plaintiff, "Anne, did you wear your target today?" (Pl.'s Decl. P 23.)

On May 3, 1993, Plaintiff and her assistant supervisor, Evelyn Blake, had a disagreement about preparing a claim file. Plaintiff, upset by the confrontation, left work early. (Pl.'s Decl. P 24.)

Two days later, on May 5, 1993, Plaintiff met with Lape, Blake, and Frank Mieczkowski, a regional manager. At the meeting, Plaintiff learned that her superiors planned to treat Plaintiff's May 3 outburst as insubordination. Their decision further upset Plaintiff. Plaintiff told Lape, Blake, and Mieczkowski that she was suffering from fear and anxiety in the wake of the Williams' threats. (Pl.'s Decl. PP 25–26.) To make matters worse, Plaintiff's coworkers spotted Williams sitting at a lunch table near the Auto Club parking lot later that afternoon. (Pl.'s Decl. P 27.)

On May 7, Plaintiff confronted Lape and Mieczkowski about Williams' presence on company property. According to Plaintiff, both Lape and Mieczkowski laughed, and Lape said that he told Williams where Plaintiff lived and the type of car she drove. (Pl.'s Decl. P 28.)

On May 10, 1993, and May 11, 1993, Plaintiff met with Dr. Rosben Gutierrez for psychological counseling. Plaintiff states in her declaration that Dr. Gutierrez diagnosed a post-traumatic stress disorder and prescribed Klonopin and Paxil. (Pl.'s Decl. P 30.)

Plaintiff continued psychological counseling sessions with Dr. Gutierrez and with Dr. Martin D. Cary through May and into June. According to Plaintiff, the side effects of the medication impaired her ability to perform her job duties. She missed a number of days of work. In mid-June, an Auto Club representative informed Plaintiff that she would have to take a leave of absence. (Pl.'s Decl. P 33.) Plaintiff commenced her leave of absence on June 15, 1993. Plaintiff never returned to work.

On July 26, 1993, Dr. J. Brand Brickman conducted a clinical psychiatric evaluation of Plaintiff. (Pl.'s Decl. P 34.) In a report dated July 30, 1993, Dr. Brickman concluded that Plaintiff had a "Temporary Total Psychiatric Disability" brought about by the Williams incident. (Pl.'s Notice of Lodgment Ex. 1 at 6.)

Dr. Brickman and his colleagues, Dr. Robert Zink and Lucinda Nerhood, L.C.S.W., counseled Plaintiff during July, August, and September. Dr. Brickman adjusted Plaintiff's medications to reduce the side effects. (Pl.'s Notice of Lodgment Ex. 1 at 7; Def.'s Notice of Lodgment Ex. 2 at 2.)

On Plaintiff's behalf, Dr. Zink and Plaintiff's workers' compensation attorney formulated a plan to make Plaintiff's return to work at the Auto Club possible and palatable. Among the items on Plaintiff's agenda were removing any reference to insubordination from Plaintiff's file, reviewing Defendant's safety procedures, and replacing Lape with another supervisor. (*See* Pl.'s Notice of Lodgment Ex. 2 at 60, 62, 68; Def.'s Notice of Lodgment Ex. 12 at 13, 24; Tsuida Decl. P 4.)

Defendant acceded to most of Plaintiff's requests, even replacing Lape with Rod Middleswart, a manager from another office. (Pl.'s Decl. PP 37–38; Tsuida Decl. PP 5–7; Middleswart Decl. P 2.) Plans for Plaintiff's return broke down, however, when Plaintiff and Carolyn Tsuida, the district office manager, did not reach a meeting of the minds about revisions to Auto Club safety procedures. (*See* Def.'s Notice of Lodgment Ex. 2 at 2.)

Plaintiff reported to Dr. Zink that her safety concerns had not been met. (*Id.*) Based on Plaintiff's continued concerns about her health, Dr. Brickman concluded in a September 20, 1993, report that Plaintiff could not return to work at the Auto Club. (*Id.* at 4.) Dr. Brickman's September 20, 1993, report, however, portrays Plaintiff as a patient on the mend. Dr. Brickman notes in the report that Plaintiff informed him that she felt "progressively more functional again" and that she was much less apprehensive. His report indicates that Plaintiff was sleeping better, enjoyed improved relations with her husband, had traveled with her family, and was going to Jazzercize classes. (*Id.* at 2.) Dr. Brickman also reports that upon psychological retesting, Plaintiff showed "substantial improvement in [her] mental state." Dr. Brickman diagnosed "Adjustment Disorder with anxiety and depression, in remission" and "Atypical Panic Disorder, in remission." (*Id.* at 3.) Importantly, Dr. Brickman found for the first time in his September 15, 1993, report that Plaintiff's psychiatric disability had become permanent and stationary. (*Id.*)

Dr. Brickman's report concludes with a discussion of Plaintiff's prospects for future employment:

> Concerning whether she can return to her usual and customary employment, I do not believe that this individual has significant restrictions concerning meeting the public in settings other than the Auto Club. However, her experiences with her employer following the recent threats at work make it impossible for her to return to work with the Automobile Club as an employee.

> I do believe she could meet the public in most settings: her concerns with security seem to be rather specifically associated with the Automobile Club, and have to do in part with the fact that other employees have been assaulted at the Automobile Club in the last few years. (*Id.* at 4) (emphasis in original).

During a December 15, 1994, deposition, Dr. Brickman reiterated his assessment that Plaintiff could hold a job that required public contact. (Def.'s Notice of Lodgment Ex. 11 at 21–22.) In fact, Dr. Brickman added that at the time he issued September 15 report, he believed that Plaintiff could return to the Auto Club if she did not have to have public contact there. (*Id.* at 21.) Dr. Brickman also stated during his deposition that he did not believe Plaintiff was limited in any of her major life activities as of the time he last saw her. (*Id.* at 23.)

Nevertheless, in light of Dr. Brickman's September 15, 1993, finding that Plaintiff could not return to her job at the Auto Club, Plaintiff's workers' compensation lawyer, Randall Mason, met with a workers' compensation adjuster, Diane Klatt, and Defendant's senior employment relations consultant, Kimberly Klink. Mason, Klatt, and Klink agreed that Defendant would provide vocational rehabilitation services to Plaintiff to prepare Plaintiff for a new line of work. (Def.'s Notice of Lodgment Ex. 10 at 125; Def.'s Notice of Lodgment Ex. 13 at 109–110.)

Plaintiff began her vocational rehabilitation in November 1993. Plaintiff received bookkeeping training. On February 24, 1994, Plaintiff told her vocational rehabilitation counselor that she had lined up a client for her new bookkeeping business. Plaintiff's vocational rehabilitation counselor then ended Plaintiff's vocational training. (Def.'s Notice of Lodgment Exs. 5–7.)

Plaintiff learned on March 4, 1994, that she had been "resigned" by Defendant as of February 28, 1994. (Pl.'s Decl. P 45.)

Plaintiff filed a claim for disability discrimination with the Equal Employment Opportunity Commission ("EEOC") in June 1994. On June 17, 1994, Plaintiff met with EEOC Investigator Raul Green for an interview. (Pl.'s Decl. P 46.) Green states in his declaration that Plaintiff admitted that her condition was temporary and did not affect her normal day-to-day functions outside of work. (Green Decl. P 5.) Green informed Plaintiff that she was not a qualified individual under the ADA. (Green Decl. P 6.) The EEOC "terminated its process" with respect to Plaintiff's claim and sent her a right to sue letter on June 27, 1994. (Pl.'s Compl. Ex. B.)

II. Discussion.

A. Summary Judgment Standard.

Fed. R. Civ. P. 56(c) provides that summary judgment is appropriate if the "pleadings, depositions, answers to interrogatories, and admissions on file, together with the affidavits, if any, show that there is no genuine issue as to any material fact and that the moving party is entitled to judgment as a matter of law." One of the principal purposes of the rule is to dispose of factually unsupported claims or defenses. *Celotex Corp. v. Catrett*, 477 U.S. 317, 323–24, 91 L.Ed. 2d 265, 106 S.Ct. 2548 (1986).

B. Plaintiff's ADA Cause of Action.

The ADA prohibits covered entities from discriminating against people with disabilities:

No covered entity shall discriminate against a qualified individual with a disability because of the disability of such individual in regard to job application procedures, the hiring, advancement, or discharge of employees, employee compensation, job training, and other terms, conditions, and privileges of employment. 42 U.S.C. § 12112(A).

Under the ADA, the term "disability" means "(A) a physical or mental impairment that substantially limits one or more of the major life activities of such individual; (B) a record of such impairment; or (C) being regarded as having such an impairment." 42 U.S.C. § 12102(2). The regulations promulgated by the EEOC to implement the ADA define "major life activities" as "functions such as caring for oneself, performing manual tasks, walking, seeing, hearing, speaking, breathing, learning, and working." 29 C.F.R. § 1630.2(i).

1. Plaintiff's actual disability theory.

Plaintiff contends she was actually disabled under the ADA. The EEOC provides a list of three factors to be considered in determining whether an individual is actually "substantially limited" in a major life activity: 1) the nature and severity of the impairment; 2) the duration or expected duration of the impairment; and 3) the permanent or longterm impact, or the expected permanent or longterm impact of or resulting from the impairment. 29 C.F.R. § 1630.2(J)(2).

According to the EEOC Technical Assistance Manual for the ADA, temporary, nonchronic impairments that do not last for a long time and that have little or no longterm impact usually are not disabilities. 1 EEOC Technical Assistance Manual § 2.2(a)(iii), reprinted in Americans with Disabilities Act Manual (BNA) § 90:0501 (1992). A broken leg, for example, would not be a disability under the ADA unless it did not heal properly and resulted in a permanent impairment significantly limiting the person's ability to walk. *Id.*

The EEOC has provided additional factors to be considered when a plaintiff argues that his or her impairment substantially limits the major life activity of working:

The term "substantially limits" means significantly restricted in the ability to perform either a class of jobs or a broad range of jobs in various classes as compared to the average person having comparable training, skills and abilities. The inability to perform a single, particular job does not constitute a substantial limitation in the major life activity of working. 29 C.F.R. § 1630.2(J)(3) (i) (emphasis in original); *see also* 1 EEOC Technical Assistance Manual § 2.2(a)(iii) (no "substantial limitation" if person is limited from performing particular job for one employer).

In *Bolton v. Scrivner Inc.*, 3 AD Cases 1089, 1092 (10th Cir. 1994), the Tenth Circuit found that summary judgment for the defendant was appropriate where the plaintiff failed to produce any evidence to suggest that his foot injuries restricted him from performing an entire class of jobs. The *Bolton* court noted the absence of evidence on any of the factors that a court may consider when an individual claims substantial limitation in the major life activity of working. *Id.* at 1091–92 (discussing 29 C.F.R. § 1630.2(J)(3)(ii)). The court found that the plaintiff had failed to present any evidence concerning his vocational training, the geographical area to which he had access, or the number and type of jobs demanding similar training from which the plaintiff would be disqualified. *Id.*

The ADA defines disability in substantially the same terms as the Rehabilitation Act of 1973. *Bolton*, 3 AD Cases at 1091. In fact, Congress intended the relevant case law under the Rehabilitation Act to apply to the term "disability" in the ADA. *Id.* (citing the legislative history of the ADA).

Federal courts applying the Rehabilitation Act repeatedly have found that individuals do not have disabilities as defined by the Rehabilitation Act when their physical or mental impairments prevent them from performing particular jobs but do not preclude them from obtaining other satisfactory employment. For example, in *Jasany v. United States Post Office*, 755 F.2d 1244 (6th Cir. 1985), the Post Office fired the plaintiff after the plaintiff developed eye problems from working at a particular machine. The Sixth Circuit found that the plaintiff failed to show that his eye problems substantially limited one of his major life activities. *Id.* at 1250. Although the eye problems prevented the plaintiff from working at the offending machine, the plaintiff failed to show that his eye problems decreased the plaintiff's "ability to obtain satisfactory employment otherwise." *Id.* at 1248. *See also*

Welsh v. City of Tulsa, 977 F.2d 1415, 1417 (10th Cir. 1992) ("While the regulations define a major life activity to include working, this does not necessarily mean working at the job of one's choice."); *Maulding v. Sullivan*, 961 F.2d 694, 698 (8th Cir. 1992) (where sensitivity to chemicals precluded lab work but did not limit employment as a whole, plaintiff not disabled); *Elstner v. Southwestern Bell Telephone Co.*, 659 F.Supp. 1328, 1343 (S.D. Tex. 1987) (finding that knee injury limited plaintiff's ability to work as pole climber but holding that injury did not substantially limit life activities).

Defendant disputes Plaintiff's assertion that she was "disabled" under the ADA. According to Defendant, Plaintiff has not presented any evidence showing an impairment that substantially limited any of her major life activities, including working. Defendant, by contrast, has supplied ample evidence showing the absence of any impairment that substantially limited any of Plaintiff's major life activities. For example, Defendant relies on Dr. Brickman's September 15, 1993, report and portions of his deposition transcript. In his report, Dr. Brickman concluded that Plaintiff did not have significant restrictions preventing her from performing essentially the same job for an employer other than the Auto Club. Dr. Brickman added in his deposition that at the time he last saw Plaintiff, he believed that she could have returned to work at the Auto Club if she could have been assigned to a position not requiring contact with the public. In an effort to show that a genuine issue of material fact does exists about whether her psychological problems rose to the level of a disability under the ADA, Plaintiff points to four sources: 1) Plaintiff's own declaration; 2) the declaration of Plaintiff's husband, Dan Muller; 3) the declaration of Jane Amsler, Ph.D; and 4) Dr. Brickman's August 20, 1993, report.

In her declaration, Plaintiff makes statements that fall into three categories. First, Plaintiff indicates at two places in her declaration that two psychiatrists found that she had psychological problems. At paragraph 30, Plaintiff states that Dr. Gutierrez diagnosed a "post-traumatic stress disorder." (Pl.'s Decl. P 30.) Later, at paragraph 34, Plaintiff states that Dr. Brickman continued her "Temporary Total Disability Status." (Pl.'s Decl. P 34.) In both cases, however, the psychiatrists offered their evaluations at the height of Plaintiff's anxiety, the summer of 1993. Dr. Brickman found in September 1993 that Plaintiff's condition had improved substantially and that she was ready to begin working again, though not necessarily for the Auto Club. Plaintiff's declaration does not contradict Dr. Brickman's assessment that Plaintiff's psychological disorders were in remission as of September 1993.

Second, Plaintiff states in her declaration that Mr. Williams' threats "impacted" her ability to do her job. (Pl.'s Decl. PP 24, 33, 47.) Even if the Williams incident prevented her from returning to her job as a claims adjuster for Defendant, Plaintiff still would not necessarily have had a disability under the ADA. Plaintiff's psychological impairment would not rise to the level of a disability as defined by the ADA unless it significantly restricted Plaintiff's ability to perform either a class of jobs or a broad range of jobs in various classes. As noted above, "The inability to perform a single, particular job does not constitute a substantial limitation in the major life activity of working." 29 C.F.R. § 1630.2(j)(3)(i).

Third, explaining her meeting with Raul Green of the EEOC, Plaintiff states in her declaration that the Williams incident "impacted" her relationship with her husband and her children and that it "impacted" her life. (Pl.'s Decl. PP 47–48.) Plaintiff's sweeping statements are insufficient to create a genuine issue of material fact. That Williams' threats affected Plaintiff does not necessarily mean that they led to psychological problems that, in turn, substantially limited her major life activities.

Plaintiff's husband, Dan Muller, makes two statements of note in his declaration, neither of which raises an issue of material fact. First, he states that "beginning in June 1993, my wife was placed on heavy doses of prescribed medication. Her condition impaired her vision, prevented her from driving, and substantially impaired her ability to take care of our three children. She was sleeping nearly seventeen hours per day." (Dan Muller Decl. P 3.) Mr. Muller's statement, however, does not contradict Dr. Brickman's statement in his September 15, 1993, report that he took Plaintiff off her medication in September 1993. In other words, Plaintiff might have suffered side effects from medication in the summer of 1993, but there is no indication that the side effects of the medication stayed with Plaintiff after September 1993. Second, Mr. Muller states in an oblique and conclusory manner that his marital relations with his wife have suffered. (Dan Muller Decl. P 4.) Mr. Muller does not state the cause of the decline in his marital relations, nor does he say when the Mullers' marital relations first were "affected substantially." Plaintiff also fails to point to any authority or to offer any analysis suggesting that loss of consortium is a "disability" as contemplated by the ADA. The declaration of Jane Amsler, Ph.D., also fails to raise a genuine issue of material fact. First, Amsler states that "it does appear that ANNE MULLER suffered from extreme anxiety and depression as a consequence of the events on the job in April of 1993." (Amsler Decl. P 3 (emphasis added).) In addition, Amsler suggests, though she does not state as a matter of fact, that at least for some period of time, Plaintiff could not take care of herself or her children. (Amsler Decl. P 4.) Amsler does not state how long Plaintiff's anxiety and depression lasted, nor does she say anything to contradict Dr. Brickman's September 15, 1993, assessment that Plaintiff's psychological problems had declined by mid-September and that Plaintiff had begun to put her life back together. Amsler states that Plaintiff now is afraid to go out at night and adds that Plaintiff's "residual and definitely limiting anxiety affects her daily functioning now." (Amsler Decl. P 7.) Amsler fails to make any specific statements about whether Plaintiff's anxiety substantially limited her ability to engage in major life activities. Amsler also fails to offer any insight into Plaintiff's condition in late 1993 or early 1994, the time surrounding Plaintiff's vocational rehabilitation and ultimate termination by Defendant.

Finally, Dr. Brickman's August 20, 1993, report does not indicate that Plaintiff had a permanent or even longterm impairment that substantially limited her ability to work. Dr. Brickman speculates in the August 20, 1993, report that Plaintiff might need "a different job placement, conceivably even some other sort of employment where she no longer had to deal with the public." (Pl.'s Notice of Lodgment Ex. 4 at 1). Dr. Brickman, however, states in the August 20, 1993, report that Plaintiff remained "Temporarily Totally Psychiatrically Disabled" and recommends that she be continued on disability for two more weeks.

Plaintiff's psychiatric disability became permanent and stationary less than one month later, and at that time, Dr. Brickman found that Plaintiff's impairment did not substantially limit her ability to hold down a job requiring contact with the public. Dr. Brickman's August 20, 1993, report does not create a genuine issue of material fact because it does not suggest anything about the severity of Plaintiff's impairment once it became permanent and stationary. Plaintiff's reliance on the August 20, 1993, report is like a person who suffered a broken leg relying on an x-ray of the fractured bone one week after the doctor placed it in a cast to show that he was disabled.

The evidence on which Plaintiff relies suffers from two shortcomings. First, the evidence regarding the diagnosis of Plaintiff's psychological problems comes from the period before her condition became permanent and stationary. As a result, the evidence fails to dispute Defendant's evidence showing that Plaintiff's psychological impairment was of limited duration and did not substantially limit a major life activity. Second, the statements on which Plaintiff relies to show a substantial limitation on a major life activity do not say anything about Plaintiff's ability or inability to engage in any particular major life activity. That the Williams incident "impacted" Plaintiff's life is insufficient to show a disability under the ADA.

Plaintiff falls especially short in her efforts to show a substantial limitation on her ability to work. Plaintiff has not pointed to any evidence showing that her psychological impairments prevented her from holding a job in the same class as the one she held at the Auto Club before her termination. That Plaintiff did not want to return to the insurance industry does not demonstrate that her impairments met the standard for "disability" under the ADA. Plaintiff has offered no information about the availability in her area of claims adjuster jobs or other jobs requiring similar skills, training, and ability.

In short, Plaintiff has failed to point to evidence suggesting the existence of any genuine issue of material fact about whether she had an actual disability under § 12102(2)(A).

2.   Plaintiff's "regarded-as" theory of disability.

Plaintiff argues in her Opposition that even if she was not actually disabled, she was "disabled" under § 12102(2)(C) of the ADA because Defendant regarded her as having a disability. According to the EEOC, "The legislative history of the ADA indicates that Congress intended [the regarded-as] part of the definition to protect people from a range of discriminatory actions based on 'myths, fears and stereotypes' about disability, which occur even when a person does not have a substantially limited impairment." 1 EEOC Technical Assistance Manual § 2.2(a), reprinted in ADA Manual (BNA) § 90:0512 (1992). Plaintiff has presented no evidence to show that Defendant regarded plaintiff as a person with a disability based on myths, fears, or stereotypes.

Plaintiff argues that Defendant's efforts to accommodate Plaintiff's security concerns demonstrate that Defendant considered Plaintiff disabled. Plaintiff's argument is without merit. Federal courts repeatedly have held that an employer's decision to accommodate an employee or to place the employee on limited duty do not establish a "regarded as" claim under the ADA. For example, in *Thompson v. City of Arlington*, 838 F.Supp. 1137, 1152 (N.D. Tex. 1993), the court found that "the mere fact that [the defendant] has put [the plaintiff] on restricted duty until it satisfies itself that she is qualified to return to regular duty does not suggest that [the defendant] regards her as having an impairment of the kind contemplated by the ADA." In *Forrisi v. Bowen*, 794 F.2d 931 (4th Cir. 1986), a Rehabilitation Act case, the court affirmed summary judgment for the defendant. In *Forrissi*, the plaintiff argued that the defendant regarded him as handicapped because of his acrophobia (fear of heights). The Fourth Circuit, however, found that the plaintiff had presented no evidence to suggest that the defendant ever doubted plaintiff's ability to work in his chosen field; rather, defendant merely thought plaintiff unfit to work as a utility systems repairman above certain altitudes in its plant. *Id.* at 935. The District of New Hampshire concluded in a persuasive opinion that the proper test for a "regarded as" claim is "whether the impairment, as perceived, would affect the individual's ability to find work across the spectrum of same or similar jobs." *Partlow v. Runyon*, 826 F.Supp. 40, 44 (D.N.H. 1993). In *Partlow*, the court found that the plaintiff had failed to show that the Postal Service considered his back injury a handicap under the Rehabilitation Act: "At most, plaintiff has established that defendant regarded him as unable to satisfy the requirements of a particular mechanic's position due to his particular back problems. This does not render him handicapped under, nor does it entitle him to protection of the Act." *Id.* at 46.

In the case at hand, Plaintiff has failed to point to any evidence suggesting that Defendant considered her disabled under the ADA. Defendant's efforts to accommodate Plaintiff's safety concerns and ultimately to help her find employment outside the Auto Club do not suggest that Plaintiff has a valid "regarded as" claim. Plaintiff's workers' compensation attorney and a representative of Defendant agreed that Plaintiff should receive vocational training after Dr. Brickman stated that Plaintiff could not return to her job at the Auto Club. By its actions, Defendant never conceded that Plaintiff was unfit for work as a claims adjuster or that Plaintiff's impairment, as perceived by Defendant, would preclude her from obtaining employment consistent with her training and experience. Instead, all of the evidence before this Court shows that Defendant's efforts at accommodation were responses to Plaintiff's own concerns about her safety and her wishes to enter a new line of work.

In short, Plaintiff has failed to raise a genuine issue of material fact about whether Defendant regarded her as disabled under the ADA.

3.   Summary.

Since Plaintiff has failed to show the existence of a genuine issue of material fact on either an actual or "regarded-as" theory of disability, Defendant is entitled to summary judgment on Plaintiff's first cause of action.

C. Plaintiff's State-Law Causes of Action. (Omitted)

III. Conclusion.

For the reasons given above, Defendant's motion for summary judgment is GRANTED IN PART. Defendant is entitled to summary judgment on Plaintiff's first cause of action. Having granted summary judgment for Defendant on Plaintiff's only cause of action based on federal law, this Court declines to retain jurisdiction over Plaintiff's remaining causes of action based on state law. Plaintiff's second through fifth causes of action are DISMISSED WITHOUT PREJUDICE to Plaintiff refiling them in an appropriate state court.

IT IS SO ORDERED.

Glossary

Americans with Disabilities Act of 1990 (ADA) – federal statute protecting disabled workers from discrimination on the job because of their disabilities

disability – a physical or mental impairment that limits a major life function

job-related qualification standard – legitimate qualification necessary to perform an essential function of a particular job

mental impairment – any mental or psychological disorder or disease

Occupational Safety and Health Act (OSHA) – federal statute requiring safety measures and standards to protect employees in the workplace

physical impairment – physiological disease or condition, cosmetic disfigurement or anatomical loss

reasonable accommodation – employer requirement to make changes and modifications to assist a disabled worker to perform his or her job

Rehabilitation Act of 1973 – federal statute designed to prevent handicapped persons from being discriminated against on the job

undue hardship – ADA standard used to limit the amount of accommodation an employer must make; accommodations that create an undue hardship are not required

Exercises

1. Does being clinically obese qualify as a physical impairment under the ADA? Argue both sides.

2. What factors would indicate whether an individual is substantially impaired in a major life function? Identify and discuss various examples. In answering this question, refer to the *Muller* case.

3. Discuss whether the ADA should be amended to specify what is meant by physical and mental impairment.

4. Even if an accommodation would not constitute an undue hardship, under what circumstances do you believe it might be considered "unreasonable?"

5. Based on the *Carlson* case, determine the importance of having published employment policies and procedures for an employer accused of violating the ADA. What should these policies and procedures cover? Should anything be omitted?

Chapter Seven

PRIVACY ISSUES

Chapter Overview

Very few laws protect an individual's personal right to privacy. For the most part, the American legal system is more concerned with disseminating information than with protecting that information from being divulged.

Before analyzing the laws and concepts that affect privacy in the workplace, it is necessary to understand the difference between privacy, confidentiality, and secrecy.

The right to **privacy** is generally defined as the right of an individual to decide how much the individual will share with others of his or her thoughts, feelings, and the facts of his or her personal life.

Confidentiality, on the other hand, reflects an individual's right to prevent others with whom he or she has shared private information from disclosing that information to third persons. In the context of the law, this generally falls under the evidentiary and ethical rules that protect a client from having information he or she has given to an attorney with respect to legal representation, or anyone in that attorney's office, such as secretaries and paralegals, from being divulged without the client's consent. This evidentiary right of the client is called the **attorney-client privilege**, which will be discussed in Chapter Ten in the section on ethics.

Finally, **secrecy** refers to the information that a person refuses to share.

> *Example: An employee has just found out that she is pregnant. Until she feels confident that she will be able to carry the baby to term, she does not want to share this information with anyone other than her husband and immediate family. This is a matter of personal privacy and secrecy.*

> *Example: The pregnant employee from the previous example is now in need of medical care. She informs her insurance company but requests that it keep the information confidential, i.e., undisclosed, until she decides to inform her employer. This is an example of confidentiality; the employee has shared information with the insurer but is expecting the insurer to keep the information to itself.*

> *Example: Eventually, the pregnant employee from the preceding examples informs her employer of her physical condition so that she may avail herself of her rights under the Pregnancy Act previously discussed. The employee has now revealed her secret to her employer; however, she retains the right to privacy about the ongoing course of her pregnancy.*

Because of the overwhelming growth of technology and the legal requirements imposed on employers for record keeping over the past few decades, it has become more and more difficult for employees to keep information about themselves private. Much personal information is readily accessible and, in many instances, legally required to be divulged to employers. Technology and record keeping have worked to erode most personal privacy in the workplace. As a general statement, it may be said that an employee has a highly limited right to privacy in today's work environment.

This chapter will examine the laws and situations that affect privacy in the workplace and will discuss various employment practices that an employee may consider to be an invasion of privacy.

The Right to Privacy

Although there is no explicit Constitutional guarantee to privacy, several courts have looked to various sections of the Bill of Rights to ascertain whether there are certain situations in which a citizen should be afforded a degree of privacy.

Typically, courts have focused on the Fourth Amendment protection against unreasonable searches and seizures to prevent the government from gathering personal information about its citizens. This protection is, however, fairly limited because of the various laws that require government to maintain records about its citizens. Also, there are many governmentally guaranteed rights that citizens can only enjoy if the government is made aware of information necessary to extend that right.

> **Example:** *An employee is permanently injured on her job. She now wishes to receive disability benefits under Social Security, but to obtain these benefits she must be willing to divulge to the government all of the information regarding her work and medical history. A conflict arises due to the individual's need to share personal information about herself to receive governmental aid.*

A right to privacy has sometimes been found in the First Amendment rights of liberty and the pursuit of happiness, but these arguments have generally been found to be weak. Once again, the arguments apply only to governmental action, as compared with the actions of private individuals and groups, including employers.

The **due process clause** of the Fifth Amendment has also been argued as the basis for a person's right to privacy. Due process requires that no one be deprived of life, liberty, or property without due process of law, and provides that people may not be compelled to testify against themselves. Under this concept, the government would be prevented from acquiring records about a citizen (the records being property) without first obtaining legal authorization. As do other Bill of Right arguments, these concepts apply only to government action.

> **Example:** *An applicant for employment is required by the prospective employer to provide a detailed financial history. The applicant refuses, saying it is a violation of the Due Process Clause of the Fifth Amendment. Unfortunately, due process does not apply in this private situation.*

As can be seen, most of the arguments with respect to privacy do not apply to private employment situations. Very few limitations are placed on private employers with respect to gathering and maintaining information about their employees. Currently there are three areas that create general threats to personal privacy in the workplace:

1. *Governmental Record Keeping*

Legislative mandates require the government to maintain many records regarding individual citizens. Health information, necessary for the control of diseases and epidemics, as well as for the allocation of funds for medical research, require continual governmental surveillance. Educational records to determine literacy and adherence to the Civil Rights Act also are maintained, as well as tax and employment records to document benefits and adherence to Title VII mandates. All of this information, because of federal computer databases, is now readily available to all agencies of the federal, many state and local governments, and the persons who work for such agencies.

> **Example:** *A daycare center is looking for employees. To maintain its state license, it is required to do background checks on all employees, specifically looking for criminal activity or evidence that the applicant is suspected of child abuse. Because of governmental record keeping, this information is now easily available.*

2. *Commercial Organizations That Maintain Records in the Furtherance of Their Business Activities*

These establishments include:

- credit bureaus that maintain financial information about anyone who has ever applied for credit;

- health organizations, such as hospitals and insurance companies, that gather physical and mental health information;

- businesses that must maintain records pursuant to various federal and state statutes, such as the Civil Rights Act, the ADA, OSHA, and Social Security laws;

- direct marketing services that maintain extensive computer databases about potential customers.

All of this information is gathered in the regular course of business, and most citizens have little or no recourse in keeping this information private.

> *Example: An employee wishes to enjoy the health insurance benefits provided by her employer and may need some accommodation made for her because of a hearing disability. To take advantage of these rights and privileges, she must be willing to divulge personal information about herself.*

3. *Private Access to Computer Databases*

Although this category may represent illegal and unauthorized use of stored information, the reality is that there are many people who, because of modern technology, are able to access personal information about other persons.

> *Example: An employee wants to find out about a coworker. Because of her computer knowledge, she is able to access various databases and discover facts about the coworker that the coworker had expected would remain private. Even though this method of information gathering is illegal, the result is that the information is divulged.*

All of these situations may erode a person's expectation of privacy.

Federal Statutes Regarding Privacy and Disclosure of Information

Under the **Federal Reports Act**, federal agencies are required, with some exceptions, to secure approval from the Office of Management and Budget before collecting information that concerns ten or more people. This provision is intended to minimize governmental record keeping, but it also permits federal agencies to acquire information about vast numbers of citizens once the approval has been given. Once acquired, this information forms part of the government's database.

Because of the growing concern over individual rights and the vast amount of information maintained by the government about private citizens, Congress enacted the **Freedom of Information Act (FOIA)**. The FOIA mandates disclosure to the public of information held by the government except in situations in which disclosure would be a "clearly unwarranted invasion of personal privacy." This statute was designed to minimize governmental secrecy. Much governmentally maintained information may now be disclosed by requesting the release of the records under the procedures detailed in the FOIA. Since the promulgation of FOIA, many states have enacted similar statutes covering state governmental records.

Unfortunately, governmental records regarding one individual will generally contain information about many, and once accessed under the Freedom of Information Act, the information may then be generally disseminated. As a general rule, unless a third party can demonstrate that he or she has suffered substantial damages as a result of the disclosure, it is unlikely that individual will be able to maintain a lawsuit to limit the disclosure of the material.

> **Example:** *A law firm represents an employee who is being discriminated against based on her having AIDS. As part of the firm's evidence gathering, it requests government research regarding AIDS in the workplace and thereby acquires information about specific individuals. The citizens whose personal information was being maintained by the government have now had their personal data revealed to third persons without their consent. However, there is little these individuals can do unless they can demonstrate actual financial harm as a result of the dissemination of this personal information.*

The government agency that maintains the record determines whether disclosure would constitute an "unwarranted invasion of personal privacy"—the individuals in question are not consulted. Once the decision has been made to release the record, the information is public.

In response to the reaction occasioned by the Freedom of Information Act's disclosure of government records, in 1974, Congress passed the Privacy Act. **The Privacy Act of 1974** safeguards the public from unwarranted collection, maintenance, and use and dissemination of personal information contained in agency records by allowing an individual to participate in ensuring that his records are accurate and properly used. To that end, the Privacy Act requires any agency that maintains a "system of records" to publish at least annually a statement in the *Federal Register* describing that system. Such notice must include, among other things, "the name and location of the system," the "categories of users and purposes of their use," and "the policies and practices of the agency regarding storage, retrievability, access controls, retention, and disposal of records." [1]

In addition, any agency that maintains a system of records must allow a person about whom records have been kept to review the record and have a copy made of all or any portion thereof in a form "comprehensible" to the individual.[2]

The Privacy Act, unlike the Freedom of Information Act, does not have disclosure as its primary goal. Rather, the main purpose of the Privacy Act's disclosure requirement is to allow individuals on whom information is being kept the opportunity to review the information and request that the agency correct any inaccuracies. Agencies are, however, authorized to promulgate rules to exempt certain records within a system from disclosure.

This is not to suggest that an agency may simply refuse to acknowledge that it maintains a system of records and thereby insulate itself from the reach of the Privacy Act. To the contrary, if there is evidence that an agency in practice retrieves information about individuals by reference to their names, the mere fact that the agency has not acknowledged that it operates a system of records will not protect it from the statutory consequences of its actions.

Recently, a **Work Place Privacy Bill** was introduced in Congress but has failed to pass. The purpose of the proposed bill was to provide employees in the private sector similar guarantees that

---

[1] 5 U.S.C. § 552a(e)(4)
[2] 5 U.S.C. § 552a(d)(1)

citizens are afforded against government intrusion. Because there is no specific guarantee of privacy in the workplace, many employment practices invade the privacy of employees.

In 1986, Congress passed the **Electronic Communication Privacy Act** to protect against computer piracy. To be covered by the statute, a person must have an **e-mail** address (a computer address for receiving information). The statute does not apply, however, if the e-mail addressee has been given prior notice that his or her e-mail will be monitored. This can have tremendous impact in the workplace where employees send and receive e-mail on a constant basis.

Note that there is an exception for e-mail and computer work performed by a union representative in his or her union capacity. Under labor law restrictions, the computer information may not be monitored by an employer even if the employer pays for the service and has given notice of its intention to monitor its employee's e-mail. Note also that if the employee pays for his or her own computer online service, the employer is prohibited from monitoring that communication as well.

> **Example:** *An employee is looking for a new job and has given his work e-mail address for employment agencies and prospective employers. His employer accesses his e-mail, discovers that he is looking for a new job, and fires him. The employee complains of a violation of the Electronic Communication Privacy Act, but the employer defends by citing a section of the Employee Handbook, given to all its employees when they start work, that states that the employer will monitor e-mail. The employee is without recourse, because under these circumstances the Act will not apply.*

In the same vein as the FOIA, the **Fair Credit Reporting Act** was passed to give people access to their own credit records to ensure that misinformation is not maintained. This Act limits such access to the individual concerned, but credit information is available to potential creditors anytime the individual requests credit.

> **Example:** *An individual is turned down for a personal loan and is informed by the bank that the loan was denied because of his poor credit history. This individual has an excellent credit history and, so, under the Fair Credit Reporting Act requests his credit records from the credit agency. When he sees the record, he discovers that the agency has included another individual's credit history in his file. Pursuant to the statute, he can now have his credit record corrected.*

Employment Practices as Invasions of Privacy

At the present time, there is only one federal statute that specifically concerns privacy issues in the workplace: the **Employee Polygraph Protection Act of 1988**, which, except in limited situations, prohibits employers from requiring employees to submit to polygraph examinations (lie detector tests). Apart from this statute, employers are free to gather information at will about their employees.

Several employer practices in widespread use may be considered as an invasion of their employees' right or expectation of privacy. These practices include

- *Maintenance of administrative records.* All employers gather basic personal information from all employees in the normal course of business, including names and addresses, age, marital status, previous employment, educational background, and so forth. Most people are so used to the dissemination of this data that they do not consider it an invasion of privacy.

Example: A new employee arrives for the first day of work. She reports first to the personnel office to fill out a basic employee form that includes her name, address, telephone number, date of birth, marital status, Social Security number, dependents, and a person to contact in case of emergency. By voluntarily completing this form, the employee has given up her expectation of privacy, but not necessarily her expectation that the information will be kept confidential.

- *Acquiring intelligence reports.* Certain types of jobs require that the employee receive a security clearance. Such positions may include security guard, prison guard, childcare worker, and so forth. As a job requirement, usually for licensing and bonding, an employee must be willing to grant the employer the right to acquire all of his or her criminal and credit records. Once again, the individual's right to keep the information private must be relinquished as a job requirement, but this does not relinquish the employee's expectation of confidentiality.

Example: An applicant for a job as a prison guard is required to permit the state prison officials to check all of her records to get a security clearance. This will probably require her to file a sample of her fingerprints as well. To get the job, she must give up her right to privacy.

- *Maintaining statistical records.* To meet the mandate of having affirmative action plans under Title VII, as well as to document activities for the ADA and the taxing authorities, employers must keep many statistical records about employees concerning race, religion, national origin, age, marital status, dependents, disabilities, and medical history. Most of these statistics are now encoded into computer databases, which means that unauthorized acquisition of the underlying information from which the records were summarized may be possible. Regardless, the records must be maintained to meet the requirements of federal and state laws.

Example: An employer uses a computerized accounting system to maintain payroll and tax records. All income information about its employees, as well as other personal information, must be maintained so that the employee can receive the appropriate pay and have all appropriate taxes withheld (see Chapter Ten). An employee wants to see how much her fellow workers are earning, and is able to access the employer's database. Even though this access is illegal and unauthorized, simply maintaining the records means that unauthorized persons may discover this "private" information.

- *Maintaining and monitoring telephone use.* Employers are permitted by law to monitor all use of company property, including telephones. This means that employers may monitor both incoming and outgoing telephone calls. Because the employer is paying for the telephone, and the employee is generally not permitted to make personal calls at work, the employer legally has the right to listen in on calls. However, there are some exceptions to the employer's right with respect to telephone usage:

1. An employer may not monitor, record, or listen to conversations made on pay phones on the employer's premises.
2. The employer may not listen to an employee's voice mail messages.

Example: While an employee is away from his desk at a meeting, he receives several telephone calls, and messages are left on his voice mail. The employer may not have access to the actual voice mail, but it may maintain records similar to caller ID that identify the telephone number from which the call to the employee was made.

- *Computer monitoring.* As mentioned above, with limited exceptions, an employer may use software to see what its employees are doing on the computer. Remember, the Privacy Act of 1974 only applies to intrusions by governmental employers.

- *Creating system analyses.* As an incident of strategic and financial planning, most modern businesses are involved in statistical analysis. They maintain statistical information to determine current effectiveness and future needs with respect to cash flow, training programs, marketing strategies, and general office planning. These plans are based, in part, on employee information, and employers are given free rein to use such information as they wish.

Example: As part of a business plan developed by an employer to acquire additional financing, the employer utilizes data regarding the education, disabilities, and other information about its current employee pool. Several employees are upset because, even though no names are used, enough information is included in the plan so that individual employees can be easily identified. The employees have no right to keep such information private, and the employer's use of the data is legitimate.

Chapter Summary

An employee's right to privacy has progressed through many legal stages. Originally, after it was realized that the government was maintaining vast records on individual citizens, assertions of a right to privacy were attempted constitutionally by means of the Bill of Rights, specifically the First, Fourth, and Fifth Amendments. As a corollary to this attempt to limit government recordkeeping, citizens demanded to know what information was being maintained about them, and so the Freedom of Information Act (FOIA) was passed, permitting access to government records.

Eventually, people realized that the dissemination of information permitted by the FOIA might invade the privacy of persons appearing in the records along with the person who was requesting the record, and an attempt was made to limit access by means of the Privacy Act of 1974.

In all discussions regarding privacy, it must be remembered that there is a legal distinction between governmental record keeping and private record keeping. The current laws pertain only to the government and the government's invasion of citizens' privacy. The laws do not apply to private employers and their employees.

Basically, private employers are free to gather and maintain information about their employees without restraint; however, the employer may be limited in its use of the information if the employee has a legitimate expectation of confidentiality with respect to the information divulged. In other words, the employee may be required to relinquish private information to the employer, but the employer may not have the right to distribute the information at will or without a legitimate business purpose.

Edited Judicial Decisions

Henke v. U.S. Dept. of Commerce & National Science Fdn. concerns governmental recordkeeping, the Privacy Act, and what constitutes a "record." *Romero-Vargas v. Shalala* discusses disclosure of confidential information by the Social Security Administration regarding immigrant status.

HENKE v. U.S. DEPT. OF COMMERCE & NATIONAL SCIENCE FOUNDATION
____ F.3d ____ (D.C. Cir. 1996)

WALD, Circuit Judge. The issue in this case is whether a Department of Commerce's Advanced Technology Program ("ATP") maintains a "system of records" containing "records" about appellee Wanda Henke, within the meaning of the Privacy Act, 5 U.S.C. § 552a (1994) ("Act"). Henke is the president and co-owner of Dynamic In Situ Geotechnical Testing, Inc. ("Dynamic"), a company which develops earthquake engineering technology. Between 1990 and 1992, Dynamic submitted three applications for competitive high-technology grants from the ATP, each of which was reviewed by technology and business experts as well as members of the ATP staff, and each of which was denied funding. Although the ATP provided Henke with oral summaries of the reviewers' comments, it declined to release copies of the actual reviews or evaluations. Henke then filed a request under the Privacy Act, seeking disclosure of the reviews. The ATP continued to refuse to disclose the reviews, claiming that it did not maintain a "system of records" within the meaning of the Privacy Act because it did not systematically file and retrieve information about individuals indexed by their names. Henke, however, argues that the ATP's groups of paper files and computer databases fell within the Act's definition.

Under the ATP's computer system, when grant proposals are received, an ATP employee enters administrative information (e.g., name of company, address, telephone number, e-mail address, technology area of the proposal, name of contact person) into a database for that proposal. In each of Dynamic's three proposals, Henke had listed herself as Dynamic's contact person, and her name was entered in that field. Henke thus argues that a system of records existed because it was possible for an ATP employee to enter "Wanda Henke" into the computer, have the computer search for every proposal in which Henke was listed as a contact person, and obtain information which was arguably "about" Henke (since she happened to be one of two scientists at Dynamic). The ATP acknowledged that while it could theoretically retrieve information this way, it did not *in practice* use the system that way, but instead used the computer databases for routine administrative purposes, such as organizing the peer reviews by the type of technology involved....

BACKGROUND

A. The Privacy Act

The Privacy Act of 1974 "safeguards the public from unwarranted collection, maintenance, use, and dissemination of personal information contained in agency records...by allowing an individual to participate in ensuring that his records are accurate and properly used." *Bartel v. F.A.A.*, 725 F. 2d 1403, 1407 (D.C. Cir. 1984). To that end, the Act requires any agency which maintains a "system of records" to publish at least annually a statement in the Federal Register describing that system. Such notice must include, among other things, "the name and location of the system," the "categories of individuals on whom records are maintained in the system," the "categories of users and purposes of their use," and "the policies and practices of the agency regarding storage, retrievability, access controls, retention, and disposal of records." 5 U.S.C. § 552a(e)(4). In addition, any agency which maintains a system of records must, upon request by any individual to gain access to his record or to any information pertaining to him which is contained in the system, permit him...to review the record and have a copy made of all or any portion thereof in a form comprehensible to him.... 5 U.S.C. § 552a(d)(1).

The Privacy Act—unlike the Freedom of Information Act—does not have disclosure as its primary goal. Rather, the main purpose of the Privacy Act's disclosure requirement is to allow individuals on whom information is being compiled and retrieved the opportunity to review the information and request that the agency correct any inaccuracies. *See* 5 U.S.C. § 552a(d)(2) (permitting individual to request amendment of her record due to inaccurate, irrelevant, or incomplete information). Agencies are, however, authorized to promulgate rules to exempt certain records within a system from disclosure, such as "investigatory material compiled for law enforcement purposes...[or] investigatory material compiled solely for the purpose of determining suitability, eligibility, or qualifications for Federal civilian employment, military service, Federal contracts, or access to classified information." 5 U.S.C. § 552a(k).

B. Advanced Technology Program

The Department of Commerce's Advanced Technology Program was established in 1990 to "improv[e] the competitive position of the United States and its businesses" by making grants to American businesses to assist in the development of high-risk technologies. 15 U.S.C. § 278n; 15 C.F.R. Part 295. The ATP program accepts grant proposals only from businesses (or joint ventures involving a business) and submits those proposals to technical and business experts who review them to determine whether the project has "the potential for eventual substantial widespread commercial application," and whether the applying company has "the requisite ability in research and technology development and management in the project area in which the grant, contract, or cooperative agreement is being sought." 15 U.S.C. § 278n(d)(10); 15 C.F.R. § 295.3. Based on these recommendations and the program's budget constraints, the ATP makes a final decision on funding, approving approximately ten percent of all proposals.

The ATP maintains information about these proposals both in paper files and in a collection of computer databases—neither of which the ATP has recognized as a "system of records." Each of the paper files is labeled with a unique proposal number which identifies the year of the competition, the specific competition number within that year, and the order in which the proposal was received (e.g., "93-2-0018"). Each paper file contains the grant proposal itself, any business or technical expert reviews, documentation from the ATP staff, debriefing worksheets, administrative checklists, and copies of correspondence with the business. In short, the paper file contains the comprehensive record of the proposal. The only way these files are indexed and retrieved is by their proposal number.

In addition, the ATP maintains for each individual competition a separate computer database, organized around approximately 70 different "fields." When a proposal arrives, an ATP employee enters into those fields administrative information about the proposal such as the name of the organization, its mailing address, its e-mail address, its telephone number, its fax number, whether it is a for-profit organization, the Congressional district of the business, whether the proposal contains proprietary information, the type of technology involved in the proposal, whether it is a new or revised proposal and—of greatest import here—the name of a "technical contact" at the applying organization.

These databases are designed to allow searching by fields. Thus, for example, if the ATP wished to compile a list of every proposal submitted from Tennessee's Third Congressional District, an ATP employee could go into each database, enter the code for that district, and pull up a screen with all of the administrative information for each of those proposals. Similarly, the ATP could use the databases to sort the proposals according to technology area, which would help the program facilitate its technical reviews. The computer databases contain only administrative information and do not contain the text of the grant proposals, technical reviews, or any of the other information contained in the ATP's paper files. However, if an authorized ATP employee were to perform a computer search and retrieve a proposal's number, the employee could make note of that number, go to the paper files, and obtain that information. [Between 1990 and 1992, Henke submitted three proposals to ATP, all of which were denied. She then requested access to the files under the FOIA. ATP refused to disclose the information saying that it was not a record within the meaning of the Privacy Act.]

II. DISCUSSION

A. The Meaning of a "System of Records"

We start with "the fundamental canon that statutory interpretation begins with the language of the statute itself." *Pennsylvania Dep't of Public Welfare v. Davenport*, 495 U.S. 552, 557–58 (1990). In every case, however, we must recognize that "the meaning of statutory language, plain or not, depends on context," *King v. St. Vincent's Hosp.*, 502 U.S. 215,221 (1991), a concern which is brought into high relief here by the fact that the determination that a system of records exists triggers virtually all of the other substantive provisions of the Privacy Act, such as an individual's right to receive copies and to request amendment of her records.

In this case, both Henke and ATP argue that the statute's main meaning supports their respective constructions. Henke argues that the Act's language clearly supports the district court's conclusion that an agency maintains a system of records where is has the *capability* to retrieve information about an individual which is indexed under her name. The ATP argues the opposite, claiming that the Act's statement that a system exists if information keyed to an individual "is retrieved" by the agency means that unless an agency has an actual *practice* of retrieving information by an individual's name, there is no system of records.

Henke's textual argument is unconvincing, for it does not take into account Congress' definition of a system of records as a "group of records...from which information *is retrieved* by the name of the individual...." 5 U.S.C. § 552a(a)(5) (emphasis added). Henke's argument would be stronger if Congress had used words which more clearly suggested that retrieval *capability* would be enough to create a system of records—something individual Members of Congress had in fact attempted to do in other bills introduced before the enactment of the Privacy Act. The Records Disclosure Privacy Act of 1974, for example, would have applied where an agency "maintains records...which *may be retrieved* by reference to, or are indexed under such person's name...." H.R. 12206, 93d Cong., 2d Sess. (1974) (emphasis added). And another bill introduced later that year would have applied to information which was "computer-*accessible* or manual-*accessible*," words clearly connoting retrieval *capability*. H.R. 13872, 93d Cong., 2d Sess.(1974) (emphasis added). But in the Privacy Act itself, Congress used the words "is retrieved," which suggests strongly that a group of records should generally not be considered a system of records unless there is actual retrieval of records keyed to individuals.

Not surprisingly, therefore, this court and others have previously concluded that retrieval capability is not sufficient to create a system of records. *See, e.g., Bartel v. F.A.A.*, 725 F. 2d at 1408 n. 10 ("To be in a system of records, a record must... *in practice* [be] retrieved by an individual's name or other personal identifier.") (emphasis added); *Baker v. Dep't of Navy*, 814 F. 2d 1381, 1383 (9th Cir.) (deferring to a Navy regulation stating that a "system of records is...[a]group of records from which information 'is,' as opposed to 'can be' retrieved by the name of the individual"), *cert. denied*, 484 U.S. 963 (1987). While *Bartel* did not focus on the definition of a system of records, our statement there tends to deflate Henke's claim that under the plain language of the statute, retrieval capability is enough to transform a group of records into a system of records.

The ATP's construction, on the other hand, is more consistent not only with the language of the statute but with the policies underlying the Act. As discussed above, the ATP's interpretation takes into account of Congress' use of the words "is retrieved" in the statute. Moreover, as the ATP points out, under Henke's theory that mere retrieval capability creates a system of records, an agency faces the threat of being found retrospectively to be maintaining a system of records it did not even know existed, simply by dint of a potential use it neither engaged in nor contemplated. This, in turn, would create serious compliance problems for the agency, because if it had not recognized that it maintained a system of records, and had, therefore, not published notice of its system in the Federal Register, then neither would it have followed the procedures necessary to invoke the exemptions in the Privacy Act which Congress intended to protect disclosure of national security information, confidential law enforcement information, or other information from confidential sources. *See* 5 U.S.C. §§ 552a(j), (k). Indeed, were we to find that the ATP was maintaining a system of records here, the agency would not be entitled to invoke exemption (k)(5) of the Act, which protects the disclosure of "investigatory material compiled solely for the purpose of determining eligibility for ...Federal contract," because not knowing that it has a system of records keyed to technical contacts, the ATP has never published the necessary rules to invoke this exemption. Cf. *Henke v. Dep't of Commerce*, No. 95-5181, F. 3d (D.C. Cir. 1996) (NSF has acknowledged that it has a system of records and has promulgated the necessary rules to invoke the section (k)(5) exemption).

This is not to suggest that an agency may simply refuse to acknowledge that it maintains a system of records and thereby insulate itself from the reach of the Privacy Act. To the contrary, if there is evidence that an agency *in practice* retrieves information about individuals by reference to their names, the mere fact that the agency has not acknowledged that it operates a system of records will not protect it from the statutory consequences of its actions. On the other hand, there is no magic number of incidental or *ad hoc* retrievals by reference to an individual's name which will transform a group of records into a *system of records* keyed to individuals.

One factor in deciding whether such a system exists, obviously, is the *purpose* for which the information on individuals is being gathered, an approach which is consistent with Congress' distinction between a mere group of records and a *system* of records. Thus, as in the case with the ATP program, where information about individuals is only being gathered as an administrative adjunct to a grant-making program which focuses on businesses and where the agency has presented evidence that it has no practice of retrieving information keyed to individuals, the agency should not be viewed as maintaining a system of records. On the other hand, where an agency—such as the FBI—is compiling information about individuals primarily for investigatory purposes, Privacy Act concerns are at their zenith, and if there is evidence of even a few retrievals of information keyed to individuals' names, it may well be the case that the agency is maintaining a system of records. We hold, therefore, that in determining whether an agency maintains a system of records keyed to individuals, the court should view the entirety of the situation, including the agency's function, the purpose for which the information was gathered, and the agency's actual retrieval practices and policies.

B. Applying This Test

The final question is whether the ATP was in fact maintaining a system of records with respect to Henke. As we have suggested above, the fact that the ATP's purpose in requesting the name of a technical contact was essentially administrative and was not necessary to the conduct of any of the ATP's core programmatic purposes weighs strongly against allowing a few isolated incidents of retrieval to transform the group of records contained in its paper files and computer databases into a system of records about Henke. The ATP gives grants to businesses, not to individuals, and does not maintain its computer database in order to retrieve information on individuals.

Henke has not seriously disputed the ATP's assertion that an applicant's prospects for receiving a grant will not turn on who it names as a technical contact, nor does she dispute the ATP's claim that the "technical contact" designated by the company applying for an ATP grant need not be responsible for directing any part of the project. As the ATP argues, "[t]he company could chose anyone—any scientist, technician, patent expert, an outside consultant who may have assisted in preparing the proposal....The ATP program takes no notice, one way or the other, of any individual characteristics of the "contact" person chosen." Appellant's Reply Brief at 8. Indeed, in 1990, the first year of the ATP competitions, the ATP did not ask applicants for a "business" or "technical" contact, but instead asked them only to designate "the person to be contacted on matters involving this application."

Henke does argue that in her experience, technical contacts are likely to be scientists, and thus reviews which focus on the quality of a company's "staff" are likely to be "about" the technical contacts. Even if this assertion is true, the record indicates conclusively that the ATP's purpose in requesting the name of a technical contact is essentially administrative and is not even necessary for the conduct of the ATP's operations. Put another way, the ATP program's substantive interests would not be affected (though it might run a bit less efficiently) if it only requested a phone number or fax number as a contact point rather than the *name* of a contact person. Consequently, we find that in the absence of any evidence that the names of contact persons are used regularly or even frequently to obtain information about those persons, the ATP does not maintain a system of records keyed to individuals listed in the contact person fields of its databases.

III. CONCLUSION

We find that the ATP does not currently maintain a "system of records" with respect to Henke for the purposes of the Privacy Act. Accordingly, we vacate the judgment of the district court and remand the case for the district court to enter summary judgment in favor of the Department of Commerce.

ROMERO-VARGAS v. SHALALA
907 F.Supp. 1128 (N. D. Ohio 1995)

BACKGROUND

Plaintiffs brought this action under the Privacy Act of 1974, 5 U.S.C. § 552a, alleging that a Social Security Administration ("SSA") employee improperly disclosed confidential information from the Social Security records of approximately sixty Hispanic employees working for Harold and Betty Freeworth. The material facts are not in dispute.

The facts underlying this case arise out of an earlier case, *Carrada v. Rainbow Tomato, Inc.*, 3:94 CV 7329. Plaintiffs are among a group of migrant farmworkers who brought suit against Harold and Betty Freeworth on June 23, 1994, alleging violations of the Migrant and Seasonal Agricultural Worker Protection Act and the Fair Labor Standards Act. Plaintiffs obtained a series of temporary restraining orders, beginning on June 23, 1994, to prevent the Freeworths from discharging them in retaliation for bringing the suit. That lawsuit ultimately settled.

On July 7, 1994, while *Carrada* was pending, Betty Freeworth telephoned the Social Security Office in Defiance, Ohio, and requested verification of each plaintiff's Social Security number as part of an attempt to investigate every plaintiff's immigration status. She talked with an SSA claims development clerk, Laurie Wilhelm, who checked the names and Social Security numbers Freeworth gave her, and indicated in each case whether the number was valid or invalid.

When Freeworth called the Social Security office, she identified herself to Wilhelm as Plaintiffs' employer. Wilhelm did not verify Freeworth's identity beyond Freeworth's statement that she was an employer. Wilhelm did not ask Freeworth the reason she was requesting the information. Wilhelm confirmed mismatches of names and Social Security numbers, as well as positive matches. Where the Social Security numbers turned out to belong to children or deceased persons, Wilhelm gave Freeworth this information as well. Each of these actions violated the guidelines published in the Social Security Program Operations Manual System (POMS).

Plaintiffs brought the instant suit, claiming that these violations of Social Security guidelines also constitute a violation of the Privacy Act of 1974 and its applicable Regulations. Defendants respond that these guidelines are not binding on Social Security employees; they argue further that even if there was a violation, it was not willful or intentional, and therefore cannot be remedied under the Privacy Act. Both sides have moved for summary judgment.

DISCUSSION

A. Summary Judgment. (Omitted)

B. The Privacy Act of 1974

The Privacy Act of 1974 ("the Act") regulates the collection, maintenance, use and dissemination of information by federal agencies "in order to protect the privacy of individuals identified in information systems maintained by [these] agencies." Section 2(a)(5), Publ. L. 93–579, reprinted in 1974 U.S.C.C.A.N. 2178. It provides that: "no agency shall disclose any record which is contained in a system of records by any means of communication to any person, or to another agency, except pursuant to a written request by, or with the prior written consent of the individual to whom the record pertains, unless disclosure of the record would be...(3) for a routine use...5 U.S.C.A. § 552a(b) (West 1977 & Supp. 1995). If an agency intentionally or willfully violates this section, or any rule promulgated under it, in such a way as to have an adverse effect on an individual, the aggrieved individual may bring a civil action against the agency, and may recover (a) the greater of $1,000 or the individual's actual damages, and (b) reasonable attorney fees and costs. 5 U.S.C.A. § 552(g)(1)(D) & (g)(4) (West 1977 & Supp. 1995).

The question presented by this case is whether, on the facts given above, the Social Security Administration intentionally or willfully violated Plaintiffs' rights in such a way as to have an adverse effect on them. To make this determination, the Court must answer three questions:

1. Was the Privacy Act of 1974 violated?
2. If so, was the violation intentional or willful?
3. Were Plaintiffs adversely affected?

C. Was the Privacy Act of 1974 Violated?

The Act requires a federal agency to obtain the written consent of an individual before it discloses information about that individual to a third party. There is an exception to this consent requirement when disclosure is for a routine use. The parties agree that Wilhelm disclosed information about Plaintiffs to Freeworth without Plaintiffs' consent. They disagree about whether disclosure of Social Security numbers to an employer under the circumstances described above constitutes a "routine use."

Each federal agency that maintains a system of records is required to publish annually in the Federal Register a notice of its records system, including notice of "each routine use of the records contained in the system, including the categories of users and the purpose of such use." 5 U.S.C.A. § 552a(e)(4)(D) (West 1977). The SSA has established two routine uses allowing disclosure to an individual's employer without the individual's consent. Disclosure of the information held in System 09-60-0058, Master Files of SSN Holders and SSN Applications, is allowed as follows: "employers are notified of the SSNs of employees in order to complete their records for reporting wages to SSA pursuant to the Federal Insurance Compensation Act and section 218 of the Act." 60 FR13442, 13443 (March 13, 1995). Employers may also have access to the information held in System 09-60-0059, Earnings Recording and Self-Employment Income System, "for correcting and reconstructing State employee earnings records and for social security purposes." 58 FR 48525, 48526 (September 16, 1993). The Regulations do not allow disclosure to employers for any other purpose.

In this case, Freeworth did not seek to obtain the Social Security numbers in order to meet the requirements of FICA or to reconstruct employee earnings records. She did not represent to Wilhelm that she was so doing. It is clear, therefore, that SSA violated the Privacy Act of 1974 when the information was disclosed.

D. Was the Violation Intentional or Willful?

In order to prevail, however, Plaintiffs must demonstrate more than a simple violation of the Act. They must show that the violation was "intentional or willful." The legislative history of the Act indicates that Congress intended the standard to be "viewed as only somewhat greater than gross negligence." Analysis of House and Senate Compromise Amendments to the Federal Privacy Act, 120 Cong. Rec. 40,405, 40,406 (1974), reprinted in Legislative History of the Privacy Act of 1974, at 990 (1976). While the Sixth Circuit has never had occasion to define the standard precisely, the law is well settled in other Circuits that the Act imposes liability whenever the agency "commit[s] the act without grounds for believing it to be lawful, or by flagrantly disregarding others' rights under the Act." *Albright v. United States*, 235 U.S. App. D.C. 295, 732 F.2d 181, 189 (D.C. Cir. 1984); *see also Wilborn v. Department of Health & Human Servs.*, 49 F.3d 597, 602 (9th Cir. 1995); *Britt v. Naval Investigative Serv.*, 886 F.2d 544, 551 (3d Cir. 1989); *Andrews v. Veterans Admin. of the United States*, 838 F.2d 418, 424–25 (10th Cir. 1988). This Court must therefore ask whether Wilhelm disclosed the Social Security numbers to Freeworth without grounds for believing the disclosure to be lawful, or with flagrant disregard for Plaintiffs' rights under the Act.

Plaintiffs have suggested that this Court should find that Wilhelm intentionally and willfully violated the Privacy Act if she violated the applicable guidelines for Social Security employees, published in the Program Operations Manual System. These guidelines, while not having the force of law, [(*Schweiker v. Hansen*, 450 U.S. 785, 789–90, 101 S.Ct. 1468, 1471–72, 67 L.Ed. 2d 685 (1981)], can give this Court insight into the level of safeguards SSA considers necessary to protect individuals' rights under the Privacy Act.

Defendant, on the other hand, invites this Court to look to the "spirit of the law," apart from the written guidelines, and ask whether Wilhelm could reasonably have believed she was disclosing information for a purpose compatible with the purpose for which the record was collected. *See* 20 C.F.R. § 401.310 ("routine use" is any disclosure which is compatible with the purpose for which the record was collected).

If the Court adopts Plaintiffs' view, it must find a willful violation of the Act. Wilhelm violated several POMS guidelines when she gave Freeworth information about Plaintiffs' Social Security numbers. First, Wilhelm violated both the federal regulation, *supra*, and a POMS guideline when she disclosed information to more than "the extent necessary for correction or reconstruction of earnings records or for Social Security tax purposes." GN 03310.045.B.2.a. Second, she violated several guidelines relating to the release of information by telephone. Only a positive verification of an employee's Social Security number may be given to an employer by telephone. GN 03360.005.A.7.a. Wilhelm gave both positive and negative verifications of the employees' Social Security numbers. The employer must provide the name, Social Security number, date of birth, and sex before a match can be confirmed. *Id.* Wilhelm disclosed information with only a name and Social Security number. Because of the difficulty of proving identity, personal information may not be disclosed to employers based on a telephone request. GN 03360.005A.7.b. Wilhelm informed Freeworth that some of the Social Security numbers Freeworth gave her were assigned to children. Third, Wilhelm failed to follow prescribed procedures for verifying

Freeworth's identity. In cases where the caller is not an SSA employee, the claims development clerk is to ask the caller to provide his or her Employer Identification Number (EIN), and verify the EIN by using the Alpha Access to Employer Identification System (AEQY). GN 3360.005B.4.g. If the caller's identity cannot be verified, the clerk cannot disclose any information, but must send the information by mail to the person about whom the request is made. GN 03360.005B.2.a. Wilhelm admitted that she accepted Freeworth's word that Freeworth was an employer and made no independent attempt to verify Freeworth's identity.

The Court need not adopt Plaintiff's extreme position, however, to find that Wilhelm disclosed information without grounds for believing the disclosure to be lawful, or with flagrant disregard for Plaintiffs' rights under the Act. Wilhelm's actions indicate a blatant disregard not only for the specifics of the POMS guidelines, but for the policies underlying the guidelines and the law they are meant to effectuate. Wilhelm disclosed confidential information to an unknown voice on the telephone, with no attempt to confirm Freeworth's identity. She made no attempt to discover the purpose for which the information was requested. She disclosed information she could not legally disclose, even had she confirmed that she was talking with an employer.

Defendant argues that Wilhelm acted in accordance with the customary procedure she has employed during her eleven and a half years of employment with SSA. Wilhelm's supervisor has testified that these procedures are customarily followed by SSA employees in the six-state region that includes Ohio. If this is so, this Court can only conclude that SSA employees in this region have a custom and practice of violating both SSA guidelines and the Privacy Act.

The statute and regulations are clear. Disclosure without the written consent of the person whose Social Security number is being disclosed is permitted only for routine uses of that information. The only routine uses for which employer can obtain that information are in order for the employer to comply with FICA, or to correct employee earnings records. The Act places an affirmative duty on federal agency employees with access to confidential information carefully to safeguard that information. This is not, as Defendant claims, a case in which a federal employee made an effort to comply with the statute and fell short of a picayune regulation hidden in the small print of a voluminous manual. It is a case in which no effort whatsoever was made to protect Plaintiffs' privacy rights. The Court finds that Defendant's violation of the Act was intentional and willful.

E.   Were Plaintiffs Adversely Affected?

The statute requires that Defendant's violation cause an adverse effect on Plaintiffs. The Sixth Circuit has never addressed the question of what constitutes an adverse effect in the context of the Privacy Act of 1974.

One court has taken a restrictive approach, holding that a plaintiff must show actual pecuniary loss in order to have standing to bring a claim under the Privacy Act. *See DiMura v. Federal Bureau of Investigation*, 823 F.Supp. 45, 47 (1993).

The better reasoned view, taken by the overwhelming majority of courts, is that emotional distress caused by the fact that the plaintiff's privacy has been violated is itself an adverse effect, and that statutory damages can be awarded without an independent showing of adverse effects. E.g., *Wilborn v. Department of Health & Human Servs.*, 49 F.3d 597, 603 (9th Cir. 1995); *Rorex v. Traynor*, 771 F.2d 383, 387 (8th Cir. 1985); *Albright v. United*

States, 235 U.S. App. D.C. 295, 732 F.2d 181, 186 (D.C. Cir. 1984); *Johnson v. Department of the Treasury, IRS*, 700 F.2d 971 (5th Cir. 1983); *Fitzpatrick v. IRS*, 665 F.2d 327, 331 (11th Cir. 1982); *Parks v. United States; IRS*, 618 F.2d 677, 682–83 (10th Cir. 1980); *Hrubec v. National R.R. Passenger Corp.*, 829 F.Supp. 1502, 1506; *Andrews v. Veterans Admin. of the United States*, 613 F.Supp. 1404, 1415–16 (D. Wyo. 1988).

This interpretation comports with the Supreme Court's general holding that the primary damage in "right to privacy" cases is mental distress. *Time, Inc. v. Hill*, 385 U.S. 374, 384, 87 S.Ct. 534, 540, 17 L.Ed. 2d 456 (1967). It also comports with the legislative history and purposes of the statute. The Act's remedial provisions are designed to provide a means of statutory enforcement, as well as compensation to aggrieved individuals. One purpose of the statutory damages of $1,000 is to provide an incentive for individuals who have minimal damages to sue, thereby "encouraging the widest possible citizen enforcement through the judicial process," S. Rep. No. 1183, 93d Cong., 2d Sess. 83, reprinted in 1974 U.S.C.C.A.N. 6997. As the Fifth Circuit has said: "[a] federal act affording special protection to the right of privacy can hardly accomplish its purpose of protecting a personal and fundamental constitutional right if the primary damage resulting from an invasion of privacy is not recoverable under the major remedy of 'actual damages' that has been provided by Congress." Johnson, *supra*, at 977.

The Court therefore finds that Plaintiffs were adversely affected by Defendant's unlawful disclosure. Plaintiffs are entitled to statutory damages of $1,000 each.

CONCLUSION

For the above reasons, Plaintiffs' Motion for Summary Judgment is granted.

Glossary

attorney-client privilege – evidentiary rule protecting from disclosure all information given by a client to an attorney in the course of legal representation

confidentiality – the expectation that disclosed information will not be divulged to third persons

due process – constitutional guarantee against arbitrary taking of life, liberty, or property by the government

e-mail – computer address for receiving information

Electronic Communication Privacy Act – federal statute designed to protect computer privacy

Employee Polygraph Protection Act – federal statute prohibiting employers from requiring employees to take lie detector tests

Fair Credit Reporting Act – federal statute permitting a person to have access to his or her credit records

Federal Reports Act – statute requiring government agencies to obtain authorization from the Office of Management and Budget before maintaining records on 15 or more persons

Freedom of Information Act (FOIA) – federal statute permitting access to government records

privacy – the expectation that personal information will not be disclosed without the person's consent

Privacy Act – federal statute designed to afford the public a limited right to privacy in the collection, maintenance and dissemination of information by the government

secrecy – information a person refuses to share

Work Place Privacy Bill – federal bill to protect privacy of employees in the workplace; it has not yet passed Congress

Exercises

1. What, if any, checks do you think should be established to protect an employee's privacy in the workplace?

2. Obtain a copy of the Work Place Privacy Bill and analyze its provisions.

3. List the procedures outlined in the FOIA to request a governmental record about yourself.

4. What is your opinion of the exception to the employer's right to monitor computers for union representatives? How can an employer determine when an employee is using the computer for union or nonunion purposes?

5. Weigh the detriments of the loss of personal privacy against the benefits gained by the loss. Be specific in your answer to indicate government and private benefits.

Chapter Eight

**REGULATIONS FOR PREVENTING AND
HANDLING SEXUAL HARASSMENT**

Chapter Overview

The problem of sexual harassment in the workplace has gained much media attention. Although the problem is significant, there is almost no federal legislation expressly dealing with it. Claims of sexual harassment in the workplace are usually dealt with as sex discrimination under Title VII of the Civil Rights Act. Most of the law in the area has evolved from judicial interpretation of sex discrimination. The Supreme Court has said in *Meritor Savings Bank v. Vinson*[1] that sexual harassment constitutes sex discrimination in violation of Title VII. This is true because the employee has been singled out because of his or her sex.

For the employee, sexual harassment in the workplace can be physically and emotionally upsetting. It can destroy the worker's job performance and create an atmosphere of tension and hostility that demoralizes the entire company. If the employer does not have a written policy prohibiting sexual harassment before an employee files a claim of sexual harassment, the employer may be held liable for any injury the worker suffers.

> *Example: A senior partner in a law office has been making unwanted sexual advances to a new associate and has indicated that the associate's position with the firm will be affected by her willingness to cooperate. The associate is upset and confides to several other people in the firm. In a short time, most of the legal staff is aware of the problem and an atmosphere of tension is created in the office.*

> *Example: In the above example, the associate finally decides to file a sexual harassment claim with the managing partner of the law office. The associate is claiming severe mental distress causing her to seek counseling. The firm has not yet established a written policy or outlined procedures to combat sexual harassment in the office. If the claim is found to be justified, the law office itself may be responsible for all damages and injuries the associate suffered.*

The most effective method of combating sexual harassment in the workplace is for the employer to establish a specific policy prohibiting it and to create a formalized procedure for investigating and solving complaints of sexual harassment. These policies should include training and sensitivity programs for all employees.

This short chapter will focus on the definition of sexual harassment, the implications of sexual harassment for the workplace, and suggested procedures and policies for dealing with sexual harassment.

---

[1] 477 U.S. 57 (1986)

Sexual Harassment Defined

In its guidelines, the **Equal Employment Opportunity Commission** (EEOC), the government department created to investigate claims of discrimination under Title VII of the Civil Rights Act, has defined **sexual harassment** as "unwelcome sexual advances, requests for sexual favors, and other verbal or physical conduct of a sexual nature." Under this definition, sexual harassment can arise when:

- Submission to the conduct is made a term or condition of employment (***quid pro quo harassment***).

- Submission or rejection of the sexual advance is used as a basis for employment decisions.

- The complained of conduct has the effect of interfering with work performance or creating a hostile work environment.

Sexual harassment applies equally to males as well as females, homosexuals as well as heterosexuals.

Example: A male paralegal is applying for a job at a law firm. His prospective employer is a female partner. The partner indicates to the applicant that the job will involve much travel. She advises the applicant that to save money she always shares a hotel room with her paralegals. She tells the applicant that, if he is unwilling to agree to these arrangements, there are many other applicants for the position. This is an example of sexual harassment used as a condition of employment.

Example: A male supervisor in a factory keeps "girlie" calendars in his office, as well as pictures of nude women. Women comprise 28 percent of his workforce, and the pictures offend them. The supervisor says he doesn't care, that it is his office and his staff. The pictures create a tense atmosphere for the women. This example of sexual harassment interferes with work performance and creates a hostile work environment.

Not only is sexual harassment in the workplace illegal, it also has a deleterious effect on work performance, productivity, and profit.

Implications of Sexual Harassment at Work

Unwelcome sexual advances create an atmosphere of tension and hostility in the workplace, are unprofessional, and violate public law and policy.

A **hostile work environment** exists when an employee can show that:

1. he or she was subjected to sexual advances, requests for sexual favors, or other verbal or physical conduct of a sexual nature,
2. this conduct was unwelcome, and

3. the conduct was sufficiently severe or pervasive to alter the conditions of the victim's employment and create an abusive working environment.

The EEOC guidelines describe hostile work environment harassment as "conduct [which] has the purpose or effect of unreasonably interfering with an individual's work performance or creating an intimidating, hostile, or offensive environment."[2]

> *Example: A factory loading dock employs one male supervisor and twenty workers, four of whom are women. The male workers continually tell off-color jokes and make explicit sexual references about the women employed by the company. The supervisor is aware of the situation but does nothing. These statements have made the female workers feel uncomfortable, and they feel tense every time they arrive for work. As a consequence of these verbal assaults, the women cannot concentrate on work, and accidents occur, harming the entire operation.*

On the other hand, in order for the conduct to be considered harassment, it must be both unwelcome and consistent. If the employee who eventually complains of harassment at first welcomed the advances and found them complimentary, sexual harassment may not have occurred. The determination would be based, in part, upon what a reasonable person would believe under similar circumstances.

If the employee welcomed the sexual advance, it is a defense to the charge of sexual harassment. However, as in the example noted above, once the employee no longer finds the advances welcome, if the conduct continues, it may turn into sexual harassment.

> *Example: A female manager finds one of her male employees very attractive and makes a mild flirtatious remark to him. He refuses, saying that he is already involved with someone. If the manager does not repeat her conduct, nor penalize the employee because of the rejection, no sexual harassment has occurred. It was an isolated incident that has no effect on the employee's job.*

> *Example: A manager and his secretary begin to date. After three months, the manager decides that the secretary is not the woman of his dreams and calls the relationship off. After the breakup, the secretary continues to leave sexually explicit notes and photographs on the manager's desk and continues to make sexual advances to him. This is an example of unwelcome sexual advances that create a hostile work atmosphere. What was once welcome has become unwelcome and now constitutes harassment. Note that supervisors may be harassed by their underlings as well as the reverse.*

It is not a defense to the employer's liability if it claims the subject employee failed to complain of the conduct and therefore the employer had no actual knowledge of the harassment. It is the employer's legal responsibility to maintain a policy prohibiting sexual harassment and to monitor the workplace to ensure that such conduct does not occur. Thus, an employer can be held

---

[2] 29 C.F.R. Sec. 1604.11(a)(3)

responsible for failing to be vigilant about a work environment where sexual harassment is occurring. A failure to complain by the employee does not indicate that no sexual harassment is occurring—the employee may fear reprisals if a complaint is made. Therefore, as will be discussed in the next section, it is the employer's responsibility to see that adequate safeguards and procedures exist for investigating and resolving a claim of sexual harassment.

> *Example: An employee is being sexually harassed at the workplace, and the employer has not provided any specific procedures for resolving such matters. The employee says nothing, but looks for another job. Once he has obtained other employment, he files a claim of sexual harassment, seeking damages. The fact that he did not file a claim while he was still employed at the place where the alleged harassment occurred is not a defense for the employer.*

An employer can be held liable for the sexual harassment of nonemployees if they were sexually harassed by its employees while conducting business with the company and the employer knew, or should have known, about the situation. This liability extends to spouses of employees, customers, clients, and suppliers.

> *Example: A corporate vice president constantly makes sexual advances to the wife of one of his assistants at corporate parties and functions. He tells her that if she does not submit to him, her husband's career with the company will be short-lived. This is a case of sexual harassment directed at the spouse of an employee, for which the company may be liable. The conduct took place at corporate functions in front of other officers and employees.*

> *Example: The representative of a supplier is constantly harassed when she goes to a particular customer's office. The buyer's representative makes lewd jokes and comments and continually taunts her in a sexual manner. When she complains to a vice president at the buyer's company, he does nothing. She then complains to her supervisor, who also refuses to act. In this instance, both companies may be liable for the harassment of the supplier's representative.*

Procedures for Dealing with Sexual Harassment

Dealing with sexual harassment in the workplace involves two distinct problems. First, the employer must establish a policy to try to prevent sexual harassment *before* it takes place. Second, should an employee claim that he or she is a victim of sexual harassment, the employer must have established procedures for investigating the charges and solving the problem.

As stated above, an employer may be held liable if it has not disseminated a written policy prohibiting sexual harassment in the workplace before a claim has been filed against it. The policy should define sexual harassment according to the EEOC guidelines as outlined above, detail exactly how complaints are to be filed and describe what internal investigative procedures will be used to substantiate the claim. If the employees are either unaware of the types of conduct that constitute sexual harassment or the procedures for dealing with such problems, it is more likely that these types of problems will occur.

> *Example:* An employee was unaware that having suggestive photographs and materials at his own workstation might constitute sexual harassment of a coworker who must share the same space. Unless sexual harassment is defined and explained, a person may unwittingly cause another person to suffer.

> *Example:* An employee is being sexually harassed by her supervisor. She has no idea whom to tell or how to go about resolving the problem, because in the normal course of business all problems are brought to the supervisor, who is the source of this particular problem. If the employer has no policy established to process these complaints, the employee would have no method of resolving the problem.

Merely having a method of reporting alleged sexual harassment does not in and of itself alleviate the problem. If the method instituted by the employer to resolve the problem is ineffective, confrontational, or provides no remedies, the procedure may aggravate rather than alleviate the problem.

> *Example:* An employer has established a procedure for processing sexual harassment complaints. The procedures require that the complainant present his or her charges and proof directly to the alleged harasser in front of their direct supervisor. Most employees are too intimidated to face a harasser directly with no counsel or support, so this method of processing the complaint is thereby ineffective.

The procedures established by an employer should provide assistance and counseling for both the victim and the harasser. They should also provide that charges of sexual harassment will be investigated and evaluated by totally impartial persons. Specific remedies should be detailed, including potential suspension or termination of the offender. If the allegations prove to be unjustified, disciplinary action may be warranted against the complaining party.

> *Example:* An employee who has not been promoted charges his supervisor with sexual harassment. He claims that the supervisor told him that if he did not have sex with her, he would never be promoted. The employee files a claim pursuant to the company's established procedures. After an investigation is made, the charges are proved false. The company may now take disciplinary action against the employee who made the false charges against his supervisor.

There is an old saying that "an ounce of prevention is worth a pound of cure," and this adage applies to the problem of sexual harassment in the workplace. Employers should provide organized training programs and sensitivity sessions for their employees on a regular basis to avoid potential problems of harassment in the future. Various training manuals are available, from texts to audiotapes and videotapes. They should be a part of regular employee training programs.

Finally, all allegations of sexual harassment should be taken seriously and fully investigated. All parties, as well as any witnesses, should be interviewed, and applicable documentation should be reviewed. The investigator should remain impartial until a final determination can be made. No procedures will be effective if the investigation is slipshod.

> ***Example:*** *An employee files a claim of sexual harassment against a coworker. The person who is put in charge of the investigation takes an immediate liking to the complainant and fails to question other workers or to take note of what the accused worker says. In this instance, any determination would be biased.*

Chapter Summary

Sexual harassment in the workplace falls under Title VII of the Civil Rights Act. If an employee is made uncomfortable because of direct or implicit sexual advances or comments, discriminatory and unlawful sexual harassment may have occurred.

Employers should establish and disseminate to all employees a written policy prohibiting sexual harassment in the workplace, and procedures should be established for presenting and investigating claims of possible harassment. Special training should be given to all employees regarding sexual harassment to try to avoid the problem. Should a problem arise, the matter should be dealt with quickly, fully, and with consideration for all parties concerned. Remedies should be specified so that the established policy will be effective in its enforcement.

Most of the law with respect to sexual harassment is judicial rather than statutory. An analysis of your own jurisdiction should be made to understand various applications of sexual harassment.

Edited Judicial Decisions

The two edited decisions discuss various problems incidental to prosecuting a claim of sexual harassment. In *Ellison v. Brady*, the court discussed what test should be applied to determine whether the questioned conduct is sufficiently pervasive to constitute sexual harassment, and, if so, what remedies should be applied. The second case, *Cronin v. United Services Stations, Inc.*, highlights examples of sexual harassment that caused an employee to resign.

ELLISON v. BRADY
924 F.2d 872 (9th Cir. 1991)

I.   Kerry Ellison worked as a revenue agent for the Internal Revenue Service in San Mateo, California. During her initial training in 1984, she met Sterling Gray, another trainee, who was also assigned to the San Mateo office. The two coworkers never became friends, and they did not work closely together.

Gray's desk was twenty feet from Ellison's desk, two rows behind and one row over. Revenue agents in the San Mateo office often went to lunch in groups. In June of 1986, when no one else was in the office, Gray asked Ellison to lunch. She accepted. Gray had to pick up his son's forgotten lunch, so they stopped by Gray's house. He gave Ellison a tour of his house.

Ellison alleges that after the June lunch Gray started to pester her with unnecessary questions and hang around her desk. On October 9, 1986, Gray asked Ellison out for a drink after work. She declined, but she suggested that they have lunch the following week. She did not want to have lunch alone with him, and she tried to stay away from the office during lunch time. One day during the following week, Gray uncharacteristically dressed in a three-piece suit and asked Ellison out for lunch. Again, she did not accept.

On October 22, 1986, Gray handed Ellison a note he wrote on a telephone message slip which read: I cried over you last night, and I'm totally drained today. I have never been in such constant term oil [*sic*]. Thank you for talking with me. I could not stand to feel your hatred for another day....

When Ellison realized that Gray wrote the note, she became shocked and frightened and left the room. Gray followed her into the hallway and demanded that she talk to him, but she left the building.

Ellison later showed the note to Bonnie Miller, who supervised both Ellison and Gray. Miller said "this is sexual harassment." Ellison asked Miller not to do anything about it. She wanted to try to handle it herself. Ellison asked a male coworker to talk to Gray, to tell him that she was not interested in him, and to leave her alone. The next day, Thursday, Gray called in sick.

Ellison did not work on Friday, and on the following Monday, she started four weeks of training in St. Louis, Missouri. Gray mailed her a card and a typed, single-spaced, three-page letter. She describes this letter as "twenty times, a hundred times weirder" than the prior note. Gray wrote, in part: "I know that you are worth knowing with or without sex ... leaving aside the hassles and disasters of recent weeks. I have enjoyed you so much over these past few months. Watching you. Experiencing you from O so far away. Admiring your style and élan.... Don't you think it odd that two people who have never even talked together, alone, are striking off such intense sparks.... I will [write] another letter in the near future."

Explaining her reaction, Ellison stated: "I just thought he was crazy. I thought he was nuts. I didn't know what he would do next. I was frightened."

She immediately telephoned Miller. Ellison told her supervisor that she was frightened and really upset. She requested that Miller transfer either her or Gray because she would not be comfortable working in the same office with him. Miller asked Ellison to send a copy of the card and letter to San Mateo.

Miller then telephoned her supervisor, Joe Benton, and discussed the problem. That same day she had a counseling session with Gray. She informed him that he was entitled to union representation. During this meeting, she told Gray to leave Ellison alone.

At Benton's request, Miller apprised the labor relations department of the situation. She also reminded Gray many times over the next few weeks that he must not contact Ellison in any way. Gray subsequently transferred to the San Francisco office on November 24, 1986. Ellison returned from St. Louis in late November and did not discuss the matter further with Miller.

After three weeks in San Francisco, Gray filed union grievances requesting a return to the San Mateo office. The IRS and the union settled the grievances in Gray's favor, agreeing to allow him to transfer back to the San Mateo office provided that he spend four more months in San Francisco and promise not to bother Ellison. On January 28, 1987, Ellison first learned of Gray's request in a letter from Miller explaining that Gray would return to the San Mateo office. The letter indicated that management decided to resolve Ellison's problem with a six-month separation, and that it would take additional action if the problem recurred.

After receiving the letter, Ellison was "frantic." She filed a formal complaint alleging sexual harassment on January 30, 1987, with the IRS. She also obtained permission to transfer to San Francisco temporarily when Gray returned.

Gray sought joint counseling. He wrote Ellison another letter which still sought to maintain the idea that he and Ellison had some type of relationship.

The IRS employee investigating the allegation agreed with Ellison's supervisor that Gray's conduct constituted sexual harassment. In its final decision, however, the Treasury Department rejected Ellison's complaint because it believed that the complaint did not describe a pattern or practice of sexual harassment covered by the EEOC regulations. After an appeal, the EEOC affirmed the Treasury Department's decision on a different ground. It concluded that the agency took adequate action to prevent the repetition of Gray's conduct.

Ellison filed a complaint in September of 1987 in federal district court. The court granted the government's motion for summary judgment on the ground that Ellison had failed to state a *prima facie* case of sexual harassment due to a hostile working environment. Ellison appeals.

II. Congress added the word "sex" to Title VII of the Civil Rights Act of 1964 at the last minute on the floor of the House of Representatives. 110 Cong. Rec. 2,577–2,584 (1964). Virtually no legislative history provides guidance to courts interpreting the prohibition of sex discrimination. In *Meritor Savings Bank v. Vinson*, 477 U.S. 57, 91 L.Ed. 2d 49, 106 S.Ct. 2399 (1986), the Supreme Court held that sexual harassment constitutes sex discrimination in violation of Title VII.

Courts have recognized different forms of sexual harassment. In "quid pro quo" cases, employers condition employment benefits on sexual favors. In "hostile environment" cases, employees work in offensive or abusive environments. *A. Larson*, Employment Discrimination § 41.61 at 8–151 (1989). This case, like *Meritor*, involves a hostile environment claim.

The Supreme Court in *Meritor* held that Michelle Vinson's working conditions constituted a hostile environment in violation of Title VII's prohibition of sex discrimination. Vinson's supervisor made repeated demands for sexual favors, usually at work, both during and after business hours. Vinson initially refused her employer's sexual advances, but eventually acceded because she feared losing her job. They had intercourse over forty times. She additionally testified that he "fondled her in front of other employees, followed her into the women's restroom when she went there alone, exposed himself to her, and even forcibly raped her on several occasions." *Meritor*, 477 U.S. at 60. The Court had no difficulty finding this environment hostile. *Id*. at 67.

Since *Meritor*, we have not often reached the merits of a hostile environment sexual harassment claim. In *Jordan v. Clark*, 847 F.2d 1368, 1373 (9th Cir. 1988), cert. denied *sub nom.*, *Jordan v. Hodel*, 488 U.S. 1006, 109 S.Ct. 786, 102 L.Ed. 2d 778 (1989), we explained that a hostile environment exists when an employee can show

  (1) that he or she was subjected to sexual advances, requests for sexual favors, or other verbal or physical conduct of a sexual nature,
  (2) that this conduct was unwelcome, and
  (3) that the conduct was sufficiently severe or pervasive to alter the conditions of the victim's employment and create an abusive working environment.

In *Jordan*, we reviewed for clear error the district court's determination that an employee was not subjected to particular unwelcome advances. *Id.* at 1375. We explained that we will review *de novo* a district court's final conclusion that conduct is not severe enough or pervasive enough to constitute an abusive environment. *Id.* We affirmed the district court's judgment in *Jordan* because we did not find its factual findings clearly erroneous. *Id.* See also *Vasconcelos v. Meese*, 907 F.2d 111, 112 (9th Cir. 1990) (affirming district court's decision that the working environment was not sexually hostile because the district court's factual findings were not clearly erroneous).

We had another opportunity to examine a hostile working environment claim of sexual harassment in *E.E.O.C. v. Hacienda Hotel*, 881 F.2d 1504 (9th Cir. 1989). In that case, the district court found a hostile working environment where the hotel's male chief of engineering frequently made sexual comments and sexual advances to the maids, and where a female supervisor called her female employees "dogs" and "whores." *Id.* at 1508. Upon a *de novo* review of the facts found by the district court, we agreed that the conduct was sufficiently severe and pervasive to alter the conditions of employment and create a hostile working environment.

III. The parties ask us to determine if Gray's conduct, as alleged by Ellison, was sufficiently severe or pervasive to alter the conditions of Ellison's employment and create an abusive working environment. The district court, with little Ninth Circuit case law to look to for guidance, held that Ellison did not state a *prima facie* case of sexual harassment due to a hostile working environment. It believed that Gray's conduct was "isolated and genuinely trivial." We disagree.

We begin our analysis of the third part of the framework we set forth in *Jordan* with a closer look at *Meritor*. The Supreme Court in *Meritor* explained that courts may properly look to guidelines issued by the Equal Employment Opportunity Commission (EEOC) for guidance when examining hostile environment claims of sexual harassment. 477 U.S. at 65. The EEOC guidelines describe hostile environment harassment as "conduct [which] has the purpose or effect of unreasonably interfering with an individual's work performance or creating an intimidating, hostile, or offensive working environment." 29 C.F.R. § 1604.11 (a)(3). The EEOC, in accord with a substantial body of judicial decisions, has concluded that "Title VII affords employees the right to work in an environment free from discriminatory intimidation, ridicule, and insult." 477 U.S. at 65.

The Supreme Court cautioned, however, that not all harassment affects a "term, condition, or privilege" of employment within the meaning of Title VII. For example, the "mere utterance of an ethnic or racial epithet which engenders offensive feelings in an employee" is not, by itself, actionable under Title VII. *Id.* at 67. To state a claim under Title VII, sexual harassment "must be sufficiently severe or pervasive to alter the conditions of the victim's employment and create an abusive working environment." *Id.*

The Supreme Court drew its limiting language from *Rogers v. EEOC*, 454 F.2d 234 (5th Cir. 1971), cert. denied, 406 U.S. 957, 32 L.Ed.2d 343, 92 S.Ct. 2058 (1972), the first case to recognize a hostile racial environment claim under Title VII. The *Rogers* phrasing limits hostile environment claims to cases where conduct alters the conditions of employment and creates an abusive working environment. The EEOC guidelines, drawing upon *Rogers* and other decisions, indicate that sexual harassment violates Title VII where conduct creates an intimidating, hostile, or offensive environment or where it unreasonably interferes with work performance. 29 C.F.R. § 1604.11(a)(3).

We do not think that these standards are inconsistent. The Supreme Court used the words "abusive" and "hostile" synonymously in *Meritor*. 477 U.S. at 66. The *Meritor* Court also approved of and paid detailed attention to the EEOC's guidelines, and it implicitly adopted the EEOC's position that sexual harassment which unreasonably interferes with work performance violates Title VII. Similarly, although we only expressly incorporated the limiting language from *Rogers* in the third part of our framework in *Jordan*, that part also encompasses the EEOC's requirements in 29 C.F.R. § 1604.11(A)(3). Conduct which unreasonably interferes with work performance can alter a condition of employment and create an abusive working environment. Contra Pollack, "Sexual Harassment: Women's Experience vs. Legal Definitions," 13 *Harv. Women's Law* J. 35, 60 (1990) (arguing that the *Meritor* court opted for the strict standard enunciated in *Rogers* instead of the more lenient EEOC standard).

Although *Meritor* and our previous cases establish the framework for the resolution of hostile environment cases, they do not dictate the outcome of this case. Gray's conduct falls somewhere between forcible rape and the mere utterance of an epithet. 477 U.S. at 60, 67. His conduct was not as pervasive as the sexual comments and sexual advances in *Hacienda Hotel*, which we held created an unlawfully hostile working environment. 881 F.2d 1504.

The government asks us to apply the reasoning of other courts which have declined to find Title VII violations on more egregious facts. In *Scott v. Sears, Roebuck & Co.*, 798 F.2d 210, 212 (7th Cir. 1986), the Seventh Circuit analyzed a female employee's working conditions for sexual harassment. It noted that she was repeatedly propositioned and winked at by her supervisor. When she asked for assistance, he asked "what will I get for it?" Coworkers slapped her buttocks and commented that she must moan and groan during sex. The court examined the evidence to see if "the demeaning conduct and sexual stereotyping caused such anxiety and debilitation to the plaintiff that working conditions were 'poisoned' within the meaning of Title VII." *Id.* at 213. The court did not consider the environment sufficiently hostile. *Id.* at 214.

Similarly, in *Rabidue v. Osceola Refining Co.*, 805 F.2d 611 (6th Cir. 1986), cert. denied, 481 U.S. 1041, 95 L.Ed. 2d 823, 107 S.Ct. 1983 (1987), the Sixth Circuit refused to find a hostile environment where the workplace contained posters of naked and partially dressed women, and where a male employee customarily called women "whores," "cunt," "pussy," and "tits," referred to plaintiff as "fat ass," and specifically stated, "All that bitch needs is a good lay." Over a strong dissent, the majority held that the sexist remarks and the pin-up posters had only a *de minimis* effect and did not seriously affect the plaintiff's psychological well-being.

We do not agree with the standards set forth in *Scott* and *Rabidue*, and we choose not to follow those decisions. Neither *Scott*'s search for "anxiety and debilitation" sufficient to "poison" a working environment nor *Rabidue*'s requirement that a plaintiff's psychological well-being be "seriously affected" follows directly from language in *Meritor*. It is the harasser's conduct which must be pervasive or severe, not the alteration in the conditions of employment. Surely, employees need not endure sexual harassment until their psychological well-being is seriously affected to the extent that they suffer anxiety and debilitation. Accord, EEOC Policy Guidance on Sexual Harassment, 8 Fair Employment Practices Manual (BNA) 405:6681, 6690, (March 19, 1990). Although an isolated epithet by itself fails to support a cause of action for a hostile environment, Title VII's protection of employees from sex discrimination comes into play long before the point where victims of sexual harassment require psychiatric assistance.

We have closely examined *Meritor* and our previous cases, and we believe that Gray's conduct was sufficiently severe and pervasive to alter the conditions of Ellison's employment and create an abusive working environment. We first note that the required showing of severity or seriousness of the harassing conduct varies inversely with the pervasiveness or frequency of the conduct. *See King v. Board of Regents of University of Wisconsin System*, 898 F.2d 533, 537 (7th Cir. 1990) ("although a single act can be enough ... generally, repeated incidents create a stronger claim of hostile environment, with the strength of the claim depending on the number of incidents and the intensity of each incident.") *Accord Andrews*, 895 F.2d at 1484; *Carrero v. New York City Housing Authority*, 890 F.2d 569, 578 (2d Cir. 1989); EEOC Compliance Manual, § 615, para. 3112, C at 3243 (CCH 1988). For example, in *Vance v. Southern Bell Telephone and Telegraph Co.*, 863 F.2d 1503, 1510 (11th Cir. 1989), the court held that two incidents in which a noose was found hung over an employee's work station were sufficiently severe to constitute a jury question on a racially hostile environment.

Next, we believe that in evaluating the severity and pervasiveness of sexual harassment, we should focus on the perspective of the victim. *King*, 898 F.2d at 537; EEOC Compliance Manual (CCH) § 615, para. 3112, C at 3242 (1988) (courts "should consider the victim's perspective and not stereotyped notions of acceptable behavior"). If we only examined whether a reasonable person would engage in allegedly harassing conduct, we would run the risk of reinforcing the prevailing level of discrimination. Harassers could continue to harass merely because a particular discriminatory practice was common, and victims of harassment would have no remedy.

We therefore prefer to analyze harassment from the victim's perspective. A complete understanding of the victim's view requires, among other things, an analysis of the different perspectives of men and women. Conduct that many men consider unobjectionable may offend many women. *See, e.g., Lipsett v. University of Puerto Rico*, 864 F.2d 881, 898 (1st Cir. 1988) ("A male supervisor might believe, for example, that it is legitimate for him to tell a female subordinate that she has a 'great figure' or 'nice legs.' The female subordinate, however, may find such comments offensive"); *Yates*, 819 F.2d at 637, ("men and women are vulnerable in different ways and offended by different behavior"). *See also* Ehrenreich, "Pluralist Myths and Powerless Men: The Ideology of Reasonableness in Sexual Harassment Law," 99 Yale L. J. 1177, 1207–1208 (1990) (men tend to view some forms of sexual harassment as "harmless social interactions to which only overly sensitive women would object"); Abrams, "Gender Discrimination and the Transformation of Workplace Norms," 42 Vand. L. Rev. 1183, 1203 (1989) (the characteristically male view depicts sexual harassment as comparatively harmless amusement).

We realize that there is a broad range of viewpoints among women as a group, but we believe that many women share common concerns which men do not necessarily share. For example, because women are disproportionately victims of rape and sexual assault, women have a stronger incentive to be concerned with sexual behavior. Women who are victims of mild forms of sexual harassment may understandably worry whether a harasser's conduct is merely a prelude to violent sexual assault. Men, who are rarely victims of sexual assault, may view sexual conduct in a vacuum without a full appreciation of the social setting or the underlying threat of violence that a woman may perceive.

In order to shield employers from having to accommodate the idiosyncratic concerns of the rare hyper-sensitive employee, we hold that a female plaintiff states a *prima facie* case of hostile environment sexual harassment when she alleges conduct which a reasonable woman would consider sufficiently severe or pervasive to alter the conditions of employment and create an abusive working environment. *Andrews*, 895 F.2d at 1482 (sexual harassment must detrimentally affect a reasonable person of the same sex as the victim); *Yates*, 819 F.2d at 637 (adopting "reasonable woman" standard set out in *Rabidue*, 805 F.2d 611, 626 (Keith, J. dissenting)); Comment, Sexual Harassment Claims of Abusive Work Environment Under Title VII, 97 Harv. L. Rev. 1449, 1459 (1984); *Cf. State v. Wanrow*, 88 Wash. 2d 221, 239–241, 559 P.2d 548, 558–559 (1977) (*en banc*) (adopting reasonable woman standard for self defense).

We adopt the perspective of a reasonable woman primarily because we believe that a sex-blind reasonable person standard tends to be male-biased and tends to systematically ignore the experiences of women. The reasonable woman standard does not establish a higher level of protection for women than men. *Cf. Rosenfeld v. Southern Pacific Co.*, 444 F.2d 1219, 1225–1227 (9th Cir. 1971) (invalidating under Title VII paternalistic state labor laws restricting employment opportunities for women). Instead, a gender-conscious examination of sexual harassment enables women to participate in the workplace on an equal footing with men. By acknowledging and not trivializing the effects of sexual harassment on reasonable women, courts can work towards ensuring that neither men nor women will have to "run a gauntlet of sexual abuse in return for the privilege of being allowed to work and make a living." *Henson v. Dundee*, 682 F.2d 897, 902 (11th Cir. 1982).

We note that the reasonable victim standard we adopt today classifies conduct as unlawful sexual harassment even when harassers do not realize that their conduct creates a hostile working environment. Well-intentioned compliments by coworkers or supervisors can form the basis of a sexual harassment cause of action if a reasonable victim of the same sex as the plaintiff would consider the comments sufficiently severe or pervasive to alter a condition of employment and create an abusive working environment. That is because Title VII is not a fault-based tort scheme. "Title VII is aimed at the consequences or effects of an employment practice and not at the ... motivation" of coworkers or employers. *Rogers*, 454 F.2d at 239; *see also Griggs v. Duke Power Co.*, 401 U.S. 424, 432, 28 L.Ed. 2d 158, 91 S.Ct. 849 (1971) (the absence of discriminatory intent does not redeem an otherwise unlawful employment practice). To avoid liability under Title VII, employers may have to educate and sensitize their workforce to eliminate conduct which a reasonable victim would consider unlawful sexual harassment. *See* 29 C.F.R. § 1604.11(f) ("Prevention is the best tool for the elimination of sexual harassment.")

The facts of this case illustrate the importance of considering the victim's perspective. Analyzing the facts from the alleged harasser's viewpoint, Gray could be portrayed as a modern-day Cyrano de Bergerac wishing no more than to woo Ellison with his words. There is no evidence that Gray harbored ill will toward Ellison. He even offered in his "love letter" to leave her alone if she wished. Examined in this light, it is not difficult to see why the district court characterized Gray's conduct as isolated and trivial.

Ellison, however, did not consider the acts to be trivial. Gray's first note shocked and frightened her. After receiving the three-page letter, she became really upset and frightened again. She immediately requested that she or Gray be transferred. Her supervisor's prompt response suggests that she too did not consider the conduct trivial. When Ellison learned that Gray arranged to return to San Mateo, she immediately asked to transfer, and she immediately filed an official complaint.

We cannot say as a matter of law that Ellison's reaction was idiosyncratic or hypersensitive. We believe that a reasonable woman could have had a similar reaction. After receiving the first bizarre note from Gray, a person she barely knew, Ellison asked a coworker to tell Gray to leave her alone. Despite her request, Gray sent her a long, passionate, disturbing letter. He told her he had been "watching" and "experiencing" her; he made repeated references to sex; he said he would write again. Ellison had no way of knowing what Gray would do next. A reasonable woman could consider Gray's conduct, as alleged by Ellison, sufficiently severe and pervasive to alter a condition of employment and create an abusive working environment.

Sexual harassment is a major problem in the workplace. Adopting the victim's perspective ensures that courts will not "sustain ingrained notions of reasonable behavior fashioned by the offenders." *Lipsett*, 864 F.2d at 898, quoting, *Rabidue*, 805 F.2d at 626 (Keith, J., dissenting). Congress did not enact Title VII to codify prevailing sexist prejudices. To the contrary, "Congress designed Title VII to prevent the perpetuation of stereotypes and a sense of degradation which serve to close or discourage employment opportunities for women." *Andrews*, 895 F.2d at 1483. We hope that over time, both men and women will learn what conduct offends reasonable members of the other sex. When employers and employees internalize the standard of workplace conduct we establish today, the current gap in perception between the sexes will be bridged.

IV. We next must determine what remedial actions by employers shield them from liability under Title VII for sexual harassment by coworkers. The Supreme Court in *Meritor* did not address employer liability for sexual harassment by coworkers. In that case, the Court discussed employer liability for a hostile environment created by a supervisor.

The Court's discussion was brief, and it declined to issue a definitive rule. 477 U.S. at 72. On one hand, it held that employers are not strictly liable for sexual harassment by supervisors. *Id.* On the other hand, it stated that employers can be liable for sexual harassment without actual notice of the alleged discriminatory conduct. *Id.* It agreed with the EEOC that courts should look to agency principles to determine liability. *Id.*

We applied *Meritor* in *E.E.O.C. v. Hacienda Hotel*, 881 F.2d 1504 (9th Cir. 1989). We held that "employers are liable for failing to remedy or prevent a hostile or offensive work environment of which management-level employees knew, or in the exercise of reasonable care should have known." *Id.* at 1515–1516. Because management level employees at the hotel took no action to redress the sexual harassment of which they knew and other harassment of which they should have known, we held the employer liable. *Id.* at 1516. We have not addressed what remedial actions taken by employers can shield them from liability for sexual harassment by coworkers.

The EEOC guidelines recommend that an employer's remedy should be "immediate and appropriate." 29 C.F.R. § 1604.11(d). Employers have a duty to "express strong disapproval" of sexual harassment, and to "develop appropriate sanctions." 29 C.F.R. § 1604.11(f). The EEOC explains that an employer's action is appropriate where it "fully remedies the conduct without adversely affecting the terms or conditions of the charging party's employment in some manner (for example, by requiring the charging party to work ... in a less desirable location)." *EEOC Compliance Manual* (CCH) § 615.4(a)(9)(iii), para. 3103, at 3213 (1988).

The Fourth Circuit has required that a remedy be "reasonably calculated to end the harassment." *Katz v. Dole*, 709 F.2d 251, 256 (4th Cir. 1983). It has held that an employer properly remedied sexual harassment by fully investigating the allegations, issuing written warnings to refrain from discriminatory conduct, and warning the offender that a subsequent infraction will result in suspension. *Swentek v. USAIR, Inc.*, 830 F.2d 552 (4th Cir. 1987).

Similarly, in *Barrett v. Omaha National Bank*, 726 F.2d 424, 427 (8th Cir. 1984), the Eighth Circuit held that an employer properly remedied a hostile working environment by fully investigating, reprimanding a harasser for grossly inappropriate conduct, placing the offender on probation for ninety days, and warning the offender that any further misconduct would result in discharge. The court concluded that Title VII does not require employers to fire all harassers.

We, too, believe that remedies should be "reasonably calculated to end the harassment." *Katz*, 709 F.2d at 256. An employer's remedy should persuade individual harassers to discontinue unlawful conduct. We do not think that all harassment warrants dismissal, *Barrett*, 726 F.2d at 427; rather, remedies should be "assessed proportionately to the seriousness of the offense." *Dornhecker v. Malibu Grand Prix Corp.*, 828 F.2d 307, 309 (5th Cir. 1987). Employers should impose sufficient penalties to assure a workplace free from sexual harassment. In essence, then, we think that the reasonableness of an employer's remedy will depend on its ability to stop harassment by the person who engaged in harassment. In evaluating the adequacy of the remedy, the court may also take into account the remedy's ability to persuade potential harassers to refrain from unlawful conduct. Indeed, meting out punishments that do not take into account the need to maintain a harassment-free working environment may subject the employer to suit by the EEOC.

Here, Ellison's employer argues that it complied with its statutory obligation to provide a workplace free from sexual harassment. It promptly investigated Ellison's allegation. When Ellison returned to San Mateo from her training in St. Louis, Gray was no longer working in San Mateo. When Gray returned to San Mateo, the government granted Ellison's request to transfer temporarily to San Francisco.

We decline to accept the government's argument that its decision to return Gray to San Mateo did not create a hostile environment for Ellison because the government granted Ellison's request for a temporary transfer to San Francisco. Ellison preferred to work in San Mateo over San Francisco. We strongly believe that the victim of sexual harassment should not be punished for the conduct of the harasser. We wholeheartedly agree with the EEOC that a victim of sexual harassment should not have to work in a less desirable location as a result of an employer's remedy for sexual harassment. *EEOC Compliance Manual* (CCH) § 615.4(a)(9)(iii), para. 3103, at 3213 (1988).

Ellison maintains that the government's remedy was insufficient because it did not discipline Gray and because it allowed Gray to return to San Mateo after only a six-month separation. Even though the hostile environment had been eliminated when Gray began working in San Francisco, we cannot say that the government's response was reasonable under Title VII. The record on appeal suggests that Ellison's employer did not express strong disapproval of Gray's conduct, did not reprimand Gray, did not put him on probation, and did not inform him that repeated harassment would result in suspension or termination. *Cf. Swentek*, 830 F.2d 552; *Barrett*, 726 F.2d 424. Apparently, Gray's employer only told him to stop harassing Ellison. Title VII requires more than a mere request to refrain from discriminatory conduct. *DeGrace v. Rumsfeld*, 614 F.2d 796, 805 (1st Cir. 1980). Employers send the wrong message to potential harassers when they do not discipline employees for sexual harassment. If Ellison can prove on remand that Gray knew or should have known that his conduct was unlawful and that the government failed to take even the mildest form of disciplinary action, the district court should hold that the government's initial remedy was insufficient under Title VII. At this point, genuine issues of material fact remain concerning whether the government properly disciplined Gray.

Ellison further maintains that her employer's decision to allow Gray to transfer back to the San Mateo office after a six-month cooling-off period rendered the government's remedy insufficient. She argues that Gray's mere presence would create a hostile working environment.

We believe that in some cases the mere presence of an employee who has engaged in particularly severe or pervasive harassment can create a hostile working environment. *See Paroline v. Unisys Corp.*, 879 F.2d 100, 106–107 (4th Cir. 1989). To avoid liability under Title VII for failing to remedy a hostile environment, employers may even have to remove employees from the workplace if their mere presence would render the working environment hostile. Once again, we examine whether the mere presence of a harasser would create a hostile environment from the perspective of a reasonable woman.

The district court did not reach the issue of the reasonableness of the government's remedy. Given the scant record on appeal, we cannot determine whether a reasonable woman could conclude that Gray's mere presence at San Mateo six months after the alleged harassment would create an abusive environment. Although we are aware of the severity of Gray's conduct (which we do not consider to be as serious as some other forms of harassment), we do not know how often Ellison and Gray would have to interact at San Mateo.

Moreover, it is not clear to us that the six-month cooling-off period was reasonably calculated to end the harassment or assessed proportionately to the seriousness of Gray's conduct. There is evidence in the record which suggests that the government intended to transfer Gray to San Francisco permanently and only allowed Gray to return to San Mateo because he promised to drop some union grievances. We do know that the IRS did not request Ellison's input or even inform her of the proceedings before agreeing to let Gray return to San Mateo. This failure to even attempt to determine what impact Gray's return would have on Ellison shows an insufficient regard for the victim's interest in avoiding a hostile working environment. On remand, the district court should fully explore the facts concerning the government's decision to return Gray to San Mateo.

V. We reverse the district court's decision that Ellison did not allege a *prima facie* case of sexual harassment due to a hostile working environment, and we remand for further proceedings consistent with this opinion. Although we have considered the evidence in the light most favorable to Ellison, because the district court granted the government's motion for summary judgment, we, of course, reserve for the district court the resolution of all factual issues.

REVERSED and REMANDED.

CRONIN v. UNITED SERVICE STATIONS, INC.
809 F. Supp. 922 (M.D. Ala. 1992)

On July 5, 1991, Steve Long, the general manager and supervisor of the convenience stores owned by United Service, hired Cronin as a cashier at the company's Day Street store. A few days after Cronin began work, the manager of the store resigned. Long offered the position to John Webster, the store's assistant manager, but he turned the job down. Long then offered the position to Cronin, who had had previous experience managing a convenience store. Cronin accepted the position, and Webster remained at the store as the assistant manager.

Webster, however, continually interfered with Cronin's management of the store. He verbally abused her, made sexual advances, and harassed her when she was trying to work. For example, one day shortly after Cronin began working at the store, Webster approached Cronin, put his arms around her waist, and said to customers present in the store, "Hey, this is our new manager, Katie, and she hates niggers." Cronin responded, "John, you know that's not true." Webster then said, "So, you like black dick then?" Cronin became, in her words, "extremely embarrassed" and "at a loss for words." She quickly left the store. Another time, Webster asked Cronin to go out and "have a good time with him," but she refused. While Cronin worked at the store, Webster would frequently approach her from behind, put his arms around her shoulders, touch her neck, and sing softly into her ear. When he did this, Cronin asked Webster not to touch her. On one such occasion, Webster touched Cronin on her shoulders and moved his hands down to her waist. When Cronin pulled away from him, Webster started to laugh. Cronin asked him what he was doing. Webster responded, "I just wanted a good feel."

Cronin attempted to institute several changes in the management procedures of the store. Cronin encountered resistance to these changes from Webster. Webster frequently called Cronin a "dumb, old stupid woman." He also told her that a woman could not handle being the manager of the store and that he had made a mistake in letting her take the position. In addition, Webster attempted to undermine Cronin's actions as manager. For example, shortly after Cronin took over as manager, she set up a meeting for all the employees. When no one showed up, Cronin discovered that Webster had told everyone there was no need for a meeting. Webster also informed the employees that they should call him, not Cronin, about problems in the store, and he changed employee schedules without consulting with Cronin. On one occasion, Webster pulled a gun on Cronin and told her that he was an undercover police agent. On another occasion, when Webster was off-duty, he spent the entire day harassing Cronin. He repeatedly walked in and out of the store and made numerous phone calls to Cronin.

Although Webster warned Cronin not to contact either Long or Ben McNeill, the owner of United Service, Cronin attempted several times to speak to Long about Webster's behavior. Long, however, either put her off or did not return her calls. Cronin then began taking notes to document Webster's actions and to have a list of things to discuss with Long when she had the opportunity.

Finally, on July 25, Webster's behavior culminated in an altercation in the Day Street store parking lot where his verbal abuse was accompanied by an attempt to assault Cronin physically. Earlier that day, when Cronin was out of town, Webster had fired an employee at the store. When Cronin later tried to question Webster about this, Webster shouted profanity and sexual remarks at her. Along with other profanity, Webster called Cronin a "white ass bitch."

He then raised his arm to hit her. Another employee at the store caught Webster's arm before it struck Cronin, although the keys Webster had in his hand scratched Cronin's arm. If Webster had not been stopped by a coworker, he would have seriously injured Cronin. Cronin fired Webster on the spot, and Webster retorted that no one could fire him. Cronin told him that if he did not leave the premises she would call the police. Webster then threatened Cronin by telling her that he knew where she lived. Cronin became, in her words, "scared that he might really hurt me."

The next day, on July 26, Long met with Cronin, Webster, and several other employees to discuss the incident. At that meeting, Cronin handed Long the notes she had been keeping about Webster's behavior toward her. She also told Long that she was afraid of Webster and that she would never work with any man who tried to hit her. Long looked at Cronin's notes, laughed, folded up the notes, and put them in his pocket. Shortly thereafter, Long transferred Webster to another United Service store.

Less than three weeks later, on August 16, Long showed up at the Day Street store along with Webster. Long informed Cronin that he was reassigning Webster to the store to deal with the store's inventory shortages. Long added that, "I don't expect that you will have a problem with [Webster]." Prior to this announcement, Long had not discussed with Cronin his intentions to reassign Webster to the store. Cronin immediately resigned her position at the store because she was afraid of Webster and could not further tolerate his sexual harassment. Webster replaced Cronin as manager of the store.

Cronin filed an administrative charge of sex discrimination with the Equal Employment Opportunity Commission. The Commission issued a "right-to-sue" letter, and Cronin timely filed this lawsuit under Title VII.

Three black women were also sexually harassed by Webster. Barbara Barlow was the manager of United Service's Court Street store when Webster was hired there as a cashier, before he went to the Day Street store. Webster asked her out several times, telling her, in her words, "how good he was in bed." Barlow made it clear to him that she was not interested. Webster also frequently put his arms around her, although Barlow would push him away. Barlow never mentioned Webster's behavior or sexual comments to Long because she did not think that he would do anything about it.

Sophie Colquist, who worked as a cashier at the Day Street store under Webster for several months after Cronin resigned, suffered harassment from Webster. When Colquist was in back of the counter running the cash register, Webster would stand behind her and stare at her rear end. He frequently told Colquist, "I like the way you're shaped," and "I like your butt." He also said, "I would like to try you," which Colquist understood to mean that he would like to have sex with her. On several occasions, Webster made these remarks about Colquist's appearance in front of her daughter. He also asked Colquist out several times, even though she told him that she was married and not interested. Webster's comments made Colquist, in her words, "feel uneasy" and "embarrassed." Webster eventually left the store as manager, but on December 31, 1991, he dropped by the store to wish Colquist a happy new year. While Colquist's daughter was present, Webster exposed his penis to Colquist and told her that he wanted her "to feel it" and to meet him after work. Colquist told him to leave the store. Colquist was reluctant to report Webster's remarks and behavior to management because she was afraid that her husband would find out and go after Webster himself.

Victoria Robertson, another female employee, had similar experiences while working as a cashier under Webster at the Day Street store. Webster frequently touched her, in her words, "wherever he could, my breasts, arms, legs, and behind." He also asked Robertson to have sex with him or "to give him some." Webster often offered to do Robertson's shift reports in return for sex. Almost every day Robertson worked at the store, Webster made sexual advances to her, and, in her words, "he always tried to kiss me." Robertson was reluctant to report this harassment to management because she did not believe that anything would be done about it. Webster repeatedly told her, "I am the best manager Steve [Long] has. He won't do anything to me." Then one day Webster exposed his penis to her. After this, Robertson complained to Long about Webster's behavior. Long did not take her complaints seriously; he laughed and thought it was funny that Webster had exposed himself. However, soon after that, Webster was discharged from the Day Street store and rehired by Long at a store Long had personally leased from United Service.

II. CLAIM OF SEXUAL HARASSMENT

Cronin claims that as an employee of United Service she was subjected to sexual harassment that was so severe and so pervasive that it created a hostile and abusive working environment in violation of Title VII. From the evidence presented, the court agrees.

A. When an employee has been sexually harassed, that employee has been discriminated against on the basis of sex. *Meritor Savings Bank v. Vinson*, 477 U.S. 57, 64, 106 S.Ct. 2399, 2404, 91 L.Ed. 2d 49 (1986); *Steele v. Offshore Shipbuilding, Inc.*, 867 F.2d 1311, 1315 (11th Cir. 1989). This is true because the employee has been singled out because of her sex. Sexual harassment, therefore, is a form of sex discrimination and as such falls within Title VII's prohibition of employer discrimination "against any individual with respect to his compensation, terms, conditions, or privileges of employment, because of such individual's ... sex." 42 U.S.C.A. § 2000e-2(a)(1)

Courts have recognized two forms of sexual harassment that are actionable under Title VII. The first type, known as "*quid pro quo* harassment," takes place "when an employer alters an employee's Job conditions as a result of the employee's refusal to submit to sexual demands." *Steele*, 867 F.2d at 1315; *see also Vinson*, 477 U.S. at 65, 106 S.Ct. at 2404–05. The second type, known as "hostile environment harassment," occurs when there is conduct that "has the purpose or effect of unreasonably interfering with an individual's work performance or creating an intimidating, hostile, or offensive environment." *Vinson*, 477 U.S. at 65, 106 S.Ct. at 2404–05; *accord Steele*, 867 F.2d at 1315.

Cronin claims that she suffered the second type of sexual harassment while working for United Service. To establish "hostile environment harassment," a plaintiff need not demonstrate a "tangible loss" of "an economic character," *Vinson*, 477 U.S. at 64, 106 S.Ct. at 2404–05; *see also Huddleston v. Roger Dean Chevrolet, Inc.*, 845 F.2d 900, 905 (11th Cir. 1988) (per curiam). A plaintiff need only show that the conduct is "sufficiently severe or pervasive 'to alter the conditions of [the victim's] employment and create an abusive working environment.'" *Vinson*, 477 U.S. at 67, 106 S.Ct. at 2405, quoting *Henson v. City of Dundee*, 682 F.2d 897, 904 (11th Cir. 1982). Therefore, while the effect on the employee must be more than *de minimis*, the employee need not show that she was required to seek psychiatric assistance or that she was incapacitated from performing her job in order to demonstrate that she was adversely and unreasonably affected by the harassment. *See Ellison v. Brady*, 924 F.2d 872, 878 (9th Cir. 1991). Moreover, the severity and pervasiveness of the conduct does not turn merely on how many or how few incidents there are; a court must examine "not only the frequency of the incidents, but the gravity of the incidents as well." *Vance v. Southern Bell Tel. & Tel. Co.*, 863 F.2d 1503, 1511 (11th Cir. 1989). Finally, the gravamen of any sexual harassment claim is "that the alleged sexual advances were 'unwelcome.'" *Vinson*, 477 U.S. at 68, 106 S.Ct. at 2406. The focus of the court should be on whether the complainant "by her conduct indicated that the alleged sexual advances were unwelcome." *Id.*

However, the Supreme Court has explicitly held that an employer may not be held "automatically liable" for all sexual harassment inflicted, or suffered, by its employees. *Vinson*, 477 U.S. at 72, 106 S.Ct. at 2408. Lower courts must consider the circumstances of each particular case before imposing liability. *Id.* Relying on *Vinson*, the Eleventh Circuit Court of Appeals has concluded that employers may be held directly liable for any illegal harassment that either it or its agents may have practiced on its employees. *Sparks v. Pilot Freight Carriers, Inc.*, 830 F.2d 1554, 1557–58 (11th Cir. 1987). Under the law of the Eleventh Circuit, an employer may also be held indirectly liable for sexual harassment. To establish indirect liability, the plaintiff must show under the theory of *respondeat superior* that the employer "knew or should have known of the harassment in question and failed to take prompt remedial action." *Sparks*, 830 F.2d at 1557, quoting *Henson*, 682 F.2d at 905; *see also Huddleston*, 845 F.2d at 904. Indirect liability reaches those situations where the person who engaged in the unlawful conduct is not the plaintiff's "employer" or "agent" as these terms are used in Title VII, but is, for example, "one of plaintiff's coworkers or [is] a supervisor with no authority over plaintiff." *Sparks*, 830 F.2d at 1558 A plaintiff can prove that the employer knew of the harassment by showing that the harassment was open or pervasive enough to charge the employer with constructive knowledge. *Vance*, 863 F.2d at 1512. A plaintiff may also prove an employer's knowledge by showing that she complained to higher management. *Huddleston*, 845 F.2d at 904. Of course, there must be some avenue by which an employee can make the employer aware of the illegal conduct. An employer should not be able to avoid indirect *respondeat superior* liability by simply not giving its employees an opportunity to come forward with their claims of harassment. *See Vinson*, 477 U.S. at 72–73, 106 S.Ct. at 2408; *Vance*, 863 F.2d at 1513–14.

B.   Applying the above principles, the court is convinced that Cronin was sexually harassed by Webster and that the harassment was sufficiently severe and pervasive to alter the working conditions and create an abusive working environment at United Service's Day Street store. As found by the court, Webster said to Cronin, or in her presence, during the very brief period she worked for the store, such things as, "Hey, this is our new manager, Katie, and she hates niggers," and, "So, you like black dick then?"; he frequently approached her from behind, put his arms around her shoulders, touched her neck, and sang softly into her ear; he touched her on her shoulders and moved his hands down to her waist, commenting that he "Just wanted a good feel"; and he called her a "white ass bitch." The court is also convinced that Cronin indicated to Webster that his advances were not welcome and that Webster knew his advances were unwelcome. The evidence indicates that Cronin "did not solicit or incite" Webster's conduct and that she "regarded the conduct as undesirable or offensive." *Henson v. City of Dundee*, 682 F.2d 897, 903 (11th Cir. 1982). Cronin refused to go out with Webster and she repeatedly asked him not to touch her. Furthermore, as noted previously, Cronin took notes about Webster's behavior and attempted to complain to Long about Webster's actions. Finally, when Webster tried to strike her, Cronin fired him on the spot.

The court has thus far focused on harassment which has sexual overtones. However, to be actionable under Title VII, the conduct giving rise to a hostile or offensive work environment need not consist of sexual advances or have clear sexual overtones. *Bell v.*

Crackin Good Bakers, Inc., 777 F.2d 1497, 1503 (11th Cir. 1985). For example, conduct of a nonsexual nature that ridicules women or treats them as inferior can constitute prohibited sexual harassment. *Sims v. Montgomery County Comm'n*, 766 F. Supp. 1052, 1073 (M.D. Ala. 1990) (Thompson, J.). Threatening and bellicose conduct related to a person's sex can also be considered as sexual harassment. *Bell*, 777 F.2d at 1503. As previously stated by the court, Webster frequently called Cronin a "dumb, old stupid woman"; he told her that a woman could not handle being the manager of the store and that he had made a mistake in letting her take the position; he attempted to undermine her actions as manager; and he threatened and attempted to physically injure her.

Webster's comments and behavior were derogatory and insulting to women generally, and overtly demeaning to Cronin personally. Without question, Webster's conduct indicates a lack of respect for women and reflects an attitude that women are to be viewed as only objects of ridicule, abuse, or sexual pleasure. Moreover, Webster's threatening and bellicose conduct directly created the hostile and offensive working environment at the store. The court concludes that but for the fact that Cronin was a woman, she would not have been subject to such harassment.

The court further finds that this combination of sexual overtures, demeaning comments, and physical abuse created an environment that adversely and unreasonably affected Cronin's "psychological well-being" and her "ability to do [her] job." *Vance*, 863 F.2d at 1510–11, quoting *Davis v. Monsanto Chemical Co.*, 858 F.2d 345 (6th Cir. 1988), cert. denied, 490 U.S. 1110, 109 S.Ct. 3166, 104 L.Ed. 2d 1028 (1989). Webster's harassment interfered with Cronin's ability to fulfill her duties as manager, particularly her ability to complete her paperwork, to organize the employees at the store, and to institute changes in the management of the store. After Webster's attempt to strike her in the parking lot, Cronin specifically told Long that she was afraid of Webster and was unwilling to work with him. Indeed, the prospect of Webster returning to the store forced Cronin to quit immediately her position.

C. The court further concludes that United Service is indirectly liable under the theory of *respondeat superior* for the sexual harassment of Cronin by Webster. The court finds that Long, the company's general manager and supervisor, not only knew about the harassment, but laughed about it and was utterly unresponsive in remedying the situation. Long failed to take prompt remedial action against Webster. Compare with *Steele v. Offshore Shipbuilding, Inc.*, 867 F.2d 1311 (11th Cir. 1989).

Defendants contend that neither Cronin nor any other female employee at United Service ever complained that Webster was sexually harassing them. Long maintains that Cronin at no time mentioned Webster's sexual misconduct, not even during their meeting after the July 25 altercation in the parking lot. Long further contends that he did not believe there was a fight in the parking lot. When he transferred Webster, it was only to avoid further problems, not because he believed Cronin's version of events or to remedy a hostile environment at the store. Long also denies receiving any notes taken by Cronin documenting Webster's behavior. Finally, defendants contend that if any sexual harassment did exist, any employee could have spoken to McNeill at any time. According to defendants, McNeill had an open door policy and was more than willing to speak with employees about matters of concern to them.

The court rejects defendants' arguments for two reasons. First, the court finds that Cronin did make management aware of Webster's sexual harassment and the hostile working environment at the Day Street store. As general manager of United Service, Long had supervisory powers over all the stores, including the Day Street store. At their meeting on July 26, Cronin informed Long that Webster had called her a "white ass bitch" and that he attempted to hit her. Cronin also specifically told Long that she was afraid of Webster and that she was unwilling to work with him. In addition, Cronin handed Long the notes she had been keeping that documented Webster's behavior. However, Long's response was only to look at the notes and laugh, and fold them up and put them in his pocket. The evidence thus clearly indicates that Long was made aware of the hostile environment at the Day Street store, in general, and of Webster's conduct, in particular. But Long chose to ignore the situation, rather than address it; he considered the situation to be simply funny. The court therefore finds that, rather than discounting Cronin's version of what happened or even making an attempt to determine whether Cronin or Webster was telling the truth, Long simply did not view Cronin's allegation that Webster had sexually harassed her as charging improper conduct and thus as worthy of a full investigation.

Second, even if Cronin did not complain to anyone about Webster's conduct, United Service cannot insulate itself from liability by claiming that it was not made aware of the harassment. The Supreme Court and the Eleventh Circuit have suggested that an employer may be insulated from a claim of hostile environment harassment if the employer has an explicit policy against sexual harassment and if it has effective grievance procedures calculated to resolve claims of sexual harassment and to encourage victims of harassment to come forward. *See Vinson*, 477 U.S. at 72–73, 106 S.Ct. at 2408–09; *Sparks*, 830 F.2d at 1560. But the evidence here indicates that United Service has no explicit and unequivocal policy against sexual harassment. In fact, it has no policy at all. The policy and procedure manual distributed to all employees contains no provisions regarding sexual harassment. It does not mention the issue of sexual harassment and in no way alerts employees to their employer's interest in correcting the problem. Indeed, the manual does not address the issue of discrimination in any form.

Furthermore, United Service does not have procedures which are "calculated to encourage victims of harassment to come forward." *Vinson*, 477 U.S. at 73, 106 S.Ct. at 2408 (emphasis added). Ben McNeill, the owner of the company, may have been willing to speak to employees who approached him about sexual harassment, but this passive management style is not an adequate means of addressing the problem of sexual harassment. Neither McNeill nor Long ever took any affirmative steps to make it clear that they were available to hear complaints of sexual harassment or to encourage employees to come forward with their complaints of such harassment. Moreover, there was no formal mechanism or procedure through which Cronin or any other employee could file a complaint about sexual harassment.

Indeed, the evidence reflects that United Service, and in particular Long, consciously tolerated, if not encouraged, sexual harassment. When Cronin complained to Long about her harassment, he laughed and did not take her allegations seriously. Similarly, when Robertson complained that Webster had exposed himself to her, Long found the incident funny.

D. The defendants sought to impeach Cronin by showing that she had failed to be honest in her answers to questions posed to her before trial, in particular about experiences unrelated to her employment with United Service. The court agrees that Cronin at times attempted to mislead counsel for the defendants. However, the court is equally convinced that Webster and Long were not fully truthful in their testimony before the court, and in particular in their testimony about harassment and abuse of female employees and the handling of complaints about such harassment. Because none of the principal witnesses has been completely truthful, the court must admit that it has been left in a quandary regarding some of the facts in this case. Nevertheless, having reflected on all the evidence and having found the testimony of some witnesses to be in part true, *see* E. Devitt, C. Blackmar, M. Wolff & K. O'Malley, "Federal Jury Practice and Instructions: Civil and Criminals' § 15.01 (4th ed. 1992) (a witness may be believed in whole or in part); Pattern Jury Instructions of the District Judges Association of the Eleventh Circuit, Civil Cases, Basic Instruction Three (1990) (same), the court is clearly and firmly convinced of one ultimate fact: that Webster sexually abused and harassed Cronin as described by the court.

The defendants emphasized that Webster was Cronin's subordinate—that is, he was the assistant manager while Cronin was the manager. This fact, while relevant, does not preclude the court from finding that Cronin was a victim of sexual harassment. Unlike *quid pro quo* harassment where harassment is directly linked to employment opportunities, *see generally Henson*, 682 F.2d at 908–13, hostile environment harassment, as explained previously, concerns conduct that creates a hostile, offensive, or abusive work environment. This type of environment can be the product of a supervisor harassing a subordinate or a subordinate harassing a supervisor, or of harassment between two equal co-employees.

The defendants sought to show that Cronin was abused at home by her boyfriend, and thus could not have viewed harassment at work as unwelcome. This argument is entirely without merit. That Cronin may have been abused at home in no way means that Cronin deserved abuse at work, that she "welcomed" Webster's abuse, or that she could not possibly be affected by Webster's actions because she was used to such abuse. In this case, the main issues for the court are determining what occurred at work and whether Cronin and Webster acted reasonably at work. Cronin's experiences at home have no general bearing on whether Cronin was subjected to sexual harassment at work. Abuse of a plaintiff in other settings, such as at home, should not be routinely admitted in cases charging sexual harassment in the workplace. Indeed, a court should be careful not to allow one party to a lawsuit to pry so far into the personal and private life of the other party that the litigation itself becomes a tool of abuse and harassment and thus victimizes the latter party in the very manner that Title VII seeks to prohibit. Therefore, absent a showing of a particularized relevance and need to delve into the deeply private sexual life of a party, a court should not allow it. The defendants did not make such a showing in this case.

The defendants suggest that Cronin disliked Webster because he is black and that her accusations against him were racially motivated. Cronin's actions toward Webster and resulting charges against him were not racially inspired. To the contrary, the court is convinced that Webster's conduct—in particular, his statements "So, you like black dick then" and "white ass bitch"—had a distinct racial bent, although motivated predominantly by a sexual bias. The court should censure Webster, not Cronin, for racial bias.

III. CONSTRUCTIVE DISCHARGE

To prove constructive discharge, the employee must demonstrate that her working conditions were so intolerable that a reasonable person in her position would be compelled to resign. *Steele*, 867 F.2d at 1317. If the intolerable working conditions are the result of a hostile environment caused by sexual harassment, then the constructive discharge violates Title VII. *Id.* Under this demanding standard, Cronin was constructively discharged.

As noted previously, when Long and Cronin met on July 26 to discuss Cronin's altercation with Webster in the parking lot of the Day Street store, Cronin informed Long that she was afraid of Webster and that she would not work with a man who tried to hit her. However, on August 16, without first soliciting any views from Cronin or even giving her any warning, Long appeared at the store, along with Webster, and informed Cronin that he was reassigning Webster to the Day Street store.

According to Long, he was not concerned about bringing Webster back because he did not believe any incident had occurred. The evidence, as stated however, reflects that Long did not care whether Webster had harassed Cronin; Long viewed much of Webster's offensive conduct as tolerable if not funny. Long further maintains that it was necessary to bring Webster back to deal with severe inventory shortages at the store. But no evidence was presented that Webster had any particular expertise in dealing with inventory shortages.

In fact, all of the United Service stores that Webster worked for experienced shortages while he was employed there. Moreover, the credible evidence does not support the defendants' contention that Long had firm and accurate information on August 16 that the inventory shortages at the Day Street store were so severe as to warrant that Cronin receive assistance in managing the store.

The court is thus led to the conclusion that the alleged inventory shortage problem was used as a pretext to bring Webster back to the store in order to force Cronin to quit. Cronin's complaints about Webster were simply a nuisance for United Service; reassigning Webster to the store provided a convenient means to get rid of Cronin, particularly because Cronin had made it clear to Long that she would not work with Webster. This strategy proved quite successful. For Cronin, once she learned that Webster was to be reassigned to the store, she had no other option. To prevent herself from again being subjected to Webster's sexual harassment, she was forced to resign.

Moreover, Cronin's resignation from her employment in the face of Webster's return to the Day Street store was reasonable. What she confronted was unbearable: Webster had sexually harassed and abused her in the past, and it appeared that he would continue to do so with Long's blessing. Her working conditions were so intolerable that a reasonable person in her position would have been similarly compelled to resign. The court, therefore, concludes that Cronin was constructively discharged in violation of Title VII.

IV. RELIEF

The court is thus convinced that Cronin was subjected to sexual harassment while employed by United Service and that she was constructively discharged in violation of Title VII. As a victim of sex discrimination, Cronin is entitled to appropriate relief. First, she is presumptively entitled to back pay and other back benefits she would have received had she not been constructively discharged. *Lengen v. Dept. of Transp.*, 903 F.2d 1464, 1468 (11th Cir. 1990).

Because the defendants have not overcome this presumption, the court will award Cronin back pay and other benefits. The court will give the parties an opportunity to agree upon the appropriate amount of back pay and other benefits Cronin should receive. If the parties cannot reach an agreement on this issue, then the court will itself determine, after an additional hearing, how much Cronin should receive in back pay and other back benefits.

Second, Cronin is presumptively entitled to immediate reinstatement to a managership with United Service. *Nord v. United States Steel Corp.*, 758 F.2d 1462, 1470 (11th Cir. 1985). However, the court cannot determine from the current record whether a management position is now available and, if not, how soon one will become available. The court will therefore give the parties an opportunity to resolve this issue. If the parties cannot reach an agreement on this issue, then the court will itself determine, after an additional hearing, the reinstatement issue.

Third, Cronin is entitled to an injunction prohibiting the defendants from discriminating against her because of her sex, for, "where there is abundant evidence of consistent past discrimination injunctive relief is mandatory absent clear and convincing proof that there is no reasonable probability of further noncompliance with the law," *Lewis v. Smith*, 731 F.2d 1535, 1540 (11th Cir. 1984). Cronin is also entitled to an injunction prohibiting the defendants from retaliating against her because she brought this lawsuit. 42 U.S.C.A. § 2000e-3(a).

Fourth, in light of the evidence that not only Cronin but three other women were also sexually harassed and forced to work in a hostile environment and in light of the fact that in the future Cronin should be able to work in an environment free of sexual discrimination, the court is compelled to enter an injunction requiring the defendants to take affirmative steps to rid United Service of its sexually hostile atmosphere. The court will require the defendants to fashion and implement, within 60 days, policies and procedures with regard to sex discrimination, including sexual harassment. *See Sims*, 766 F.Supp. at 1080. The policies and procedures must include, at a minimum, the following aspects: a prohibition of all forms of sexual discrimination, including sexual harassment, at United Service; effective grievance procedures calculated to resolve claims of sexual discrimination and to encourage victims of sexual discrimination, including sexual harassment, to come forward with their complaints; and a program to educate all employees of United Service about the law and their obligations under the law regarding sexual discrimination, including sexual harassment. *Id.*

Finally, Cronin is entitled to recover reasonable attorney's fees and expenses. 42 U.S.C.A. § 2000e-5(k). The court will give the parties an opportunity to agree to such fees and expenses.

An appropriate judgment will be entered in accordance with this memorandum opinion.

Glossary

hostile environment harassment – sexual harassment that creates an unfriendly workplace

quid pro quo **harassment** – sexual harassment used as a requisite to obtain job benefits

sexual harassment – unwelcome sexual advances, requests for sexual favors, and other unwelcome verbal or physical conduct of a sexual nature

Exercises

1. Do you think statutes should be enacted to deal specifically with sexual harassment? Why or why not?

2. Find a recent case in your jurisdiction concerning sexual harassment in the workplace and discuss it.

3. Compile a bibliography of available employee training material concerning sexual harassment in the workplace.

4. Based on the *Cronin* case, what are the rights inherent in bringing a sexual harassment claim? What explanation can you offer for why juries frequently give large damage awards for these cases?

5. In the *Elkins* case, the court declared that the plaintiff must prove that her harasser knew or should have known that his conduct was unlawful. Why? Do you agree or disagree? What is the standard of proof?

Chapter Nine

APPLYING EMPLOYMENT LAW TO HUMAN RESOURCE MANAGEMENT

Chapter Overview

The purpose of this chapter is to apply the preceding discussion of employment law to human resource management. In dealing with the basic concepts of employment law, it is not enough simply to be aware of the various laws that concern employment; one must also be familiar with the application of these laws in an everyday work situation.

Many states have enacted **right-to-work** statutes, laws that guarantee that a person who is qualified and capable of working will be able to work. However, to work, one must first be hired, and the first contact that a person has with employment law arises during the hiring process. Many methods of recruiting and screening applicants have been developed over the years, but the hiring process must adhere to the various statutes previously discussed. An employer no longer has the absolute right to hire anyone it wishes: it must be sure that its application procedures are fair and nondiscriminatory and within the parameters of any labor agreements it is subject to.

Example: An employer places a notice in the newspaper as a method of recruiting applicants for several positions it has open. The ad states that only nonunion applicants will be considered. This notice violates the labor law statutes and contracts this particular employer has with several unions.

Once an applicant is offered and accepts employment, he or she may be asked to sign a contract with the employer. Individually negotiated contracts are common among upper echelon officers and employees, whereas letters offering employment, provisions in application forms, employee benefit material, employee handbooks, and oral job promises provide the basic contract provisions governing the majority of the workforce. In the union setting, the collective bargaining agreement constitutes the contract of employment. Regardless of the form, once the contract is in effect, both the employer and the employee become subject to its terms and conditions. In addition to the contract, the employer and employee are also subject to both statutory and common law governing the employment situation.

Example: An employee signs a contract in which she promises not to divulge any information about the company to outsiders. After working several weeks, the employee is offered a better-paying job with a competitor company. She quits, taking the first employer's customer list with her when she leaves. This is a violation of the nondisclosure provision in her employment contract, for which she may be liable for monetary damages to the first employer.

At some point, it may become necessary to discharge an employee. Whereas common law gave an employer the absolute right to terminate employment at will, current law may limit an employer's ability to fire employees without legally sufficient justification.

Example: An employee is called for jury duty and is selected to be a member of the jury for a murder trial. It is estimated that the trial will take over nine months and will be televised. The employer does not want to be without the employee for that long a period of time, nor does it want the publicity that the employee's image on television may engender for the business. The employer fires the employee. In most states, this is against the law as violating public policy. An employee cannot be fired for fulfilling a legal obligation to serve on a jury. The employee can sue for reinstatement and back wages.

Much of this chapter will concentrate on management's legal responsibility in the hiring and firing process with respect to statutory and common law.

Recruitment and Hiring

The process of recruiting, hiring, managing, and firing employees is known as **human resource management** and, in larger companies, is primarily the function of a personnel director or office manager. In smaller companies this responsibility is usually borne by the owner or general manager. It is this person's job to see that appropriate people are found for specific jobs. The job of personnel management is fairly complex and beyond the scope of this text. However, it is important to note several of the functions of the personnel office that specifically relate to the laws discussed previously in this text.

Recruitment requires the personnel manager to attract the largest possible pool of potential applicants who meet the qualifications of the available positions. In order to alert the public of the job opening, a **job description** is usually formulated that specifies the minimum requirements the applicant must posses to fulfill the job functions.

The description should include the job title, a statement of the duties and responsibilities associated with the job, the educational and work background needed, and the general salary range. When drafting the job description, the personnel officer must be aware of certain standards required by federal law. For instance, under the Americans with Disabilities Act (ADA), the requirements indicated in the job description must be essential to the performance of the job and not designed to discriminate against persons with disabilities.

Example: A job description for a paralegal states that the applicant must be able to go up and down two flights of stairs easily, because the firm is located on several floors in an office building. The firm maintains a private elevator for the partners who go from floor to floor. Consequently, this job description would violate the ADA, since a disabled worker who could not climb stairs could use the elevator as an accommodation.

One of the oldest and most common methods of advertising an available position is to place a notice in a local newspaper. In this manner, the employer can draw upon a large pool of potential applicants. However, the choice of newspaper in which the advertisement is placed may be one that could give rise to a claim of discriminatory employment practices under Title VII.

Example: A company is owned by a person of Hispanic descent who wants to employ persons with a similar background. A job becomes available that does not require knowledge of the Spanish language. The employer places a notice of the job opening only in the Spanish-language newspaper in the community. This method of advertising excludes the majority of non-Hispanic persons who would not be reading this journal. This could violate Title VII.

Many companies use employment agencies to recruit applicants. Even though, on its face, the job description may appear fair, it would violate the law if the employer told the agency "off the record" of other job specifications that did not appear in the printed material. Employment agencies are subject to the same laws that apply to all employers.

Example: An employer hires an employment agency to find an applicant for a job opening. The personnel director says that the company is unwilling to hire anyone over the age of 35 because the company wants to maintain a youthful image, but the job description does not indicate any job-related reason for hiring persons of a certain age. If the employment agency screens out people over 35, both the agency and the employer have violated the Age Discrimination in Employment Act.

Almost all employers require applicants to submit résumés or complete application forms. The application form cannot ask questions that violate any of the applicant's civil rights, such as race or national origin.

Conversely, once an applicant has submitted an application or résumé, he or she is deemed to have agreed to allow the employer to check the accuracy of the statements made therein. Many employers require applicants to sign **releases**, which are statements or documents that give the employer the right to check on the accuracy of the information the applicant has provided. Additionally, many positions require security clearances and, as discussed in Chapter Seven, the employer can access various government records concerning the applicant.

Example: On his résumé, an applicant for a paralegal position states that he graduated from a specified paralegal school with a high grade-point average. The applicant signs a release so that the information on his résumé can be verified. The employer discovers that the applicant never graduated from the school; in fact, he flunked out. When the applicant is turned down for the job, he files a claim of discrimination. The employer can defend by showing that the applicant lied about his background. The law works to protect both parties in the employment process.

An employer should check all of the information appearing on an applicant's résumé or application, including all references. If an employer does not do a careful check of the applicant's qualifications, and the applicant is subsequently hired and injures a third person because of his or her incompetence, the employer may be personally liable for **negligent hiring**, even if the injury resulted from a nonwork-related task.

> *Example: An employer does not fully check the background of a job applicant whom he hires as a maintenance worker at a preschool. After the employee physically abuses two of the children at the school, it is discovered that she had been incarcerated for child abuse. The employer will be liable to the children because he was negligent in not checking the employee's background and placing the employee in a situation that would make the injury to the children more likely to occur. Note that this is the employer's own negligence, not a case of respondeat superior.*

At some point in the recruitment and hiring process, the applicant will be interviewed and perhaps asked to demonstrate his or her skills by taking a test. The interview must be handled in a fair and nondiscriminatory manner, and all applicants must be asked similar questions. The employer cannot use the interview to discriminate against protected categories of individuals.

> *Example: A law firm is looking for a new associate attorney, and one of the applicants is a 30-year-old woman who is about to graduate from law school. During the interview, the interviewer asks the applicant if she has any children, why not, what she will do about work if she becomes pregnant, and what form of birth control she uses. None of these questions are asked of male applicants. The firm is guilty of sex discrimination under Title VII.*

Any test that is given must be specifically job-related and test the essential skills necessary to perform the job. The test cannot be geared so that it will discriminate against people by creating situations that never, or rarely, occur on the job just to have a basis for denying employment to persons in a protected category. Examples of these types of discriminatory testing practices have appeared in earlier chapters.

> *Example: A law firm requires that applicants for paralegal positions carry a 50-pound stack of books. The firm claims that paralegals are required to carry heavy books between the office library and the attorneys' offices; thus, this is an essential job function. However, the firm has wheeled carts available, and paralegals are rarely, if ever, asked to carry that many books at one time. The firm is using this test to screen out women and the disabled. This violates Title VII and the ADA.*

Performance Evaluations

Once an applicant has been hired, the employer should provide feedback to the employee on a periodic basis to indicate how well or poorly the employee is fulfilling his or her job functions. It is prudent for employers to establish and maintain written documentation of these evaluations, and many employers now use performance evaluation forms that document each job function performed by the employee. The employee should be afforded the opportunity to review the evaluation, comment on it, and add any written statements he or she wishes. If, at a later date, the employee claims that he or she has been unlawfully discriminated against, either in promotion or discharge, these records can constitute evidence to support or refute the parties' contentions.

> *Example:* A paralegal has just been fired from a law firm after working for the firm for more than 20 months. The paralegal claims that she is being discriminated against because she is a woman. In its defense, the law firm provides copies of the performance evaluations prepared for the paralegal. The evaluations were made every six months. The employee saw and signed them, and failed to make any statements at her evaluation conferences about the evaluations' accuracy. It appears that she was late for work more than half of the time, refused to work overtime, and produced less work than any other paralegal in the firm. These evaluations provide evidence that the firm fired the paralegal for just cause.

Employment Contracts

Once an applicant has been hired, he or she usually enters into a contractual relationship with the employer. The contract may be either express or implied. An **express contract,** either written or oral, is formed by the explicit manifestations of the parties. Only certain types of contracts must be in writing to be enforceable. If the employment is intended to last more than one year, it should be in writing. An **implied contract** comes about not by the words of the parties, but rather, by their actions.

> *Example:* When an applicant accepts employment as a paralegal with a law firm, the firm tells the paralegal what his duties will be, what his compensation will be, and what hours he is expected to work. The oral offer of employment and statements about duties and promises regarding compensation, along with providing the employee a place to work, combine to form a contract between the parties.

A written employment contract can be either individually negotiated and signed by the employer and the employee or it can take the form of an **employee handbook**. Individually negotiated contracts are usually used for upper echelon employees. Many times an employer will use an offer letter to outline the terms of employment for employees who do not have specifically negotiated contracts. Also, an employee handbook can be a contract between the employer and all of its employees, as well as a statement of general company policies and procedures. This chapter will concentrate on the contract aspect of the handbook, whereas the next chapter will discuss the handbook as a method of disseminating company policy.

Regardless of the format, most employment contracts contain certain provisions that are peculiar to the employment situation. For a complete discussion of contract law, a text on that subject should be consulted. This section will discuss only those contract provisions that directly relate to employment:

1. *Consideration.* Consideration is the bargain element of the contract. To be a valid contract, both parties must give and receive something of legal value. In employment law, this means that the employee will render services for which he or she will be compensated, and the employer will provide compensation for the services it receives from the employee.

> *Example: A paralegal agrees to provide services for a litigation attorney in return for a salary of $500 per week, to be paid by the attorney each week the services are performed. This represents the consideration of the contract, the reason why the parties have come together.*

A written contract of employment should specify all of the employee's duties, including any authority the employee will have to act on behalf of the employer, plus any limitation on that authority. This clause should specify, if necessary, days, hours, and the physical location of the employment. Refer back to the chapters dealing with master-servant and principal-agent relationships, as well as federal wage and hour restrictions.

> *Example: An employer contracts for a manager for one of its plants. The contract specifies that the employee's title is plant manager. His duties are specified, and his authority to act on behalf of the company is limited to hiring and firing personnel and directing operations at one specified plant. The job opening is for a night manager, and so his hours are given as midnight to 8 a.m. at the specified plant.*

In return, the employer should specify all of the compensation the employee will receive, including any special benefits to which he will be entitled, such as profit sharing, stock options, health and retirement benefits, etc.

> *Example: "Employee shall be paid a salary of $____ per week, payable monthly on the first work day of each month, for all work performed up to 40 hours in every 7-day period. Any work performed by the employee over the 40 hours per week shall be compensated at a rate of one and one-half his or her contractual weekly rate, divided by 40, per extra hour worked. If the employee works more than ten consecutive hours in any one 24-hour period, he or she shall be entitled to a meal allowance of $10 payable in cash on the day in question."*

2. **Duration.** The contract should state a specified duration, if one is contemplated. If not, the contract will be deemed to stay in effect or become at will unless some specified ground for termination is met. Contracts that provide for an annual salary are generally construed to remain in effect for one year. Almost all individually negotiated employment contracts contain a duration provision.

3. **Terminology.** Under general contract law, all words used in a contract are to be construed according to their ordinary meaning and usage. Consequently, if the parties intend to give a special meaning to any term, the meaning must be specifically stated in the contract. Most contracts contain a section that gives these definitions.

> *Example: "As used herein, the term 'manager' applies to any employee whose duties include supervising the work of at least ten other employees."*

4. **Delegation and Assignment. Delegation** refers to the legal ability of a party under a contractual duty to have someone else perform that duty on his or her behalf. The contracting

party always remains liable under the contract and is held accountable for the delegate's performance. **Assignment** is the legal ability of a party to transfer his or her rights under a contract to a third person. Because assignment concerns rights, not obligations, the effect of the assignment may be to terminate the contracting party's rights.

> *Example: A client hires a law firm to represent her in an employment discrimination case. The attorney assigned to the case has a paralegal help him with some of the research involved. The attorney delegates some of his duties to the paralegal; if the paralegal fails to perform or performs poorly, the attorney is the one who remains liable.*

An employment contract should indicate if, and under what circumstances, the parties may assign or delegate. Note that contracts for personal services, those that depend upon the ability of a particular person, may not be assigned without the other contracting party's consent.

> *Example: A company entices away an executive from its major business rival. In the employment contract, the executive grants the company the right to assign his contract to any "successor in interest," a person who acquires the company's rights. One year later, the company is taken over by its rival, the one from whom the executive was lured away. He is now working for his old employer. He has contractually agreed to let his personal services be assigned.*

5. *Covenant Not to Compete.* A **covenant not to compete** is a specific contractual provision in which an employee agrees not to compete with the employer. These clauses are held to be valid and enforceable, provided that the period of the restriction is for a reasonable period of time, covers only a limited geographic location that would directly compete with the employer, and its enforcement would not prohibit the employee from earning a livelihood in his or her profession during the stated period. This type of provision is known as a **restrictive covenant**; it limits what the employee may do. These restrictions typically apply only to upper echelon and key personnel with special knowledge critical to the employer.

> *Example: An associate with a law firm has signed a contract that contained a covenant not to compete. The covenant specifies a 2-year period and indicates a geographic location of a 2-mile radius around the firm. When the lawyer leaves, she cannot open her own office within the 2-mile restriction for 2 years. She is free, however, to practice law anywhere else during that period.*

6. *Proprietary Covenants.* These contractual provisions concern ownership of patents, copyrights, and marks developed by the employee during his or her employment for the company. The covenant also includes **work products**, anything produced by the employee as part of his or her job. The employment contract should specify who holds title to such property.

Example: A research scientist is employed by a drug manufacturer. The scientist's employment contract states that all patentable discoveries made by the scientist as a part of her work shall belong absolutely to the employer. However, under the compensation section of the contract, the employer agrees to pay the scientist 20 percent of all royalties and license fees it receives because of any patents developed by the scientist. In this fashion, the contract benefits both parties.

7. *Confidentiality*. Some information that an employee learns about an employer is meant to be kept confidential and cannot be divulged by the employee to third persons. The requirement of confidentiality applies to customer lists, trade secrets, personnel data, and all other material the employer expects to be kept confidential. Even though such material is protected by the common law, employment contracts will often have separate provisions concerning confidentiality.

8. *Grounds for Termination*. To avoid claims of unlawful discrimination and to alert the employee about expected behavior, most employment contracts include clauses detailing the grounds under which the contract may be terminated. Usual provisions include commission of a felony, incarceration, physical or mental illness making job performance impossible, acts of moral turpitude, poor work evaluations, and so forth. If the employer can document a discharge based on one of the grounds specified in the contract, the employee's ability to maintain a lawsuit based on unlawful discharge is lessened. Many of these clauses also contain provisions permitting termination without cause upon timely written notice. Whenever these clauses exist, it is a good idea to indicate what compensation, if any, the employee may be entitled to upon departure, including rights to employee benefit and pension plans.

9. *Waivers*. A **waiver** is the legal relinquishment of a right. In contract law, if a party is owed some duty under a contract, and the other side fails to perform, the injured party could either sue or waive his or her right to the performance of that duty. The party who failed to perform is thereby relieved of that contractual obligation. In an employment contract, this provision should indicate which provisions may be waived, how such waiver is to be effectuated, and whether the waiver is only for one specified performance or for all such performances required under the contract. Once a contractual right has been waived it cannot be reasserted.

Example: "No delay or failure on the part of ____ to fulfill any of these provisions shall operate as a waiver of such or of any other right, and no waiver whatsoever shall be valid unless in writing and signed by the parties, and only to the extent therein set forth."

10. *Remedies*. Many employment contracts state what each party will be entitled to if the other side fails to meet his or her contractual obligations. This relief is known as **remedies**. Remedies may include a dollar amount, if financial injury can be shown, or may provide for enforcement of specific contractual provisions such as a covenant not to compete. By having these provisions in an employment contract, each side knows in advance to what extent each will be liable if he or she fails to perform.

> **Example:** *"In the event of breach of any of the provisions of this agreement, damages shall be limited to $___ exclusive of attorneys' fees and court costs."*

11. ***Alternative Dispute Resolution.*** Because litigation is usually time-consuming and expensive, many contracts provide for alternate methods of solving contractual disputes. The two most common methods are **arbitration** and **mediation**, both of which have been discussed in Chapter Three, Employment Law and Labor Unions, but are equally applicable to nonunion employment situations.

The preceding is a short list of some of the most typical provisions that appear in employment contracts. Remember, these provisions can (and do) appear in both individually negotiated contracts and employee handbooks. Both employers and employees are legally bound to adhere to the contracts they have agreed to, as well as statutory law. Union contracts are a subset with their own special set of rules and provisions and are not discussed here.

Termination

The common-law concept of employment at will, whereby an employer was totally free to fire any employee at any time for any reason, has been limited by various statutes enacted over the last century. With respect to human resource management, this means that before an employee can be fired, the employer must be able to document the reason for the discharge and be able to prove that the termination was not occasioned by any unlawful discriminatory practice.

Generally, employees may only be fired for **just cause**. Just cause means that the employee has violated some established work rule and has been given the opportunity to reform before the termination. In this context, employee handbooks and performance evaluations are the formal methods of establishing and documenting valid grounds for termination. Typically, there are three areas of performance that form the basis of terminating an employee for just cause:

1. ***Poor job performance.*** Assuming that the employee is aware of his or her duties and the standard expected by the employer in performing those duties, the employee's continued failure to meet these standards would justify termination. However, the employee should be forewarned of his or her poor performance and be given some opportunity to improve before being fired.

> **Example:** *A paralegal has been employed by a law firm for about two years. She has constantly turned work in late, and the work she does turn in is of poor quality, especially when compared to the work product of other paralegals at the firm. She has received three performance evaluations during her employment. Her shortcomings have been described to her, but she has failed to improve. When she is fired, the firm can demonstrate that she was fired for just cause.*

2. ***Disciplinary Reasons.*** If an employee has created problems in the workplace because of temperament or unethical conduct and the company's policies with respect to the conduct have been disseminated to the employee by means of an employee handbook or performance

evaluations, the employee can be fired for just cause. The law does not require an employer to continue to employ a disruptive worker.

> *Example:* *A law firm represents a well-known public figure. A paralegal in the office breaches the client's confidentiality by selling private information about the client to a tabloid newspaper. The firm is justified in firing the paralegal because of unethical conduct.*

3. *Economic Conditions.* If the economic climate changes and the employer is forced to restructure or downsize because of lost income, some employees will have to be laid off. An employee may be discharged if the basis for the termination is economic and if the employer is careful not to discriminate against employees who fall into the various protected categories

> *Example:* *A law firm loses its major client and must now reduce its workforce. The firm discharges five paralegals. To determine which paralegals are to be discharged, the firm establishes a policy of first firing the most recently hired. Because the method of determining who must go is even-handed and nondiscriminatory, these terminations would be justified.*

Whenever an employee is discharged, the employer has certain obligations imposed by law. First, the employer may be responsible to pay **unemployment compensation** for the discharged worker. Many jurisdictions permit even persons who were discharged for cause to receive some limited benefits. Next, the discharged employee may still be eligible to receive certain pension and insurance benefits. The company must inform the employee of these rights, and the employer is obligated to see that the discharged employee receives all such rights to which he or she may be entitled. Finally, under many state right-to-work statutes the employer may be liable to the employee for damages. In this context, it is necessary to examine the appropriate statutes of the jurisdiction in question.

Under the various federal statutes previously discussed, there are many grounds for which an employer may not discharge an employee without incurring liability. Grounds that cannot be used to terminate employment include:

•   *Unlawful Discrimination.* An employer may not discharge an employee if the employer can be shown to be discriminating against a protected category of worker. The protected categories are enumerated in Title VII, the ADA, the ADEA, the Pregnancy Leave Act and the Family and Medical Leave Act. No discharge may constitute discrimination under one or more of these acts.

> *Example:* *An employer has been forced to hire Hispanic workers under the affirmative action requirements of Title VII. The employer does not like Hispanics and continually finds reasons for firing these workers. If this practice of discriminating against Hispanics in the firing process can be documented, the employer has violated the law.*

Note that it is not unlawful discrimination under Title VII to require certain dress codes and standards of behavior, even if some distinction is made between the sexes (short hair styles for men, for example), provided that the employer's policy is disseminated to employees and applied equally to all workers.

- *Retaliation.* An employer cannot fire an employee because the employee has asserted rights against the employer or because the employee refuses to commit a crime in furtherance of the employer's interests. Likewise, an employer cannot fire an employee for whistle-blowing. **Whistle-blowing** refers to an employee making public an employer's illegal or unethical activities. An employee cannot be forced to engage in unlawful activity at the employer's request.

> *Example: An employee is injured on the job and files a workers' compensation claim. The employer retaliates against the employee by firing her. This is an unlawful discharge.*

> *Example: An employee is asked to lie on his time sheet to enable the employer to bill the client for additional work. The employee refuses, and he informs the client that she should look over her bills very carefully. The employee is fired. This is an unlawful discharge; the employee cannot be required to commit fraud to further the employer's interests.*

- *Contractual Grounds.* If there is a valid employment contract in existence between the employer and the employee, and the contract has specified grounds for termination, the employer may discharge the employee only for the grounds so indicated in the agreement. If the employer fires the employee for any other reason, this would breach the contract and render the employer liable under the agreement.

> *Example: An employment contract specifies that the contract will be terminated if the employee is found guilty of committing a felony. The employee, a bad driver, acquires a dozen traffic tickets, and the employer uses this as the basis for firing the employee. This is a breach of contract, because multiple speeding tickets do not constitute a felony.*

- *Constructive Discharge.* **Constructive discharge** results when an employee is still officially employed but experiences a change in working conditions so severe or so distasteful that he or she is forced to quit. If this pattern of behavior is used to mask an unlawful employment practice, the employer can be held liable for unlawful discharge.

> *Example: To get rid of its black employees, an employer puts all of its black personnel in its worst facility with a poor heating and cooling system and no hot water. The employer makes only half-hearted attempts to fix the physical problems. Eventually the black employees quit. The employer's actions constitute a constructive discharge, for which it may be held liable under Title VII.*

- *Circumstances Personal to the Employee.* If an employee experiences some personal problems or engages in a lifestyle of which the employer disapproves, the employer may not use these reasons as the basis for discharging the employee, provided these problems or lifestyle do not interfere with the employee's work performance.

Example: An employee fails to make alimony and child support payments, and his ex-wife obtains a court-ordered garnishment of his wages. The employer is upset at the employee's irresponsibility, but the garnishment cannot be used as a reason to fire the worker.

Chapter Summary

Human resource management involves overseeing the personnel policies of a business. Because of national policy as enumerated in various statutes, employers are no longer given a free rein with respect to their employment practices. Employers, for the most part, can no longer hire and fire at will, and must now show that they adhere to all legal employment requirements and document their practices.

In the hiring and interview process, the Civil Rights Act requires employers to seek qualified applicants from all segments of society and prohibits them from discriminating against persons in the protected categories in their hiring and recruitment policies. To this end, employers must make conscious attempts to publicize job openings to attract a wide range of applicants, and they are strictly prohibited from using criteria that would discriminate against persons in protected categories.

Once hired, all employees should be made aware of their rights and obligations. The dissemination of this information may take the form of an employee handbook or an individually negotiated employment contract. Both parties are held to the terms of their employment agreement and may be liable to the other for a breach of any one of its provisions.

Finally, employers have less freedom than in the past to fire employees without just cause. They may not discriminate against persons who fall into the protected categories in their termination decisions. All decisions with respect to termination should be documented and, if the cause for the termination is the employee's own conduct, the employee should be made aware of the problem and given the opportunity to rectify the situation before his or her dismissal.

Edited Judicial Decisions

McDonald v. Santa Fe Trail Transportation Co. discusses potential problems under Title VII when an employer discharges workers. *United States v. City of Warren* concerns the government's attempt to enjoin a municipality from using an "eligibility" list in its hiring process for firefighters.

McDONALD v. SANTA FE TRAIL TRANSPORTATION CO.
427 U.S. 273 (1976)

I.   Petitioners, both white employees of respondent transportation company, were discharged for misappropriating cargo from one of the company's shipments, but a Negro employee, who was also charged with the same offense, was not discharged. After subsequent grievance proceedings pursuant to a collective-bargaining agreement between the company and respondent union and complaints filed with the Equal Employment Opportunity Commission (EEOC) secured no relief, petitioners brought an action against respondents, alleging that in discharging petitioners, while retaining the Negro employee, respondent company had discriminated against petitioners on the basis of race, and that respondent union had acquiesced in this discrimination by failing properly to represent one of the petitioners in the grievance proceeding, all in violation of Title VII of the Civil Rights Act of 1964, which prohibits the discharge of "any individual" because of "such individual's race," and of 42 U.S.C. § 1981, which provides that "[all] persons ... shall have the same right ... to make and enforce contracts ... as is enjoyed by white citizens...." The district court dismissed the complaint on the pleadings, holding, *inter alia*, that § 1981 is inapplicable to racial discrimination against whites, and that the facts alleged by petitioners failed to state a claim under Title VII. The Court of Appeals affirmed. Held:

1. Title VII, whose terms are not limited to discrimination against members of any particular race, prohibits racial discrimination in private employment against white persons upon the same standards as racial discrimination against nonwhites.

    (a) Title VII has been so interpreted by the EEOC, whose interpretations are entitled to great deference, and its conclusion accords with uncontradicted legislative history.

    (b) That petitioners' dismissal was based upon the commission of a criminal offense does not preclude them from seeking relief under Title VII. *McDonnell Douglas Corp. v. Green*, 411 U.S. 792. While respondent employer may decide that participation in a theft of cargo may warrant not retaining a person in its employment, this criterion must be "applied alike to members of all races," or Title VII is violated. Crime or other misconduct may be a legitimate basis for discharge, but it is not a basis for racial discrimination.

    (c) Respondent union, as well as respondent company, is subject to liability under Title VII, since the same reasons that prohibit an employer from discriminating on the basis of race among culpable employees apply equally to the union, regardless of whether the union, under the circumstances, may find it necessary to compromise in securing retention of some of the affected employees. Whatever factors such a compromise may legitimately take into account in mitigating discipline of some employees, under Title VII race may not be included.

2. Section 1981 prohibits racial discrimination in private employment against white persons as well as nonwhites, and this conclusion is supported both by the statute's language, which explicitly applies to "all persons," and by its legislative history. While the phrase "as is enjoyed by white persons" would seem to lend some support to the argument that the statute is limited to the protection of nonwhite persons against racial discrimination, the legislative history is clear that the addition of the phrase to the statute as finally enacted was not intended to eliminate the prohibition of racial discrimination against whites.

II. Title VII of the Civil Rights Act of 1964 prohibits the discharge of "any individual" because of "such individual's race," § 703 (a)(1), 42 U.S.C. § 2000e-(a)(1). Its terms are not limited to discrimination against members of any particular race. Thus, although we were not there confronted with racial discrimination against whites, we described the Act in *Griggs v. Duke Power Co.*, 401 U.S. 424, 431 (1971), as prohibiting "[d]iscriminatory preference for any [racial] group, minority or majority" (emphasis added) n6. Similarly the

EEOC, whose interpretations are entitled to great deference, *id.* at 433–434, has consistently interpreted Title VII to proscribe racial discrimination in private employment against whites on the same terms as racial discrimination against nonwhites, holding that to proceed otherwise would: "constitute a derogation of the Commission's Congressional mandate to eliminate all practices which operate to disadvantage the employment opportunities of any group protected by Title VII, including Caucasians." EEOC Decision No. 74-31, 7 FEP 1326, 1328, CCH EEOC Decisions P 6404, p. 4084 (1973)].

This conclusion is in accord with uncontradicted legislative history to the effect that Title VII was intended to "cover white men and white women and all Americans," 110 Cong. Rec. 2578 (1964) (remarks of Rep. Celler), (1964), and create an "obligation not to discriminate against whites," *id.*, at 7218 (memorandum of Sen. Clark). *See also id.*, at 7213 (memorandum of Sens. Clark and Case); *id.*, at 8912 (remarks of Sen. Williams). We therefore hold today that Title VII prohibits racial discrimination against the white petitioners in this case upon the same standards as would be applicable were they Negroes and Jackson white.

Respondents contend that, even though generally applicable to white persons, Title VII affords petitioners no protection in this case, because their dismissal was based upon their commission of a serious criminal offense against their employer. We think this argument is foreclosed by our decision in *McDonnell Douglas Corp. v. Green*, 411 U.S. 792 (1973).

In *McDonnell Douglas*, a laid-off employee took part in an illegal "stall-in" designed to block traffic into his former employer's plant, and was arrested, convicted, and fined for obstructing traffic. At a later date, the former employee applied for an open position with the company, for which he was apparently otherwise qualified, but the employer turned down the application, assertedly because of the former employee's illegal activities against it.

Charging that he was denied re-employment because he was a Negro, a claim the company denied, the former employee sued under Title VII. Reviewing the case on certiorari, we concluded that the rejected employee had adequately stated a claim under Title VII. *See id.*, at 801. Although agreeing with the employer that "[n]othing in Title VII compels an employer to absolve and rehire one who has engaged in such deliberate, unlawful activity against it," *id.*, at 803, we also recognized:

> "[T]he inquiry must not end here. While Title VII does not, without more, compel rehiring of [the former employee], neither does it permit [the employer] to use [the former employee's] conduct as a pretext for the sort of discrimination prohibited by [the Act]. On remand, [the former employee] must ... be afforded a fair opportunity to show that [the employer's] stated reason for [the former employee's] rejection was in fact pretext. Especially relevant to such a showing would be evidence that white employees involved in acts against [the employer] of comparable seriousness to the 'stall-in' were nevertheless retained or rehired. [The employer] may justifiably refuse to rehire one who was engaged in unlawful, disruptive acts against it, but only if this criterion is applied alike to members of all races." *Id.*, at 804.

We find this case indistinguishable from *McDonnell Douglas*. Fairly read, the complaint asserted that petitioners were discharged for their alleged participation in a misappropriation of cargo entrusted to Santa Fe, but that a fellow employee, likewise implicated, was not so disciplined, and that the reason for the discrepancy in discipline was that the favored employee is Negro while petitioners are white. *See Conley v. Gibson*, 355 U.S. 41, 45–46 (1957) n11. While Santa Fe may decide that participation in a theft of cargo may render an employee unqualified for employment, this criterion must be "applied, alike to members of all races," and Title VII is violated if, as petitioners alleged, it was not.

We cannot accept respondents' argument that the principles of *McDonnell Douglas* are inapplicable where the discharge was based, as petitioners' complaint admitted, on participation in serious misconduct or crime directed against the employer. The Act prohibits all racial discrimination in employment, without exception for any group of particular employees, and while crime or other misconduct may be a legitimate basis for discharge, it is hardly one for racial discrimination. Indeed, the Title VII plaintiff in *McDonnell Douglas* had been convicted for a "nontrivial" (n13) offense against his former employer. It may be that theft of property entrusted to an employer for carriage is a more compelling basis for discharge than obstruction of an employer's traffic arteries, but this does not diminish the illogic in retaining guilty employees of one color while discharging those of another color.

At this stage of the litigation the claim against Local 988 must go with the claim against Santa Fe, for in substance the complaint alleges that the union shirked its duty properly to represent McDonald, and instead "acquiesced and/or joined in" Santa Fe's alleged racial discrimination against him. Local 988 argues that as a matter of law it should not be subject to liability under Title VII in a situation such as this, where some but not all culpable employees are ultimately discharged on account of joint misconduct, because in representing all the affected employees in their relations with the employer, the union may necessarily have to compromise by securing retention of only some. We reject the argument. The same reasons which prohibit an employer from discriminating on the basis of race among the culpable employees apply equally to the union; and whatever factors the mechanisms of compromise may legitimately take into account in mitigating discipline of some employees, under Title VII race may not be among them.

Thus, we conclude that the District Court erred in dismissing both petitioners' Title VII claims against Santa Fe, and petitioner McDonald's Title VII claim against Local 988.

[Discussion of the Civil Rights Act of 1866 omitted.]

The judgment of the Court of Appeals for the Fifth Circuit is reversed, and the case is remanded for further proceedings consistent with this opinion.

So ordered.

UNITED STATES OF AMERICA v. CITY OF WARREN
759 F. Supp. 368 (E.D. Mich. 1991)

I. BACKGROUND.

On April 12, 1990, the Government filed a motion with this Court asking that Warren be enjoined from hiring fire personnel from the 1989 eligibility list. In its April 12 motion, the Government alleged, and continues to allege, that the 1989 eligibility list was the product of a firefighter recruitment effort by Warren that was intended to exclude blacks from employment in the City's fire department. In other words, the Government believes that the

1989 firefighter recruitment was intended to disparately treat blacks in violation of Title VII of the Civil Rights of 1964, as amended, 42 U.S.C. § 2000e, *et seq,* by keeping them from applying for firefighter jobs in the City.

As support for its disparate treatment claim as to the 1989 eligibility list, the Government points to the alleged conduct of the Mayor of Warren, Ronald Bonkowski. Specifically, the Government contends that Mayor Bonkowski refused to allow the City of Warren Police and Firefighter Civil Service Commission from implementing its alleged plan to advertise the firefighter recruitment in two media outlets geared towards blacks—the *Michigan Chronicle* newspaper and WJLB radio. This act by Mayor Bonkowski, the Government argues, was for purposes of excluding blacks from applying for positions (and eventually being hired) as firefighters in Warren.

Warren disputes the Government's contentions and first argues that Mayor Bonkowski's refusal to use the *Michigan Chronicle* and WJLB was based on valid, nondiscriminatory reasons, to wit: (1) cost-effectiveness, that is, that the City was already going to advertise in the *Free Press*, a paper the City believed reached the black community even more effectively than the *Chronicle* or WJLB; and (2) advice from private counsel for the City that a refusal to use such media in the recruitment would not violate Title VII. Additionally, Warren argues that no Title VII violation occurred as a result of the September 1989 recruitment and that even if such a violation is assumed, there can be no "victims" of such discrimination under the facts of the issue as presented by the Government.

II. DISCUSSION.

Initially, it must be stressed that the motion presently before the Court is for a preliminary injunction. This consideration is the leading guide for the Court in its disposition of this matter.

On September 24, 1990, this Court entered an order ("September 24 Order") that provided for the following:

> (1)   Warren would eliminate the 1989 eligibility list and that no additional firefighters would be hired from it.
> (2)   Warren would promptly begin recruiting for a new firefighter list and that such recruiting be approved by the Court and include advertising in the *Michigan Chronicle*.
> (3)   the Government would retain any claims it has regarding the legality of the list and could seek, at trial, any relief it believes available to it based on Warren's development and use of such list.

Warren has since "eliminated" the 1989 eligibility list—it no longer uses such list as a basis for hiring new firefighters into its Fire Department.

A. Mootness

This Court must deny the injunctive relief sought by the Government. Simply put, the September 24 Order has rendered moot the original purpose of the Government's motion — its desire to prevent Warren from hiring firefighters from the allegedly discrimination-based 1989 eligibility list.

Admittedly, Warren did make some hirings from this list before the date of the September 24 Order. However, this fact alone does not mandate the injunctive relief the Government seeks. No more hirings will ever be made from the [1989] eligibility list. Therefore, there is no need to enjoin its use. And, the September 24 Order expressly allows the Government to challenge the legality of the recruitment at trial.

[Discussion of preliminary injunction omitted.]

C. Availability of retroactive relief.

At the hearing conducted on this motion in September, 1990, a disagreement arose between the parties concerning the issue of whether, under Title VII, nonemployees who had no notice of job openings can ever be nonapplicant victims entitled to retroactive relief. Warren argues that this issue must be answered in the negative and that, as a result, the Government's motion for a preliminary injunction should be denied. The Government argues the opposite. Both parties have extensively briefed the issue in their current pleadings relating to the present motion.

As the statement of its view of the law on this issue, Warren concludes: "For a nonemployee to establish that he or she is a 'deterred' applicant, the individual must be able to show that he or she had knowledge of the employer's alleged discriminatory practice or reputation and that he or she was discouraged from applying for the job because of that practice or regulation." Defendant City of Warren's Brief as to Whether Retroactive Relief is Available in This Discrimination in Recruitment Case, at p. 8.

The basic premise Warren uses in arriving at its conclusion of law is that there can be only two kinds of victims in a Title VII discrimination case—actual victims and deterred victims. Warren states that the former are "those about whom the employer made a decision or took action (e.g., the individual who actually applied for a job and was rejected)." The latter, according to Warren, are those "who can show that [they were actually] deterred or discouraged from applying for the job by the employer's discriminatory practices." Defendant City of Warren's Brief as to Whether Retroactive Relief is Available in This Discrimination in Recruitment Case, at p. 8.

From its concept of "deterred [non]applicant" Warren goes on to interpret the Supreme Court's discussion of nonapplicant Title VII victims in the landmark Teamsters decision and its subsequent interpretation by the courts as standing for the proposition that, for purposes of Title VII, a deterred applicant can only be discriminated against if he/she knows he/she has been discriminated against (or if he/she knows the employer has a reputation of discrimination). From this, Warren proceeds to state that if the deterred applicant had no knowledge of the discrimination, he/she will not have standing to make a claim against the employer. Defendant City of Warren's Brief as to Whether Retroactive Relief is Available in This Discrimination in Recruitment Case, at pp. 7–9.

Barren's reasoning in support of its conclusion of law on this issue is seriously flawed.

In *Teamsters*, the Supreme Court set forth the bedrock standards required for nonapplicant discriminatees to make a claim under Title VII. The Court stated: "A nonapplicant must show that he was a potential victim of unlawful discrimination. Because he is necessarily claiming that he was deterred from applying for the job by the employer's discriminatory practices, his is the not always easy burden of proving that he would have applied for the job had it not been for those practices." *Teamsters*, 431 U.S. at 367–68, 97 S.Ct. at 1871 (emphasis added). The Court further stated: "Resolution of the nonapplicant's claim, however, requires two distinct determinations: that he would have applied but for discrimination and that he would have been discriminatorily rejected had he applied." *Id.*, 431 U.S. at 368, n. 52, 97 S.Ct. at 1871, n. 52.

This language does not require a "deterred" nonapplicant to have knowledge of an employer's discriminatory practice in order to make out his/her Title VII claim. All the nonapplicant need show is that "had it not been" for the employer's discriminatory practice, he/she would have applied for the job and "would have been discriminatorily rejected" for the job. *Id.* Knowledge of the employer's practice is not an element to this type of claim.

Further, the case Warren primarily relies upon as support for its conclusion as to this issue, *Robinson v. Montgomery Ward & Co.*, 823 F.2d 793 (4th Cir. 1987), cert. denied, 484 U.S. 1042, 98 L.Ed. 2d 860, 108 S.Ct. 773 (1988), does not require an element of knowledge for a nonapplicant claim. In *Robinson* the Fourth Circuit ruled that an employee who did not prove that she applied for and was qualified for a job had not established a prima facie case of discrimination under Title VII. *Id.* at 796. In so ruling, the Fourth Circuit commented:

> Since Robinson [the employee-plaintiff] did not apply [for the job], she was not rejected. Although a plaintiff, who did not apply for a position is not foreclosed from success in an employment discrimination action, in such a situation the plaintiff must establish that she was inhibited from applying because of the employer's discriminatory practices. *International Brotherhood of Teamsters v. United States*, 431 U.S. 324, 97 S.Ct. 1843, 52 L.Ed. 2d 396 (1977).

In the case at bar, the plaintiff admitted that she did not apply for the position but asserted no argument whatsoever that she was in any way inhibited from making an application by Montgomery Ward's alleged discriminatory practices. *Id.* Such language does not impose a requirement of knowledge of the employer's discriminatory practice on a nonapplicant Title VII plaintiff.

If Warren's knowledge requirement were taken to its logical end, a deterred nonapplicant could never have standing to challenge an employer's discriminatory recruitment practice where that practice was so cleverly designed and so successfully implemented that it kept the nonapplicant from even knowing of the recruitment. That is to say, even where the nonapplicant was qualified for the job, would have applied for it, and would have been discriminatorily rejected, if such nonapplicant had no knowledge of the job because of the employer's discriminatory practice, he/she could not, according to the view set forth by Warren, challenge that practice under Title VII. In sum, Warren's knowledge requirement would serve to shield the thorough discriminator from Title VII liability.

As further support for its conclusion on this issue, Warren asserts that "actual or threatened injury is essential to establish that the individual has standing to challenge the employer's actions, and the injury must be direct and individualized." Defendant City of Warren's Brief as to Whether Retroactive Relief is Available in This Discrimination in Recruitment Case, at p. 9. From this, Warren concludes that a nonapplicant cannot meet this requirement if he/she had no knowledge of the employer's discriminatory practice because he/she would have no actual or threatened injury.

This Court disagrees. The cases Warren cites as support for this assertion are distinguishable from the issue at hand—they all involve determinations of appropriate class representatives and members for purposes of class action suits or relate to general concepts of standing.

Finally, the Court finds persuasive, notwithstanding Warren's attempts to distinguish them, the cases cited by the Government in support of its basic premise that retroactive relief may be available to deterred nonapplicant victims of an employer's discrimination. Specifically, the Court finds as persuasive the primary case the Government relies upon, *EEOC v. Andrew Corp.*, 54 Empl. Prac. Dec. (CCH) P 40,166 (N.D. Ill. 1990).

The district court in *Andrew* allowed retroactive relief to be awarded to blacks who had been discriminated against by the employer with regard to recruitment and hiring. The *Andrew* court was also confronted with the employer's argument that retroactive relief should not be allowed because of the difficulty involved in determining "who, from among Blacks in the general public, would have applied to and been hired but for word-of-mouth recruitment." *Id.* at 63,784. The court rejected this argument, reasoning that the employer could not gain an advantage by the success of its discriminatory recruitment policy and the uncertainty as to victims it created. *Id.*

Although, as Warren points out, *Andrew* involved word-of-mouth recruiting as well as hiring, the court's decision that retroactive relief should be available to the victims has application to the present matter. At trial, the Government may have a difficult task showing that the 1989 firefighter recruitment disparately treated blacks. However, if the Government can prove disparate treatment, the fact that the victims of such discrimination may be difficult to ascertain should not automatically serve as a bar to the granting of retroactive relief to those victims who can meet the burden of proving they were, in fact, victims of the discrimination.

III. CONCLUSION.

The Government's motion for a preliminary injunction is denied. However, if, at trial, the Government can prove Warren disparately treated blacks with regard to the 1989 firefighter recruitment, and if victims of such disparate treatment are identified and can prove their victim status, retroactive relief may be available to them as a remedy.

An Order reflecting the above shall issue forthwith.

Glossary

alternative dispute resolution – nonjudicial methods, such as arbitration or mediation, to solve legal problems

assignment – transfer of legal rights

consideration – the bargain of a contract; something of legal value

constructive discharge – method of making the work situation so distasteful that the employee will quit; an unlawful practice

covenant not to compete – contract provision prohibiting an employee from competing with his or her employer

delegation – having someone assist in performing contract obligations

express contract – contract created by the words of the parties

human resource management – process of recruiting, hiring, managing and firing employees

implied contract – contract formed by the parties' actions rather than words

job description – statement of work duties and responsibilities

just cause – legally sufficient grounds for discharging an employee

negligent hiring – an employer hiring someone unsuitable for the job whose unsuitability results in injuries to third persons; the master is personally liable

proprietary covenant – contract clause concerning ownership or patents, copyrights, marks, and work products

release – legal relinquishment of rights

restrictive covenant – contract clause limiting what a party may do

right to work – statutory right to be gainfully employed

waiver – legal relinquishment of contract right

whistle-blowing – employee's informing the public of his or her employer's illegal or unethical conduct

work product – anything developed by an employee as part of his or her job

Exercises

1. Check your jurisdiction for right-to-work and other employment statutes.

2. Draft a sample employment contract for a paralegal.

3. Discuss how an employer could document a discharge based on just cause.

4. Discuss how labor law (Chapter Two) affects human resource management.

5. Discuss the concept of constructive discharge.

Chapter Ten

EMPLOYMENT LAW IN A REGULATED SOCIETY

Chapter Overview

In today's society, almost all aspects of employment are regulated by one branch of the government or another, and in many circumstances, it has become a requirement of the workplace that certain employment practices be documented to ensure that these practices meet the standards of federal and state laws. The various reporting requirements create documents that are now computerized and centralized for use in developing statistical analyses of the American workplace.

This chapter will focus on various areas of concern for employers in today's regulated society. The first area discussed will be the employee handbook and its use as the written statement of office policy pursuant to statutory requirements. These handbooks are used to enunciate policies designed to adhere to the dictates of federal and state statutory law.

The second section of this chapter highlights the various tax records that an employer is required to maintain and the problems that may be incidental to the keeping of these records. Many small businesses go under because of their failure to maintain appropriate tax records. This failure results in fines and penalties imposed by both federal and state taxing authorities.

Finally, the chapter discusses the procedures for filing and defending claims under the statutes discussed throughout the text. Note that this chapter does not discuss the peculiarities of labor law and union negotiations that have previously been mentioned.

Today most companies carefully tailor their human resource policies in anticipation of potential lawsuits pursuant to federal statutes. In many instances relating to employment, the modern office has become almost a war zone between employer, employee, and government.

The Employee Manual

Chapter Nine discussed the concept of the employee handbook or manual as the basis of a contractual relationship between the employer and the employees who are not subject to individually negotiated agreements. In this chapter, the focus is on the handbook as a statement of employment policy, typically designed to meet the requirements of various federal statutes.

The employee handbook declares the employer's nondiscriminatory hiring, promotion, and firing policies in accordance with the provisions of Title VII, the ADEA, the ADA, and the other statutes that affect employment. Title VII requires employers who meet its definition of "employer" to adhere to a policy of nondiscrimination and to see that this policy is disseminated to all of its employees. The simplest method of meeting this standard is to print the policy in the manual.

The manual can provide procedures for the employee to follow in case he or she feels that he or she has been unlawfully discriminated against.

As with the provisions of Title VII, the employee manual outlines the employer's policies with respect to the Americans with Disabilities Act, sexual harassment, sexual discrimination, and general standards of conduct expected of employees with respect to drugs, alcohol, and tobacco use. Having a handbook ensures that the employer is at least meeting the statement of policy requirements of the federal statutes, and also can form the basis of any complaint against the employer or employee for failing to meet the obligations stated in the manual.

The appendix on page 233 offers a checklist of categories that should be covered in an employee handbook.

Tax Reporting Requirements

In our regulated society, employers are required to retain and report information about employees' wages and earnings to the federal, state, and local taxing authorities, and to pay into the authority certain taxes that may be due thereon. In this capacity, the employers are acting both as agents for the government tax bureaus and fiduciaries for the employees; they must turn over appropriate funds to the government on behalf of their workers. Many small businesses are guilty of violating these tax reporting and payment requirements and are fined by the government. Consequently, all employers and employees must be aware of the tax burdens imposed by statute.

Employment taxes generally fall into two broad categories: one, taxes that must be withheld on behalf of the workers in anticipation of the income taxes that must be paid on their earned income; and, two, taxes imposed on the employer both with respect to income and in providing benefits for workers. Each category of tax will be discussed in turn.

Income Taxes

An employer is required to calculate the total income earned by each employee and be aware of the number of dependents and deductions to which the employee may be entitled. Employees may have their taxable income reduced by the number of dependent **deductions** they have: a tax reduction for dependents such as spouses, children, and other persons for whom the employee provides more than 50 percent of the support. The employer must be aware of these deductions to calculate the amount of taxes from the employee's paycheck that the employer must withhold.

Withholding refers to an employer's legal responsibility to collect, on behalf of the government, (with the mandatory filing out of the federal form W-2 by the employee) income taxes that the employee owes on his or her earned income. These funds must be placed by the employer in a special bank account that is turned over to the government tax offices on a quarterly basis. It is a violation of the tax laws for the employer to use these funds for its own purposes; the money belongs to the government, and the employer pays it to the government on behalf of the employee.

> *Example: A small business owner employs four workers whom she pays on a weekly basis. Although she withholds the appropriate amount from each employee, instead of depositing the funds in the appropriate bank account, she uses the money to cover her own immediate business expenses, expecting to pay the money to the government at the end of the quarter. Even if she does have sufficient cash on hand when the money is due, this action still violates the tax law.*

To make the correct calculations and to ensure that the withheld taxes are attributed to the right worker, an employer is required to know the employee's Social Security number. Also, the employer must have proof of the worker's American citizenship or status as a legal alien resident in the United States under an immigrant status that permits the alien to work (the employee must complete federal form I-9). Such proof of legal immigrant status appears on a government-issued **green card.** An employer is prohibited from employing illegal aliens or using a false Social Security number for a worker.

> *Example: A restaurant owner hires several people as waiters. The owner does not require proof of citizenship or immigration status and accepts any numbers the waiters provide as their Social Security numbers. This is a direct violation of several federal statutes.*

As discussed in Chapter Seven, "Privacy Issues," disclosing this information may be an invasion of privacy but it is a requirement of employment.

An employer must withhold taxes on its employees' earned income for federal, state and, sometimes, local taxing authorities.

In addition to income taxes that must be paid by the employer on behalf of its employees, employers are required to file income tax returns on their own earnings. Businesses are generally required to file income tax returns on a quarterly basis (four times each year) to ensure that the tax money is not used to operate the business but is paid to the government. The business is required to estimate how much income it expects to earn over the tax year and must have paid into the government at least 90 percent of the total taxes it will owe by the middle of January following the close of the tax year (December).

> *Example: A corporate employer must calculate its profit each quarter. The government requires a corporation to file tax returns on the income generated by its business (after deducting expenses) and to pay the taxes due on such profits on a quarterly basis. This requirement exists to make sure that all taxes are paid and that the business does not end up with a huge amount of money owing at the end of the tax year.*

Social Security Taxes

All employers are required to contribute to their employees' Social Security fund. This is true for all full- and part-time workers. Both the worker and the employer contribute to the fund by paying what is known as **Federal Insurance Contributions Acts (FICA)** taxes each tax period. This is not true for **independent contractors**, persons hired solely for the results to be accomplished, who are totally responsible for their own tax payments; however, the employer must retain records of such independent employment, including Social Security numbers and all amounts paid to the person.

Example: An employer has 40 full-time and ten part-time workers who are paid every two weeks. Each pay period, the employer must calculate and withhold from each worker's paycheck an amount for FICA taxes that is based on the worker's earnings. In addition, the employer must also contribute an amount calculated on tax tables to the Social Security fund on behalf of the employee.

Example: In the preceding example, once a month the employer hires an accountant to prepare the books of the company. The accountant is paid a fee of $2,000. The employer does not withhold any taxes from this amount; taxes are the individual responsibility of the independent contractor. The employer retains records of the amounts paid to the accountant and, at the end of the year, sends the accountant a statement of how much it has paid the accountant during the year. The independent contractor pays his or her own FICA taxes, which are calculated at a higher rate than an employee pays, because no one else contributes to Social Security on the contractor's behalf.

Medicare

As a subdivision of the Social Security tax, money for the employee must be paid directly into the Medicare fund. The amount of the tax depends on the worker's earnings, which is established by a schedule prepared by the Internal Revenue Service.

State Disability Insurance Tax

Many states impose a tax on employers and employees to cover the cost of disability if the worker becomes unable to work. Once again, the employer is responsible for ensuring that the appropriate amount of taxes are withheld and making its own contribution for the insurance.

Unemployment Compensation

Both the employer and the employee must contribute to unemployment compensation. Unemployment compensation guarantees that an employee who has been discharged without fault can maintain an income for a statutorily set period until he or she finds another position. These amounts are also withheld by the employer and paid over to the government, along with the employer's contribution, on the employee's behalf.

Example: Due to a loss in business, a company is forced to reduce its staff. Three employees are laid off because of the company's financial state. Because the employees have paid money into the unemployment compensation fund, they are entitled to receive fund benefits for a certain number of weeks or until they locate new jobs, whichever occurs first. Be aware, though, that to be entitled to receive unemployment benefits, the employee must have been continuously employed for a specified time and have been discharged without fault.

All of the above tax requirements are usually handled by the **payroll department** of a business that is responsible for maintaining all of the appropriate employment records, doing all of the tax calculations, and seeing that the appropriate paychecks are issued with the correct amounts withheld and deposited. There are severe penalties imposed for knowingly falsifying tax records and/or failing to deposit the withheld taxes in a fiduciary account for the government.

Employment Claims

In either prosecuting or defending a claim made against an employer by an employee or job applicant based on any of the federal statutes discussed in the text, specific procedures must be followed, as set out in each of the statutes, and documents must be produced to support all allegations or defenses. These procedures are different for private and federal employees. The procedures to be followed under each statute will be discussed in turn.

Title VII and the ADA

Both Title VII and the Americans with Disabilities Act have the same requirements for instituting a claim under of their provisions:

- *Charge.* A **charge** is a sworn written statement naming the person claiming the discrimination, the person who he or she claims is guilty of the discriminatory act, specifying the act and the basis for the discrimination (age, race, sex, etc.), and indicating the date, place and nature of the discriminatory act. The charge must be filed with the regional office of the Equal Employment Opportunity Commission (EEOC) or, if the state or local authority has an enforcement agency recognized by the EEOC, in that office. The local agency is referred to as a **deferral agency**. If there is a deferral agency, the charge must first be filed and decided there before it can be brought before the EEOC.

> *Example:* An employee is charging employment discrimination based on sex. She claims to have been denied promotion because she is a woman. Her state has a deferral agency authorized to hear such complaints and recognized by the EEOC. The employee files her charge directly with the regional office of the EEOC. The EEOC will not hear the charge; she must first file with the deferral agency.

Deferral agencies are given a 60-day period of exclusive jurisdiction during which they may investigate the charge and settle the claim. An EEOC charge may be filed within 30 days after the state agency terminates its jurisdiction. If the state agency has not terminated its jurisdiction within the 60 days, a charge may be filed with the EEOC, provided it is within 300 days of the alleged discriminatory act. In other words, the deferral agency has an initial 60-day period to settle the claim, but if it does not settle the claim within this time, the charging party may bring the matter before the EEOC. He or she must do so within 300 days of the alleged discriminatory act.

> *Example: A discharged employee is claiming that she was fired because of her race. Two months after her dismissal, she files a charge with her state deferral agency. The agency investigates the matter and, after 20 days, decides that there is no valid basis for the claim. The employee may now bring the matter before the EEOC within 30 days of the deferral agency's decision.*

Some jurisdictions have agreements with the EEOC that permit filings directly with the EEOC. This automatically terminates the state's authority. In these states, the employee may file a charge directly with the EEOC, if he or she wishes, within 300 days of the alleged occurrence and thereby bypass state action. Each jurisdiction must be checked to determine whether this is possible in that state.

● *The Discriminatory Act.* The act complained of must fall within the boundaries of Title VII or the ADA, and it must be supported by sufficient facts and documentation to give rise to a reasonable belief of its truth. Supporting evidence may be in the form of affidavits of parties who witnessed the occurrence, as well as work records. These proofs need not be part of the charge but must exist to substantiate the allegations.

● *The EEOC Charge.* The EEOC has exclusive jurisdiction over the charge for a period of 180 days. The EEOC must notify the party charged with the discriminatory act and must determine whether or not there is **reasonable cause** to proceed. The EEOC must attempt to form some agreement between the parties, but if none can be reached within 30 days of the charge being filed, the EEOC may institute a complaint in court. If the employer is a government agency, the EEOC refers the matter over to the U.S. Attorney General for enforcement. No statute of limitations exists for the EEOC's investigation and mediation effort, but no court suit may be filed within the first 30 days of the EEOC's jurisdiction to permit the EEOC to reach a settlement between the parties. There is also no statute of limitations for when the EEOC or the attorney general may institute suit in court.

> *Example: A charge is filed with the EEOC, and the charged party absolutely refuses to attempt any reconciliation. The EEOC must still wait at least 30 days before filing a suit in court.*

● *Right-To-Sue Notice.* If the EEOC or the attorney general decides after the 180-day period that it will not file suit, or the 180-day period expires with no action having been taken, the charging party may file suit in court him- or herself. However, before the suit is instituted, the charging party must receive from the EEOC a **Right-to-Sue Notice**. This document states that the EEOC has found no violation and the 180-day period has elapsed. This Right-to-Sue Notice is a prerequisite for the charging party to file suit in court. The charging party has 90 days from the date he or she receives the Right-to-Sue Notice in which to file a claim in court. These suits are filed in federal court because they are based on a federal statute.

> *Example: The EEOC is still investigating a charge 180 days after it was filed. The charging party wishes to file suit in court and receives a Right-To-Sue Notice from the EEOC. Within 90 days of receipt of the Notice, the charging party may file suit in federal court.*

Rule 23 of the Federal Rules of Civil Procedure permits class action suits under Title VII. A **class action** is a suit in which numerous plaintiffs are alleging injuries resulting from a single action by the same defendant. To streamline the judicial process, these claims may be adjudicated together as a class action. Under Title VII, to maintain a class action, at least one member of the class must have followed the procedures described above; the other members may join the action when suit is filed and do not have to follow the EEOC claim procedures.

If the charged employer is a federal agency, as opposed to a private employer, the procedure for charging unlawful discrimination is different. Every federal agency is required to maintain its own EEO office, and the charging party must file the charge with his or her own agency's EEO counselor. Only after an initial investigation has been completed by the agency may the charging party institute suit in the federal district court.

> *Example: An IRS federal agent claims he is being discriminated against in job promotion because of his national origin. Before he can file suit in federal court, he must first file a charge with the IRS Equal Employment Opportunity Office and must exhaust all internal IRS administrative remedies.*

Age Discrimination in Employment Act

Under the ADEA, any suit claiming violation of the statute's provisions must begin within two years of the alleged discriminatory act. The EEOC has jurisdiction over claims of discrimination under the ADEA, but it does not require the procedures necessary for Title VII or ADA claims. The only requirement is that the claim be filed within two years of the alleged discriminatory act. Once the charge is filed with the EEOC, the EEOC must investigate the claim, attempt to settle the matter, or file suit in court, and there is no statutory time limitation imposed for these claims as there is with Title VII and ADA charges.

The charging party may institute a private suit in federal or state court, but only 60 days after charges have been filed with the EEOC and if the EEOC has not instituted its own suit. An EEOC suit precludes the charging party from bringing his or her own action. The charge itself must contain the same information as is required under Title VII and ADA charges.

The EEOC must notify the charging party if it terminates its jurisdiction, and the charging party may then file suit within 90 days of receiving the notification.

Before filing a private suit, the injured party must file a charge with any state antidiscriminatory agency that exists, and may only file suit after 60 days from filing the charge if the state agency fails to resolve the matter. The charging party must also file an EEOC charge within 30 days of notification that the state agency has terminated its proceedings. The EEOC charge may be filed prior to, simultaneously with, or 60 days after, filing the state charge.

The charging party must wait 60 days after filing charges before commencing federal suit. This is 60 days for both the state and EEOC action, but the charges may be filed simultaneously.

Example: An employee believes that he was fired because of his age (61). He files charges with both his state agency and the EEOC on the same day. He may commence suit in federal court in 60 days if the matter has not been resolved by either authority.

The court suit must be filed within two years of the alleged discriminatory act, or three years if the act was willful. **"Willful"** is defined as either "knowing" or "conscious disregard" of the law. If more than the two years have elapsed from the alleged misconduct, the charging party may still file suit if it is within 90 days after the EEOC notifies him or her that its proceedings have been terminated.

Class actions are not permitted for claims arising under the ADEA.

The Equal Pay Act and the Fair Labor Standards Act

Both the Equal Pay Act and the FLSA permit government enforcement of their provisions by having actions filed by the Secretary of Labor. There is no requirement that charges be filed with the EEOC, even though the EEOC has the power to investigate such charges if they are reported to it.

Any suit must be filed within two years after the cause of action arose, or three years if the employer's action was willful. Suit may be brought directly without any prior agency action.

Remedies

Under the preceding federal statutes, a successful claimant may be entitled to the following remedies:

- *Injunctions*. Court orders requiring the employer to stop the unlawful practice and to restore or hire the claimant. If no position is available, the injured party must be offered the first position that becomes available and be paid **front pay** (a salary until the job opens up).

- *Back pay*. The court may award the injured party all pay he or she lost because of the unlawful act, including the value of all benefits to which the employee would have been entitled to during this period.

- *Interest*. The employer may have to pay the injured employee interest on all back pay to which he or she is entitled.

- *Consequential damages*. This is money used to compensate an injured individual for economic loss suffered because of the unlawful act, such as premiums on private health insurance lost because of the discriminatory act by the company.

- *Punitive damages*. The court may allow damages as punishment for malicious or reckless indifference to employees' rights. These damages can range from $50,000 for employers of fewer than 101 employees to a maximum of $300,000 for employers with more than 500 employees.

- *Seniority*. The court may require the employer to award the injured employee seniority rights he or she may have lost because of the unlawful act. Seniority awards employment benefits for length of employment.

- *Affirmative action*. The court can require the employer to create an affirmative action plan to rectify past discrimination under Title VII.

- *Liquidated damages*. Under the EPA and the ADEA, an injured employee may be entitled to receive an additional amount of money equal to the lost back pay liability if he or she can show the violation was willful.

- *Attorney's fees*. The prevailing party in a suit based on employment discrimination may be granted "reasonable" attorneys' fees incurred during the suit. This also applies to employers if they have successfully defended the suit.

Chapter Summary

Today's society has become so regulated that almost every aspect of life is subject to some form of government oversight. This is particularly true in the area of employment law. Adherence to all of the federal laws governing employment practices has resulted in the modern office becoming a maze of documentation, full of records and documents designed to demonstrate adherence to federal employment standards.

Nowadays, almost every employer provides its employees with an employee handbook as evidence of its policies and procedures designed to show compliance with federal laws. These manuals provide employees with specific written evidence of an employer's practices and guidelines, and may form the basis of a claim of violation of federal law if the employer does not follow its own procedures and policies.

The adage that a person can avoid everything except death and taxes is particularly true in the modern workplace. The proliferation of taxes over the past century has forced employers to become government agents in the preparation, reporting, and collection of taxes.

Finally, in today's litigious society, specific rules and regulations have been established to provide procedures for presenting claims of violations of any of the federal employment laws. Not only do the statutes create rights and liabilities for employers and employees, they dictate the manner and method of enforcing the rights through the administrative and judicial processes.

Edited Judicial Decisions

In *EEOC v. Commercial Office Products, Inc.*, the court discusses the procedures for filing a claim under Title VII. In *Favors v. Fisher*, the court discusses the use of an employment testing procedure as a racially discriminatory practice.

EEOC v. COMMERCIAL OFFICE PRODUCTS CO.
486 U.S. 107 (1988)

SYLLABUS: Under § 706(e) of Title VII of the Civil Rights Act of 1964 (Act), a complainant must file a discrimination charge with the Equal Employment Opportunity Commission (EEOC) within 180 days of the occurrence of the alleged unlawful employment practice, or within 300 days if the proceedings are initially instituted with a state or local agency having "authority to grant or seek relief." Under § 706(c), no charge may be filed with the EEOC until 60 days have elapsed from the initial filing of the charge with an authorized state or local agency, unless that agency's proceedings "have been earlier terminated."

This Court has held that, in light of § 706(c)'s deferral period, a charge must be filed with, or referred by the EEOC to, the state or local agency within 240 days of the alleged discriminatory event in order to ensure that it may be filed within Sec. 706(e)'s extended 300-day limit, unless the state or local agency terminates its proceedings before 300 days. *Mohasco Corp. v. Silver*, 447 U.S. 807. The Colorado Civil Rights Division (CCRD) and the EEOC have entered into a work-sharing agreement, which provides that each will process certain categories of charges and that the CCRD waives § 706(c)'s 60-day deferral period with respect to those charges processed by the EEOC but retains jurisdiction to act on such charges after the EEOC's proceedings conclude. Alleging that, 290 days earlier, respondent had discharged her because of her sex in violation of Title VII, Suanne Leerssen filed a charge with the EEOC, which undertook the initial charge processing pursuant to the work-sharing agreement. The CCRD informed Leerssen that it had waived its right in this regard but retained jurisdiction under the agreement. Respondent refused to comply with the EEOC's administrative subpoena, and the District Court denied enforcement of the subpoena because the EEOC lacked jurisdiction because the charge was not timely filed within § 706(e)'s 300-day period. The Court of Appeals agreed and therefore affirmed, although it rejected respondent's contention that the 300-day period was inapplicable because Leerssen had not filed the charge with the CCRD within the 180-day limitations period provided by state law.

This case raises two questions regarding the time limits for filing charges of employment discrimination with the Equal Employment Opportunity Commission (EEOC) under Title VII of the Civil Rights Act of 1964, 78 Stat. 253, 42 U.S.C. § 2000e *et seq.* The primary question presented is whether a state agency's decision to waive its exclusive 60-day period for initial processing of a discrimination charge, pursuant to a work-sharing agreement with the EEOC, "terminates" the agency's proceedings within the meaning of § 706(c) of Title VII, 78 Stat. 260, as amended in 1972, 86 Stat. 104, 42 U.S.C. § 2000e-5(c), so that the EEOC immediately may deem the charge filed. In addition, we must decide whether a complainant who files a discrimination charge that is untimely under state law is nonetheless entitled to the extended 300-day federal filing period of § 706(e) of Title VII, 78 Stat. 260, as amended in 1972, 86 Stat. 105, 42 U.S.C. § 2000e-5(e)

I.   The time limit provisions of Title VII as interpreted by this Court establish the following procedures for filing discrimination charges with the EEOC. As a rule, a complainant must file a discrimination charge with the EEOC within 180 days of the occurrence of the alleged unlawful employment practice. § 706(e), 42 U.S.C. § 2000e-5(e). N1 If a complainant initially institutes proceedings with a state or local agency with authority to grant or seek relief from the practice charged, the time limit for filing with the EEOC is extended to 300 days. *Ibid.*

In order to give states and localities an opportunity to combat discrimination free from premature federal intervention, the Act provides that no charge may be filed with the EEOC until 60 days have elapsed from initial filing of the charge with an authorized state or local agency, unless that agency's proceedings "have been earlier terminated." § 706(c), 42 U.S.C. § 2000e-5(c). The EEOC's referral of a charge initially filed with the EEOC to the appropriate state or local agency properly institutes the agency's proceedings within the meaning of the Act, and the EEOC may hold the charge in "suspended animation" during the agency's 60-day period of exclusive jurisdiction. *Love v. Pullman Co.*, 404 U.S. 522, 525-526 (1972). In light of the 60-day deferral period, a complainant must file a charge with the appropriate state or local agency, or have the EEOC refer the charge to that agency, within 240 days of the alleged discriminatory event in order to ensure that it may be filed with the EEOC within the 300-day limit. *See Mohasco Corp. v. Silver*, 447 U.S. 807, 814, (1980). If the complainant does not file within 240 days, the charge still may be timely filed with the EEOC if the state or local agency terminates its proceedings before 300 days. *See ibid.*

The central question in this case is whether a state agency's waiver of the 60-day deferral period, pursuant to a work-sharing agreement with the EEOC, constitutes a "termination" of its proceedings so as to permit the EEOC to deem a charge filed and to begin to process it immediately. This question is of substantial importance because the EEOC has used its statutory authority to enter into work sharing agreements with approximately three-quarters of the 109 state and local agencies authorized to enforce state and local employment discrimination laws. *See* § 709(b), 86 Stat. 107-108, 42 U.S.C. § 2000e-8(b) (authorizing the EEOC to "enter into written agreements" with state and local agencies to promote "effective enforcement" of the Act); Brief for Petitioner 4 (EEOC has entered into work-sharing agreements with approximately 81 of 109 authorized state and local agencies).

These work-sharing agreements typically provide that the state or local agency will process certain categories of charges and that the EEOC will process others, with the state or local agency waiving the 60-day deferral period in the latter instance. *See, e.g.,* Work-sharing Agreement between Colorado Civil Rights Division and EEOC, App. to Pet. for Cert. 48a-49a. In either instance, the non-processing party to the work-sharing agreement generally reserves the right to review the initial processing party's resolution of the charge and to investigate the charge further after the initial processing party has completed its proceedings. *See, e.g., id.,* at 47a. Whether a waiver of the 60-day deferral period pursuant to a work-sharing agreement constitutes a "termination" of a state or local agency's proceedings will determine not only when the EEOC may initiate its proceedings, but also whether an entire class of charges may be timely filed with the EEOC in the first instance.

The facts of the instant case concretely reflect what is at stake. On March 26, 1984, Suanne Leerssen filed a charge of discrimination with petitioner EEOC. She alleged that 290 days earlier, respondent Commercial Office Products Company had discharged her because of her sex in violation of Title VII. On March 30, the EEOC sent a copy of Leerssen's charge and a charge transmittal form to the Colorado Civil Rights Division (CCRD), which is authorized by the State to process charges of employment discrimination. The form stated that the EEOC would initially process the charge, pursuant to the work-sharing agreement between the EEOC and the CCRD.

The CCRD returned the transmittal form to the EEOC, indicating on the form that the CCRD waived its right under Title VII to initially process the charge. On April 4, the CCRD sent a form letter to Leerssen explaining that it had waived its right to initial processing but stating that it still retained jurisdiction to act on the charge after the conclusion of the EEOC's proceedings. If the CCRD's waiver "terminated" its proceedings, then Leerssen's charge was filed with the EEOC just under the 300-day limit. If the waiver was not a "termination," however, then the charge was not timely filed with the EEOC because the 60-day deferral period did not expire until well after the 300-day limit.

The timeliness issue was raised in this case when the EEOC issued an administrative subpoena for information relevant to Leerssen's charge. Respondent refused to comply with the subpoena, maintaining that the EEOC lacked jurisdiction to investigate the charge because it was not timely filed. The EEOC commenced an action in the United States District Court for the District of Colorado seeking judicial enforcement of the subpoena. The District Court agreed with respondent and dismissed the EEOC's enforcement action, holding that the EEOC lacked jurisdiction over Leerssen's charge because it was not timely filed.

The Court of Appeals for the Tenth Circuit affirmed. 803 F.2d 581 (1986). As a threshold matter, the Court of Appeals rejected respondent's contention that the extended 300-day federal filing period was inapplicable because Leerssen had failed to file her charge with the CCRD within the state's own 180-day limitations period. *Id.*, at 585-586. The Court of Appeals agreed with the District Court, however, that Leerssen's charge was not filed within the 300-day period and that the EEOC therefore lacked jurisdiction over the charge. The Court of Appeals reasoned that a state agency "terminates" its proceedings within the meaning of § 706(c) only when it "completely surrenders its jurisdiction over a charge." *Id.*, at 587. Because the CCRD retained jurisdiction over Leerssen's charge, reserving the right to act at the conclusion of the EEOC's proceedings, it did not "finally and unequivocally terminate its authority" over the charge as the plain language of the statute required. *Id.*, at 590. The Court of Appeals expressly disagreed with the decision of the First Circuit in *Isaac v. Harvard University*, 769 F. 2d 817 (1985). The First Circuit had upheld the EEOC's view that a waiver of the right to initially process a charge constitutes a "termination," reasoning that the language of the Act is ambiguous and that the history and purposes of the Act support the EEOC's construction. Judge McKay dissented from the opinion of the Court of Appeals in this case, arguing that the EEOC should prevail for the reasons offered by the First Circuit.

We granted certiorari to resolve the conflict between the First and the Tenth Circuits, 482 U.S. 926 (1987), and we now reverse.

II-A.   First and foremost, respondent defends the judgment of the Court of Appeals on the ground that the language of the statute unambiguously precludes the conclusion that the CCRD's waiver of the deferral period "terminated" its proceedings. According to respondent, "terminated" means only "completed" or "ended." Respondent urges that this definition is met only when a state agency, in the words of the Court of Appeals, "completely relinquish[es] its authority to act on the charge at that point or in the future." 803 F. 2d, at 589 (emphasis in original). Because the CCRD retained authority to reactivate its proceedings after the EEOC's resolution of the charge, respondent maintains that the CCRD did not "terminate" its proceedings within the meaning of the Act.

We cannot agree with respondent and the Court of Appeals that "terminate" must mean "to end for all time." Rather, we find persuasive the determination of the First Circuit that the definition of "termination" also includes "cessation in time." The First Circuit noted that this definition is included in both *Webster's Third New International Dictionary* 2359

(1976) (definition of "terminate") and *Black's Law Dictionary* 1319 (5th ed. 1979) (definition of "termination"). *See Isaac*, 769 F.2d, at 820, 821. Moreover, the First Circuit correctly observed that common usage of the words "terminate," "complete," or "end" often includes a time element, as in "ending negotiations despite the likely inevitability of their resumption" or "terminating work on the jobsite knowing that it will resume the next day." *Id.*, at 821. These observations support the EEOC's contention that a state agency "terminates" its proceedings when it declares that it will not proceed, if it does so at all, for a specified interval of time.

To be sure, "terminate" also may bear the meaning proposed by respondent. Indeed, it may bear that meaning more naturally or more frequently in common usage. But it is axiomatic that the EEOC's interpretation of Title VII, for which it has primary enforcement responsibility, need not be the best one by grammatical or any other standards. Rather, the EEOC's interpretation of ambiguous language need only be reasonable to be entitled to deference. *See Oscar Mayer & Co. v. Evans*, 441 U.S. 750, 761 (1979). The reasonableness of the EEOC's interpretation of "terminate" in its statutory context is more than amply supported by the legislative history of the deferral provisions of Title VII, the purposes of those provisions, and the language of other sections of the Act, as described in detail below. Deference is therefore appropriate.

B.   The legislative history of the deferral provisions of Title VII demonstrates that the EEOC's interpretation of § 706(c) is far more consistent with the purposes of the Act than respondent's contrary construction.

The deferral provisions of § 706 were enacted as part of a compromise forged during the course of one of the longest filibusters in the Senate's history. The bill that had passed the House provided for "deferral" to state and local enforcement efforts only in the sense that it directed the EEOC to enter into agreements with state agencies providing for the suspension of federal enforcement in certain circumstances. *See* H. R. 7152, 88th Cong., 2d Sess., § 708, 110 Cong. Rec. 2511-2512 (1964). The House bill further directed the EEOC to rescind any agreement with a state agency if the EEOC determined that the agency was no longer effectively exercising its power to combat discrimination. *See ibid.* In the Senate, this bill met with strenuous opposition on the ground that it placed the EEOC in the position of monitoring state enforcement efforts, granting states exclusive jurisdiction over local discrimination claims only upon the EEOC's determination that state efforts were effective. *See, e.g., id.*, at 6449 (remarks of Sen. Dirksen). The bill's opponents voiced their concerns against the backdrop of the federal-state civil rights conflicts of the early 1960's, which no doubt intensified their fear of "the steady and deeper intrusion of the Federal power." *See id.*, at 8193 (remarks of Sen. Dirksen). These concerns were resolved by the "Dirksen-Mansfield substitute," which proposed the 60-day deferral period now in § 706(c) of the Act. *See* 110 Cong. Rec., at 11926-11935.

The proponents of the Dirksen-Mansfield substitute identified two goals of the deferral provisions, both of which fully support the EEOC's conclusion that states may, if they choose, waive the 60-day deferral period, but retain jurisdiction over discrimination charges by entering into work-sharing agreements with the EEOC. First, the proponents of the substitute deferral provisions explained that the 60-day deferral period was meant to give states a "reasonable opportunity to act under State law before the commencement of any Federal proceedings." *Id.*, at 12708 (remarks of Sen. Humphrey). Nothing in the waiver provisions of the work sharing agreements impinges on the opportunity of the States to have an exclusive 60-day period for processing a discrimination charge. The waiver of that opportunity in specified instances is a voluntary choice made through individually negotiated agreements, not an imposition by the Federal Government. Indeed, eight work-sharing states and the District of Columbia filed a brief as *amici* in this case, explaining their satisfaction with the operation of the waiver provisions of the work-sharing agreements: "By clarifying primary responsibility for different categories of charges, work-sharing agreements benefit both the EEOC and the states." Moreover, most work-sharing agreements are flexible, permitting states to express interest in cases ordinarily waived under the agreement and to call upon the EEOC to refrain from assuming jurisdiction in such cases.

In contrast, respondent's argument that states should not be permitted to waive the deferral period because its creation reflected a Congressional preference for state as opposed to federal enforcement is entirely at odds with the voluntarism stressed by the proponents of deferral. Congress clearly foresaw the possibility that states might decline to take advantage of the opportunity for enforcement afforded them by the deferral provisions. It therefore gave the EEOC the authority and responsibility to act when a state is "unable or unwilling" to provide relief. 110 Cong. Rec. 12725 (1964) (remarks of Sen. Humphrey). This Court, too, has recognized that Congress envisioned federal intervention when "States decline, for whatever reason, to take advantage of [their] opportunities" to settle grievances in "a voluntary and localized manner." *Oscar Mayer & Co. v. Evans*, 441 U.S., at 761. As counsel for the EEOC explained, deferral was meant to work as "a carrot, but not a stick," affording states an opportunity to act, but not penalizing their failure to do so other than by authorizing federal intervention. The waiver provisions of work-sharing agreements are fully consistent with this goal.

In addition to providing states with an opportunity to forestall federal intervention, the deferral provisions were meant to promote "time economy and the expeditious handling of cases." 110 Cong. Rec. 9790 (1964) (remarks of Sen. Dirksen). Respondent's proposed interpretation of § 706(c), adopted by the Court of Appeals, is irreconcilable with this purpose because it would result in extraordinary inefficiency without furthering any other goal of the Act. The EEOC would be required to wait 60 days before processing its share of discrimination claims under a work-sharing agreement, even though both the EEOC and the relevant state or local agency agree that the State or locality will take no action during that period. Or, in an effort to avoid this pointless 60-day delay, state and local agencies could abandon their work-sharing agreements with the EEOC and attempt to initially process all charges during the 60-day deferral period, a solution suggested by respondent. Such a solution would create an enormous backlog of discrimination charges in states and localities, preventing them from securing for their citizens the quick attention to discrimination claims afforded under work sharing agreements. Or, in another scenario proposed by respondent, *see id.*, at 29, state or local agencies could rewrite their work-sharing agreements with the EEOC to provide for "termination" of state or local proceedings in accordance with respondent's definition of that term—complete relinquishment of jurisdiction. This solution would prevent a pointless 60-day delay, but it would also preclude a state's reactivation of a discrimination charge upon the conclusion of federal proceedings. Requiring that states completely relinquish authority over claims in order to avoid needless delay turns on its head the dual purposes of the deferral provisions: deference to the states and efficient processing of claims. Such a requirement "frustrates the Congressional intent to ensure state and local agencies the opportunity to employ their expertise to resolve discrimination complaints."

The most dramatic result of respondent's reading of the deferral provisions is the preclusion of any federal relief for an entire class of discrimination claims. All claims filed with the EEOC in work-sharing states more than 240 but less than 300 days after the alleged discriminatory event, like Leerssen's claim in this case, will be rendered untimely because the 60-day deferral period will not expire within the 300-day filing limit. Respondent's interpretation thus requires the 60-day deferral period—which was passed on behalf of state and local agencies—to render untimely a claim filed within the federal 300-day limit, despite the joint efforts of the EEOC and the state or local agency to avoid that result. As petitioner epigrammatically observes, a claim like Leerssen's that is filed with the EEOC within the last 60 days of the federal filing period is "too early until it is too late." Brief for Petitioner 25. This severe consequence, in conjunction with the pointless delay described above, demonstrates that respondent's interpretation of the language of § 706(c) leads to "absurd or futile results...'plainly at variance with the policy of the legislation as a whole,'" which this Court need not and should not countenance. *United States v. American Trucking Assns., Inc.*, 310 U.S. 534, 543 (1940), quoting *Ozawa v. United States*, 260 U.S. 178, 194 (1922).

C.   The EEOC's construction of § 706(c) also finds support in other, related sections of Title VII. These sections reinforce our reading of the legislative history that the 1964 Congress did not intend to preclude the operation of the waiver provisions of the work-sharing agreements now widely in force.

Section 706(d) provides that when a member of the EEOC, rather than an individual complainant, files a discrimination charge in a state or locality with concurrent jurisdiction, "the Commission shall, before taking any action with respect to such charge, notify the appropriate State or local officials and, upon request, afford them a reasonable time, but not less than sixty days... unless a shorter period is requested, to act." 42 U.S.C. § 2000e-5(d) (emphasis added). This language clearly permits state and local agencies to waive the 60-day deferral period and thus authorize the EEOC to take immediate action in cases arising under § 706(D). There is every reason to believe that Congress intended the same result in § 706(c), notwithstanding the variance in language. The legislative history of the deferral provisions reflects the legislators' understanding that the time limits of Sections 706(c) and (d) were the same. *See, e.g.,* 110 Cong. Rec. 12690 (1964) (remarks of Sen. Saltonstall); *id.,* at 15896 (remarks of Rep. Celler). Moreover, this Court already has recognized in *Love v. Pullman Co.*, 404 U.S., at 526-527, that "the difference in wording between [the two sections] seems to be only a reflection of the different persons who initiate the charge." We concluded in *Love* that "[t]here is no reason to think" that Congress meant to permit the EEOC to hold a claim in abeyance during the deferral period under § 706(d), but not under § 706(C)—even though the former section expressly authorizes such action, and the latter section does not. *Ibid.* Similarly, in the instant case, there is no reason to think that Congress meant to make the deferral period waivable by states under § 706(d) when the EEOC files a claim, but mandatory under § 706(c) when an individual files a claim.

The EEOC's interpretation of § 706(c) also finds support in provisions of the Act calling for formal cooperation between the EEOC and state and local agencies. Section 705(g)(1) gives the EEOC the power "to cooperate with and, with their consent, utilize regional, State, local, and other agencies." 78 Stat. 258, 42 U.S.C. § 2000e-4(g)(1). Section 709(b) specifies that "[i]n furtherance of such cooperative efforts, the Commission may enter into written agreements with such State or local agencies." 86 Stat. 108, 42 U.S.C. § 2000e-8(b). These sections clearly envision the establishment of some sort of work-sharing agreements between the EEOC and state and local agencies, and they in no way preclude provisions designed to avoid unnecessary duplication of effort or waste of time. Because the EEOC's interpretation of the "termination" requirement of § 706(c) is necessary to give effect to such provisions in most of the existing work-sharing agreements, we find that interpretation more consistent with the cooperative focus of the Act than respondent's contrary construction.

III.   In the alternative, respondent argues in support of the result below that the extended 300-day federal filing period is inapplicable to this case because the complainant failed to file her discrimination charge with the CCRD within Colorado's 180-day limitations period. Respondent reasons that the extended 300-day filing period applies only when "the person aggrieved has initially instituted proceedings with a state or local agency with authority to grant or seek relief" from the practice charged, § 706(e), 42 U.S.C. § 2000e-5(e), and that in the absence of a timely filing under state law, a state agency lacks the requisite "authority to grant or seek relief." The Tenth Circuit rejected this argument below, as has every other Circuit to consider the question, on the ground that the words "authority to grant or seek relief" refer merely to enabling legislation that establishes state or local agencies, not to state limitations requirements. We join the Circuits in concluding that state time limits for filing discrimination claims do not determine the applicable federal time limit.

Although respondent is correct that this Court's opinion in *Oscar Mayer & Co. v. Evans*, 441 U.S. 750 (1979), did not decide the precise issue we address today, *see* Brief for Respondent 36, the reasoning of *Oscar Mayer* provides significant guidance. In *Oscar Mayer*, we found in the Age Discrimination in Employment Act of 1967 (ADEA) context that a complainant's failure to file a claim within a state limitations period did not automatically render his federal claim untimely. We reasoned that the federal statute contained no express requirement of timely state filing, 441 U.S., at 759, and we declined to create such a requirement in light of the remedial purpose of the ADEA and our recognition that it is a "statutory scheme in which laymen, unassisted by trained lawyers, initiate the process." *Id.*, at 761, quoting *Love v. Pullman Co.*, *supra*, at 527. In the instant case, we decide the separate question whether under Title VII, untimely filing under state law automatically precludes the application of the extended 300-day federal filing period, but the reasoning of *Oscar Mayer* is entirely apposite. As we noted in *Oscar Mayer* itself, the filing provisions of the ADEA and Title VII are "virtually *in hacek verbal*," the former having been patterned after the latter. 441 U.S., at 755. Title VII, like the ADEA, contains no express reference to timeliness under state law. In addition, the policy considerations that militate against importing such a hurdle into the federal ADEA scheme are identical in the Title VII context: Title VII also is a remedial scheme in which laypersons, rather than lawyers, are expected to initiate the process.

The importation of state limitations periods into § 706(e) not only would confuse lay complainants, but also would embroil the EEOC in complicated issues of state law. In order for the EEOC to determine the timeliness of a charge filed with it between 180 and 300 days, it first would have to determine whether the charge had been timely filed under state law, because the answer to the latter question would establish which of the two federal limitations periods should apply. This state-law determination is not a simple matter. The EEOC first would have to determine whether a state limitation period was jurisdictional or nonjurisdictional. And if the limitation period was nonjurisdictional, like Colorado's in this case, the EEOC would have to decide whether it was waived or equitably tolled. The EEOC has neither the time nor the expertise to make such determinations under the varying laws of the many deferral states and has accordingly construed the extended 300-day period to be available regardless of the state filing. *See* 52 Fed. Reg. 10224 (1987). In contrast to the difficulties presented by respondent's argument, our broadly worded statement in *Mohasco Corp. v. Silver*, 447 U.S. 807 (1980), a case presenting a related issue regarding the application of the extended 300-day federal filing period, that a complainant "need only file his charge within 240 days of the alleged discriminatory employment practice in order to ensure that his federal rights will be preserved," *id.*, at 814, establishes a rule that is both easily understood by complainants and easily administered by the EEOC. We reaffirm that rule today.

Because we find that the extended 300-day federal limitation period is applicable to this case and that the CCRD's waiver of the 60-day deferral period "terminated" its proceedings within that 300-day limit, we conclude that Leerssen's claim was timely filed under Title VII. We therefore reverse the decision of the Court of Appeals and remand the case for further proceedings consistent with this opinion.

FAVORS v. FISHER
13 F.3d 1235 (8th Cir. 1994)

Nora Favors appeals from a final judgment entered in the United States District Court (n1) for the Western District of Missouri in favor of Dennis Fischer, in his official capacity as Administrator for the General Services Administration (GSA), on her claim of race discrimination. The District Court held that Favors' employer, GSA, did not intentionally discriminate against her when it denied her a promotion from Procurement Clerk to Contract Specialist. *Favors v. Fischer*, Civ. No. 88-0665-CV-W-9 (W.D. Mo. Dec. 18, 1991). For reversal, Favors argues that the District Court erred in concluding that she was not a victim of race discrimination. For the reasons discussed below, we affirm the judgment of the District Court.

I. BACKGROUND

Favors began to work for GSA in February 1980 as a Shipment Clerk in the distribution management and operations branch of the Federal Supply Service.

In 1984, she was reassigned to the position of Procurement Clerk. In April 1987, Favors applied for a position as a Contract Specialist. Following that application, she was selected as one of thirteen applicants qualified for the position. She was referred to Contract Specialist Supervisor Carl Harper for an interview, as were the other twelve qualified applicants. Two of the thirteen applicants were African-American, including Favors. Harper is a Caucasian male. Harper, as Contract Specialist Supervisor, conducted the interviews, and he asked each applicant the same ten questions designed to test their knowledge of procurement regulations.

Raymond Wessling, a Caucasian male, was selected by Harper for the position of Contract Specialist. After selecting Wessling, Harper destroyed the ten questions he asked the applicants and the answers they gave. In May 1987, Favors filed an EEOC charge based upon her failure to receive the promotion. The EEOC charge included allegations of racial discrimination against Favors and other African-American employees.

In March 1988, Favors was given a grade of "successful" on her yearly performance evaluation. Between 1986 and 1988, financial awards were given to employees who received grades of "highly successful" or "outstanding" on their yearly performance evaluations. Favors' March 1988 grade of "successful" did not entitle her to a financial award. Her 1987 grade was "highly successful," which had entitled her to a financial award.

Favors filed suit in federal district court against Fischer, in his official capacity as Administrator for GSA, under Title VII of the Civil Rights Act of 1964, 42 U.S.C. § 2000e *et seq.*, alleging that her failure to be promoted to Contract Specialist in 1987 was the result of race discrimination, and that Harper down graded her 1988 performance evaluation from "highly successful" to "successful" in retaliation for filing her prior race discrimination charge. Following a two-day bench trial, the district court entered judgment in favor of GSA on Favors' discriminatory failure to promote claim and in favor of Favors on her retaliation claim. The district court awarded Favors $261.00 in damages on her retaliation claim. Favors appeals the district court's decision in favor of GSA on her discriminatory failure to promote claim.

II. DISCUSSION

In *Texas Dep't. of Community Affairs v. Burdine*, 450 U.S. 248, 252-3, 67 L.Ed. 2d 207, 101 S.Ct. 1089 (1981) (*Burdine*), the Supreme Court established the analytical framework for a Title VII disparate treatment case. First, Favors as the plaintiff must prove by a preponderance of the evidence a *prima facie* case of discrimination. In establishing a *prima facie* case of discrimination, Favors must produce sufficient evidence to support an inference that GSA denied her a promotion to Contract Specialist for discriminatory reasons. *Craik v. Minnesota State Univ. Bd.*, 731 F.2d 465, 469 (8th Cir. 1984). The elements necessary to establish a *prima facie* case vary according to the circumstances of the alleged discrimination. *Jones v. Frank*, 973 F.2d 673, 676 (8th Cir. 1992). In the promotion context, Favors can establish a *prima facie* case of prohibited racial discrimination by showing (1) she belongs to a racial minority, (2) she applied and was qualified for a job for which GSA was seeking applicants, (3) despite her qualifications, she was rejected, and (4) after her rejection, GSA filled or sought to fill the position with persons of Favors' qualifications. The district court found that Favors established a *prima facie* case based upon race. We agree. Favors, an African-American female, applied for and were qualified for the position of Contract Specialist; she was rejected and Wessling was selected.

Once the *prima facie* case is established, GSA as the employer bears the burden of articulating a legitimate, nondiscriminatory reason for its adverse employment action. *Burdine*, 450 U.S. at 256. The district court held that GSA articulated a legitimate, nondiscriminatory reason for denying Favors the promotion. GSA asserted that the promotion decision was made solely on the basis of an objective, ten-question test, and that Wessling was promoted because he scored the highest on the test. Not promoting Favors because Wessling was more qualified is a legitimate, nondiscriminatory reason and thus GSA rebutted Favors' *prima facie* case and satisfied the second step of the *Burdine* framework.

Once GSA articulates a legitimate, nondiscriminatory reason for denying Favors the promotion, Favors has the "opportunity to demonstrate that the proffered reason was not the true reason for the employment decision," or, in other words, to prove pretext. *Burdine*, 450 U.S. at 256. In attempting to establish pretext, Favors relies on two points. First, Favors claims that GSA changed its alleged legitimate, nondiscriminatory reason for denying her the promotion. *See Estes v. Dick Smith Ford, Inc.*, 856 F.2d 1097, 1101 (8th Cir. 1988) (where an employer changes its alleged nondiscriminatory reason, that alone is strong evidence of pretext). Favors contends that Harper told her that the reason Wessling received the promotion was because Wessling would not require any training. At trial, Harper denied ever telling this to Favors because anyone hired for the position of Contract Specialist would need to be trained. Harper acknowledged that Wessling, at the GS-7 level, would only need one year's training, while Favors, at the GS-5 level, would have needed at least two years of training. However, Harper maintained that Wessling received the promotion solely because he scored higher on the ten-question test than any other applicant.

The district court stated that it did "not believe that Carl Harper told Nora Favors that Ray Wessling would need no training. That is clearly contrary to what everybody knew at the time, that the Contract Specialist position was known to be a training position." Due regard must be given to the trial court in judging the credibility of witnesses. *Anderson v. City of Bessemer City*, 470 U.S. 564, 573, 84 L.Ed. 2d 518, 105 S.Ct. 1504 (1985) (*Anderson*). "Only the trial judge can be aware of the variations in demeanor and tone of voice that bear so heavily on the listener's understanding of and belief in what is said." *Id.* at 575. "When a trial judge's finding is based on his [or her] decision to credit the testimony of one of two or more witnesses, each of whom has told a coherent and facially plausible story that is not contradicted by extrinsic evidence, that finding, if not internally inconsistent, can virtually never be clear error." *Id.* In the present case, the district court heard the oral testimony of both Favors and Harper. Harper's account of why he selected Wessling for promotion is plausible and is neither [**8] contradicted by any extrinsic evidence nor internally inconsistent. Under these circumstances, the district court's decision to credit Harper's testimony was not clearly erroneous.

Second, Favors argues that Harper's destruction of the ten-question test and results violates 29 C.F.R. § 1602 and therefore shows that GSA's articulated reason is pretextual. The regulation requires that an employer preserve "relevant personnel records" including "test papers completed by an unsuccessful applicant and all other candidates for the same position" for six months from the date of the making of the record or the personnel action, and continue preservation of all relevant records once a charge of discrimination has been filed until final disposition of the charge of discrimination. GSA argues that the ten-question test was not a personnel or employment record within the meaning of § 1602.14, but rather, merely constitutes Harper's interview notes.

We believe, and the district court so found, that the regulation encompasses the ten-question test administered by Harper and the resulting answers. Each objective question called for a single correct answer and served as a means of determining the applicant's knowledge and application of procurement rules and regulations. Harper assigned a numerical score to each response provided by an applicant. Harper's ten-question test indeed constituted a "test" within the meaning of § 1602.14. The ten-question test and answers were relied upon by Harper in selecting the Contract Specialist. The documents were "records having to do with promotion," 29 C.F.R. Sec, 1602.14(a), and are thus employment records which should have been retained by GSA for at least six months after the employment decision. Harper's destruction of the ten-question test and answers violates this federal regulation.

The district court found that because Harper violated § 1602.14 by destroying the test and records, Favors was entitled to the benefit of a presumption that the destroyed documents would have bolstered her case. *See Hicks v. Gates Rubber Co.*, 833 F.2d 1406, 1419 (10th Cir. 1987) (*Hicks*); *Capaci v. Katz & Besthoff, Inc.*, 711 F.2d 647, 661 n.7 (5th Cir. 1983), cert. denied, 466 U.S. 927, 80 L.Ed. 2d 182, 104 S.Ct. 1709 (1984). Nevertheless, the district court found that GSA presented sufficient evidence to overcome such a presumption. Harper testified that the records were not destroyed because they showed something contrary to GSA's position. Rather, Harper testified that the ten-question test and results were immediately destroyed because he anticipated using the same or similar questions again in future promotion decisions. Harper testified that he was unaware of any reason to keep the ten-question test and answers because he had never been advised by his supervisors of any federal regulations that would mandate their preservation. Harper also testified that he had previously administered similar tests on seven occasions, and it was his normal practice to immediately destroy the documents.

The district court "believed the test results were destroyed as Harper testified, because Harper had not been told to keep them and because it was best not to keep the questions around because he was going to be" using those questions again. The district court found that Harper's testimony created an inference that he did not destroy the documents in anticipation of litigation. Where two permissible views of the evidence exist, the district court's choice between them cannot be clearly erroneous. *Anderson*, 470 U.S. at 574. We cannot say that the district court's finding that GSA rebutted any presumption that the destroyed test questions and answers would have bolstered Favors' case was clearly erroneous.

Favors contends that, because Harper destroyed the ten-question test and results, she was not afforded a "full and fair opportunity" to demonstrate pretext within the meaning of *Burdine*. Favors argues that, because Harper destroyed the documents, she was deprived of her opportunity to challenge the scoring of the answers and dispute whether the questions were truly job-related.

While we do not condone Harper's destruction of the documents, we disagree with Favors' contention. Favors was provided with the opportunity to cross-examine Harper. Harper testified that Wessling correctly answered nine or ten questions, in contrast to Favors who, Harper testified, correctly answered between five and seven questions. Harper not only testified that Wessling received the highest score of the thirteen applicants, but that several other applicants received scores higher than Favors' score. Favors was afforded the opportunity to challenge Harper's veracity and reliability, and to cross-examine GSA's other witnesses. Moreover, the destruction of the ten-question test and answers entitled Favors to a presumption of pretext, which imposed upon GSA the burden of showing that the documents were destroyed in good faith. We hold that Favors was provided with a fair and full opportunity to establish pretext.

The district court found both Harper's recollection of the applicants' scores and his explanation for destroying the ten-question test and answers to be credible. Affording due regard to the district court's assessment of Harper's credibility, we hold that the district court's ultimate conclusion that Favors was not the victim of intentional discrimination is not clearly erroneous.

Accordingly, we affirm the judgment of the district court.

Glossary

back pay – Salary and employee benefits to which an injured employee may be entitled as a remedy for unlawful discrimination

charge – Claim filed pursuant to Title VII or the ADA alleging unlawful discrimination

class action – Permitted under the Federal Rules of Civil Procedure to aggregate similar claims arising out of the same occurrence

consequential damages – Monetary award to cover economic loss resulting from an unlawful act over and above mere compensation

deduction – Reduction of taxable income based on the number of persons supported by the employee

deferral agency – State agency where Title VII and ADA charges must first be filed

employee manual – Written statement of employer's policies and procedures disseminated to all employees

Federal Insurance Contributions Act (FICA) – Federal statute providing for withholding of Social Security contributions

front pay – Award to employee who proves discrimination to cover wages until a position opens up with the charged employer

hostile environment harassment – Unlawful sexual harassment that causes an uncomfortable work atmosphere

independent contractor – A person who contracts to do a piece of work according to his or her own methods and without being subject to the control of the employer except with regard to the result of the work

injunction – Court order requiring a person to do a particular act or refrain from doing a particular act

liquidated damages – Special monetary award permissible under EPA and ADEA claims

payroll department – Business office that deals with paychecks and withholding taxes

punitive damages – Court awarded remedy designed to punish an employer's willful misconduct

quid pro quo **harassment** – Form of sexual harassment in which an employee is required to submit to sexual requests to receive employee benefits such as promotions, training, etc.

reasonable cause – Standard needed to proceed with a charge of unlawful discrimination

Right-to-Sue Notice – Document issued by the EEOC as a prerequisite to the charging party being able to file a private suit in court

seniority – Employee benefits tied to length of employment

willful – Knowing or conscious [disregard]

withholding taxes – Money employers are required to keep back from employees and deposit directly to the government in anticipation of the income taxes the employee will owe on his or her earnings

Exercises

1. Determine whether the EEOC has a deferral agency relationship with your state.

2. Obtain a copy of your school's employee handbook and analyze its provisions relating to adherence to federal employment law.

3. Discuss how liquidated damages compare to punitive damages.

4. Discuss the benefits and detriments of requiring administrative action before filing a private suit in court for unlawful discrimination.

5. Discuss how you would document a discriminatory act as the basis of an ADA charge.

actual authority – Agent's ability to act resulting from direct manifestations to the agent by the principal. Contrast with apparent authority (*see* below).

ADA – Americans with Disabilities Act of 1990 (*see* below).

ADEA – Age Discrimination in Employment Act of 1967 (*see* below).

administrative law judge – Civil servant who renders decisions at administrative agency hearings.

affirmative action – Policy prescribed by Title VII to remedy past discrimination.

Age Discrimination in Employment Act of 1967 (ADEA) – Federal statute prohibiting discrimination in the workplace based on age; covers people over the age of 40.

agency by estoppel – Agency created when a person intentionally or negligently causes or allows a third person to believe that another is his or her agent.

ALJ – Administrative law judge (*see* above).

alternative dispute resolution – Nonjudicial methods, such as arbitration or mediation, to solve legal problems.

Americans with Disabilities Act of 1990 (ADA) – Federal statute protecting disabled workers from being discriminated against because of their disabilities.

apparent authority – Agent's ability to act resulting from the principal's manifestations to third persons about the agent's authority. Contrast with actual authority, above.

arbitration – The process of having a dispute resolved by an independent person outside the court process. *See* alternative dispute resolution, above.

assignment – Transfer of legal rights.

attorney-client privilege – Evidentiary rule protecting from disclosure all information given by a client to an attorney in the course of legal representation.

back pay – Salary and employee benefits to which an injured employee may be entitled as a remedy for unlawful discrimination.

BFOQ – *Bona fide* occupational qualification (*see* below).

***bona fide* occupational qualification (BFOQ)** – Permissible employer defense to charges of discrimination under Title VII and the ADEA.

boycott. Union action to bring attention to its position by refusing to work for or buy from a particular employer.

charge – Claim filed pursuant to Title VII or the ADEA alleging unlawful discrimination.

charging party – Person bringing a complaint before the NLRB or EEOC.

Civil Rights Act of 1866 – Federal statute providing equality in contract and property rights to persons of all races.

Civil Rights Act of 1964 – Federal statute prohibiting employment discrimination against employees in protected categories.

civil service – Government employment.

Civil Service Commission – Government agency with authority over government employment.

class action – Permitted under the Federal Rules of Civil Procedure to aggregate similar claims arising out of the same occurrence.

collective bargaining – Process of contract negotiation between unions and employers.

confidentiality – The expectation that disclosed information will not be divulged to third persons.

consequential damages – Monetary remedy above the standard measure for unusual losses resulting from a breach of contract.

consideration – The bargain of a contract; something of legal value.

constructive discharge – Method of making the work situation so distasteful that the employee will quit; an unlawful practice.

cool down period – The period before union action may be taken.

covenant not to compete – Contract provision prohibiting an employee from competing with his or her employer.

deduction – Reduction of taxable income based on the number of dependents supported by the employee.

deferral agency – State agency where Title VII and ADA charges must first be filed.

delegation – Having someone assist in performing contract obligations.

derivative violation – Violation of Section 8(a)(2), (3), (4) or (5) of the Wagner Act.

disability – A physical or mental impairment that limits a major life function.

diversified investments – Assets placed in various securities to minimize the risk of loss.

domestic partnership – People living in a close committed relationship without the benefit of marriage.

due process – Constitutional guarantee against arbitrary taking of life, liberty, or property by the government.

EEOC – Equal Employment Opportunity Commission (*see* below).

e-mail – Computer address for receiving information.

Electronic Communication Privacy Act – Federal statute designed to protect computer privacy.

employee benefit plan – Qualifying plan under ERISA.

employee handbook – Employer-generated document regarding employment policies and procedures disseminated to employees.

employee manual – *See* employee handbook, above.

Employee Polygraph Protection Act – Federal statute prohibiting employers from requiring employees to take lie detector tests.

Employee Retirement Income Security Act of 1974 (ERISA) – Federal statute designed to provide protection for employee benefit funds.

employer – Person who regularly employs a statutory minimum of employees for a statutory minimum number of weeks in a given year.

employment at will – Common law right of freedom of employment.

Equal Employment Opportunity Commission (EEOC) – Federal agency empowered to implement Title VII.

Equal Pay Act of 1963 – Federal statute requiring workers of opposite sexes performing equal work for the same employer to be paid equal wages.

equal work – Tasks requiring similar abilities and duties.

ERISA – Employment Retirement Income Security Act of 1974 (*see* above).

Executive Order 11246 – Applies Title VII standards to persons with government contracts.

express authority – A subset of actual authority arising out of specific instructions by the principal to the agent.

express contract – Contract created by the words of the parties.

Fair Credit Reporting Act – Federal statute permitting a person to have access to his or her credit records.

Fair Labor Standards Act (FLSA) of 1938 – Federal statute guaranteeing a minimum wage and maximum number of work hours.

Family Medical Leave Act of 1993 (FMLA) – Federal statute providing leave for employees to take care of family medical emergencies.

featherbedding – Requiring pay for work not actually performed.

Federal Insurance Contributions Act (FICA) – Federal statute providing for withholding of Social Security contributions.

Federal Reports Act – Statute requiring government agencies to obtain authorization from the Office of Management and Budget before maintaining records on 15 or more persons.

fellow servant exception – A master is not liable for the tortious acts of one servant who injures another servant.

fetal protection policy – Employer policy designed to protect fetuses from harm, allowing them to avoid hiring or placing pregnant women in areas where there may be danger for fetuses.

FICA – Social Security taxes.

fiduciary – Person held to a standard of care higher than ordinary care.

FLSA – Fair Labor Standards Act of 1938.

FMLA – Family Medical Leave Act of 1993.

FOIA – Freedom of Information Act (*see* below).

Freedom of Information Act (FOIA) – Federal statute permitting access to government records.

frolic of his own – A master is only liable for a servant's tortious acts that injure third persons if the servant was furthering the master's business and not his or her own devices when the negligent act took place.

front pay – Award to employee who proves discrimination to cover wages until a position opens up with the charged employer.

fully insured – Meeting minimum 40-quarters requirement to qualify for Social Security.

golden parachute – Special provision to protect an employee who may be discharged because of a change in the company's ownership.

good faith – Showing a clear willingness to bargain.

hostile environment harassment – Unlawful sexual harassment that causes an uncomfortable work atmosphere.

human resource management – Process of recruiting, hiring, managing, and firing employees.

implied authority – Actual authority resulting from custom and usage.

implied contract – Contract formed by the parties' actions rather than words.

independent contractor – A person who contracts to do a piece of work according to his or her own methods and without being subject to the control of the employer except with regard to the result of the work.

independent violation – Violation of Section 8(A)(1) of the Wagner Act.

injunction – Court order requiring a person to do a particular act or to refrain from doing a particular act.

job description – Statement of work duties and responsibilities.

job-related qualification standard – Legitimate qualification necessary to perform an essential function of a particular job.

just cause – Legitimate business reasons for discharging an employee.

Labor Management Reporting & Disclosure Act (Landrum-Griffin Act) – Federal statute requiring unions to disclose financial information to their members.

Landrum-Griffin Act – Popular name of the Labor Management Reporting & Disclosure Act (*see* above).

law of agency – Common law rules that define the employment relationship.

liquidated damages – Special monetary award permissible under EPA and ADA claims.

lockout – Employer keeping union workers out of the workplace to protest union's unfair labor practice.

master-servant – The basic employment relationship in which the master controls the servant's activities.

mediation. Form of negotiation that is assisted by an impartial third party called a mediator. *See* alternative dispute resolution, above.

mental impairment – Any mental or psychological disorder or disease.

minimum wage – Lowest legally permissible pay rate.

mitigation of damages – Legal obligation of injured party to lessen the amount of the award the injuring party will have to pay.

National Labor Relations Act (Wagner Act) – Major federal statute regulating union activities.

National Labor Relations Board (NLRB) – Agency established to administer the Wagner Act.

national origin – Country of a person's birthplace or ancestry.

nationality – Country to which a person owes allegiance.

negligent hiring – An employer hiring someone unsuitable for the job whose unsuitability results in injuries to third persons; the master is personally liable.

nepotism – Hiring of relatives.

NLRB – National Labor Relations Board (*see* above).

Norris-LaGuardia Act – First federal statute to legitimize unions.

Occupational Safety and Health Act (OSHA) – Federal statute requiring safety measures and standards to protect employees in the workplace.

OSHA – Occupational Safety and Health Act (*see* above).

pay rate – Salary, benefits, pensions, etc.

payroll department – Business office that deals with paychecks and withholding taxes.

partnership – An association of two or more persons engaged in business for profit as co-owners.

physical impairment – Physiological disease or condition, cosmetic disfigurement or anatomical loss.

picket – Standing in front of a workplace with signs to bring attention to a labor problem.

Pregnancy Discrimination Act of 1978 – Federal statute extending protection of Title VII to pregnant women and their husbands.

primary boycott – Boycott of employer against whom the union has a complaint.

principal-agent – Relationship in which one person is legally able to contract on behalf of another.

privacy – The expectation that personal information will not be disclosed without the person's consent.

Privacy Act – Federal statute designed to afford a limited right to privacy in the collection, maintenance, and dissemination of information by the government.

proprietary covenant – Contract clause concerning ownership of patents, copyrights, marks and work products.

protected categories – Under Title VII: race, religion, color, national origin, and sex. Under ADEA: age.

punitive damages – Court-awarded remedy designed to punish an employer's willful misconduct.

***quid pro quo* harassment** – Form of sexual harassment in which an employee is required to submit to sexual requests in order to receive employee benefits such as promotions, training, etc.

ratification – Method of creating an agency relationship retroactively by accepting the benefits of an unauthorized contract.

reasonable cause – Standard to proceed with a charge of unlawful discrimination.

reasonable accommodation – Employer requirement to make changes and modifications to assist a disabled worker to perform his or her job.

red circle – Temporary work assignment justifying a temporary pay change.

Rehabilitation Act of 1973 – Federal statute designed to prevent handicapped persons from being discriminated against on the job.

release – Legal relinquishment of rights.

religion – Moral or ethical belief.

respondeat superior – A master is liable for the tortious acts of a servant who injures third persons.

restrictive covenant – Contract clause limiting what a party may do.

Right-To-Sue Notice – Document issued by the EEOC as a prerequisite to the charging party being able to file a private suit in court.

right to work – Statutory right to be gainfully employed.

runaway shop – Employer's closing one facility, then opening up a similar facility in order to de-unionize.

same establishment – A facility owned by an employer, used to determine whether equal pay is paid to workers of different sexes performing the same work for the same employer.

secondary boycott – Boycott of an employer not in conflict with the union in hopes that the second employer will force the first employer to give in to union demands.

secrecy – Information a person refuses to share.

seniority – Employee benefits tied to length of employment.

sexual harassment – Unwelcome sexual advances, requests for sexual favors, and other verbal or physical conduct of a sexual nature.

sexual stereotyping – Assuming particular characteristics to a particular gender.

Sherman Act – First U.S. antitrust act.

Social Security Act of 1935 – Federal statute used to fund a retirement and disability account for U.S. workers.

Social Security Administration – Government agency formed to administer the Social Security Act.

Social Security number – Personal identifying number used, among other things, to determine Social Security benefits.

sole proprietorship – Business owned and managed by just one person.

staggered term – Appointment procedure for the NLRB members; each member serves a five-year term, but is appointed in different years.

strike – Union action of refusing to work for a particular employer.

Taft-Hartley Act – Continues the Labor Relations Act and, in addition, provides for an 80-day injunction against strikes.

Title VII – Federal statute prohibiting discrimination against protected categories; part of the Civil Rights Act.

undue hardship – ADA standard used to limit the amount of accommodation an employer must make; accommodations that create an undue hardship are not required.

unfair labor practice – Activities specified in Section 8 of the Wagner Act as violative of labor relations.

vicarious liability – Being held legally accountable for actions committed by other persons.

Wagner Act – Popular name of the National Labor Relations Act (*see* above).

waiver – Legal relinquishment of a contract right.

whistle-blowing – Employee's informing the public of his or her employer's illegal or unethical conduct.

wildcat strike – Strike by union members not authorized by the union.

willful – Knowing or conscious [disregard].

withholding taxes – Money employers are required to keep back from employees and deposit directly to the government in anticipation of the income taxes the employee will owe on his or her earnings.

Work Place Privacy Bill – Federal bill to protect privacy in the workplace; it has not yet passed Congress.

work product – Anything developed by an employee as part of his or her job.

workers' compensation – Formerly workmen's compensation; statutes granting recovery to workers for injury in the performance of their duties.

wrongful discharge – Terminating employment without just cause.

EMPLOYMENT HANDBOOK CHECKLIST

Taken From the Texas Workforce Commission's
Employee Handbooks From A to Z

A Word of Caution

There are no legal guidelines as to what must be covered in a policy handbook, but it should answer as many workplace questions as possible. The contents of this appendix are suggestions only and are not meant to be definitive or absolute.

This checklist should not be used in lieu of legal advice. It is always wise to have any final version of company policy reviewed by an attorney.

Absenteeism

- State the company policy on attendance, tardiness and absenteeism.

- Distinguish between exempt and non-exempt employees.

- State the consequences for violation of the policy.
    - When are written warnings warranted?
    - When can employees be terminated?
    - What happens in a no show/no call situation?

- State the procedure for notifying the employer in case of an absence.
    - Whom should the employee notify?
    - How should the notice be given, and by what time?
    - What are the consequences for failing to give proper notice?
    - What is expected in the event an employee cannot reach the contact person in the company?

- Emphasize the need to follow policy and procedure as a courtesy to other employees.

For medical leave and leave of absence, *see* "Leave."

AIDS

- State the company's policy concerning equal access to employment for individuals with disabilities.

- Explain that individuals with AIDS and others who are HIV positive are individuals entitled to protection under state and federal laws against discrimination.

- Make it clear that the company will treat employees with this disability as it would any other employee with a life-threatening disease.

- Explain how the AIDS virus is transmitted.

- State the ways in which the AIDS virus is not transmitted.

- Where relevant, discuss company policy regarding medical exams and insurance coverage with respect to this virus.

- State clearly that the company does not test for the AIDS virus.

- Advise employees that the company will maintain in the strictest confidence all medical records of any employee with this disability.

Affirmative Action

An affirmative action/equal opportunity statement might include the following:

- Recognition of the laws against discrimination with a listing of classifications of groups protected.

- A statement of the company's anti-discrimination policy.

- Statements that all recruiting, hiring, training, and promotion decisions will comply with the principle of equal employment opportunity.

Benefits

- List all benefits offered by the company. Include the policy on health insurance, workers' compensation, profit-sharing plans, pension funds and credit union participation.

- State the differences for temporary and part-time employees.

- State the policy on employee benefits in the event of an employee's separation from the company.

- State the compensation policy for holidays or overtime. *Also see* "Compensation."

Compensation

- List the company's regularly scheduled paydays.

- Describe any deductions that may be subtracted from a paycheck. (Be sure to comply with your state's payday laws.)

- State the policy for distributing payroll checks to friends or relatives. Such distribution must be designated by the employee in writing.

- Explain the company's policy on bonuses or other nonsalary payments.

- Describe the policy on overtime compensation.
    - Who is eligible?
    - Is advance permission or authorization required?
    - When is overtime permitted?
    - How should workers report hours worked over 40 per week?

- State the policy on compensatory time and any limitations. Use caution. Federal law allows only governmental employers to give compensatory time in lieu of overtime pay.

- Make it clear what happens to unused leave time.

Conflict of Interest

- State the expectation of employee loyalty.

- Make it clear that regular and full-time employees must devote their full attention to the company during working hours.

- State employees' obligations to avoid activities or interests that conflict with the interests of the company.

- Consider requiring employees to disclose potential conflicts in advance.

Discipline

- Identify conduct that may result in immediate dismissal.

- Outline employee conduct that may result in disciplinary action. Be sure to allow for changes, additions, modifications or deletions to the policy.

- State that the conduct outlined is not an exhaustive list.

- Identify the penalty to be imposed for infractions.

- Describe the company's disciplinary procedure.

- Describe the company's process of appealing any disciplinary action taken.

- Advise employees of their "Bill of Rights."

- Advise employees that all disciplinary action will be documented in writing by the company in the employees' personnel files. Make it mandatory that both employee and supervisor sign counseling documentation.

- Advise employees of their rights to have their own written accounts of incidents included in their personnel files.

- Allow for termination with no notice if the misconduct is severe enough.

Disclaimers

- State that the handbook is meant to set policy and is to be used only as a guideline.

- State affirmatively that the handbook is not intended to imply any contract or contractual rights.

- State that the employer reserves the right to change or modify the contents of the handbook at any time without prior notice to employees.

- Identify individuals who have authority to modify the handbook and specifically exclude all others.

Drugs

- Explain the company's desire to maintain a safe working environment and a drug- and alcohol-free workplace.

- State the position of the company with respect to illegal use of drugs and alcohol. Include:
  - Policy overview
  - Policy on drug tests
  - Policy on searches.

- State the requirement that all employees provide prior written acknowledgment of the policy and consent to tests and searches.

- Outline the consequences of a positive test result. Include:
  - A provision for re-test by different method in the event of a positive result.
  - A notification that positive results may lead to immediate discharge.

- Explain that a request for a search is not an accusation of illegal drug use and that refusal to submit to a search may lead to immediate dismissal.

- Outline a grievance procedure for employees who think they have been treated unfairly.

- Where applicable, explain any or all employee assistance programs.

Grievances and Complaints

- State the company policy against discrimination.

- State the company policy against retaliation.

- State the policy of the company to comply with all applicable regulations, and state and federal laws.

- State that employees who feel they have been discriminated against or who have been asked to perform an illegal act are encouraged to report such incidents to the grievance officer immediately.

- Identify the individual in the company responsible for handling all grievances.

- State the company grievance procedure.

House Rules

- List house rules clearly in the company policy.

- State the consequence or punishment for breaking house rules.

- Specify that house rules apply to *all* employees.

Leave

Military Leave

- Explain that the company provides military leave to regular, full-time employees.
- State that the company complies with state law with respect to job reinstatement.
- State that an employee must notify the employer immediately when called to active duty. Notice should include anticipated duration of service and when the employee expects to return to work.

Jury Duty

- Explain that the company recognizes leave to serve on state and federal juries.
- State that the company complies with federal and local state laws with respect to reinstatement when jury service is complete.
- Explain that an employee called for jury service must immediately notify the company.
- State that an employee is expected to return to work immediately after the case concludes or the court recesses for the day if there is a reasonable amount of time remaining in the work day.

Funeral Leave

- State whether the company provides for funeral leave.
- Identify which employees are entitled to funeral leave.
- Establish which familial relationships qualify for funeral leave. For example, immediate family only, etc.
- Explain how much time is permitted and what, if any, provisions there are for extending this time.
- State what, if any, provisions there are for taking time off without pay.
- State the policy regarding notifying the company in the case of a death in the family.

Personal Leave

- State whether the company provides personal leave.
- If so, state what constitutes "personal leave."
- Explain when personal leave can be taken and give the details on length of time allowed, procedure for requesting time, etc.

Medical Leave

- Describe the company policy concerning a prolonged medical leave of absence.
- Explain the difference between sick leave and medical leave of absence.
- Define temporary disability. **Note:** pregnancy must be treated like any other temporary disability.
- State the amount of medical leave allowed with or without pay, and explain whether an employee is first required to exhaust all unused vacation and sick leave.
- Explain whether the employee continues to accrue vacation and sick leave during a medical leave of absence.
- Discuss whether verification of the disability is required and, if so, whether the employee or the company selects the doctor.
- State the company's policy about returning to work. Include consequences for unauthorized failure to return.
- Explain the company's policy on reinstatement to the same position upon return, and what happens if that position no longer exists.

Privacy

- State the company policy on employee access to personnel files.

- State which documents are available to employees for review and which documents will not be accessible.

- Outline procedure for requesting to see a personnel file.

- State which employees will have access to such records. The policy should emphasize the company's intent to protect employees' privacy.

- Describe the company's policy on electronic surveillance.

- Explain the company's policy regarding references following separation from the company.

- Ask for the employee's written authorization, where applicable, permitting the company to give references.

Severance

- State who is eligible to receive severance pay.

- State the instances when an employee forfeits rights to severance pay (i.e.: fired for misconduct).

- State the manner in which severance will be paid.

- State if the severance is guaranteed or paid at the discretion of the employer.

Sexual Harassment

- State the company's policy against sexual harassment.

- Define sexual harassment, quid pro quo sexual harassment and hostile work environment sexual harassment.

- Advise employees of the company's grievance procedure in the event they ever feel harassment has occurred.

- Assure employees that every complaint will be taken seriously and investigated immediately.
- State the penalties for sexually harassing an employee.

- Explain that individuals involved in sexual harassment complaints will have the opportunity to give a full account of their recollection of the incident or incidents.

Termination

- State the company policy regarding at-will employment.

- If there is a probation period, define it and explain it.

- Identify those actions that may result in immediate dismissal even for a first offense. Explain that the list is not exhaustive and that items are listed by way of example only.

- List conduct likely to result in a warning and which actions may result in suspension. Explain the lists are as examples only and not exhaustive.

- Explain the company policy regarding unused vacation and sick leave. Where applicable, distinguish between voluntary and involuntary discharge.

- State the company policy regarding continuation of insurance benefits.

- Explain when a terminated employee can expect to receive a final paycheck.

Trade Secrets

- State the general company policy regarding trade secrets.

- Define a trade secret and provide examples peculiar to the company's business and industry.

- Explain that the unauthorized taking, copying or communication of the company's trade secrets constitutes a third-degree felony.

- State the company's policy requiring employees to sign an Acknowledgment of Confidentiality or a Confidentiality Agreement.

- Describe the company policy for violations of the Acknowledgment of Confidentiality or Confidentiality Agreement, including the company's right to seek immediate legal action, injunctive relief, money damages or criminal prosecution.

- Outline the company's procedures for access to and use of confidential information or trade secrets.

Vacation/Sick Leave

Sick Leave

- State which employees are entitled to sick leave (i.e., full-time vs. temporary or part-time employees). Explain the quotas.
- Explain how sick leave is accrued and describe the company's policy for carrying over sick leave and whether employees will be paid for unused sick leave upon separation from the company.
- Define the company policy for entitlement to sick leave and whether proof of illness could be required.

Vacation Leave

- State which employees are entitled to vacation (i.e., full-time vs. temporary or part-time employees).
- Explain when vacation is accrued and how it may be used.
- Describe how vacation time is accrued and whether it can be carried over to the next year. If so, explain.

- If there is a distinction between those who voluntarily separate from the company and those who are discharged, explain it. State the company policy for payment of unused vacation in the event of layoffs.

refusal to bargain in good faith, 33
violations by employer, 32
United Paperhangers Int. Union v. Misco, Inc., 45
United States v. City of Warren, 195

V

vicarious liability
   defined, 9, 25
   distinguished from negligence, 11
   in principal-agent relationship, 13
   workers' compensation, 16

W

Wagner Act. See National Labor Relations Act
waiver
   defined, 188, 200
Walker v. Secretary of the Treasury, I.R.S., 89
whistle-blowing
   defined, 191, 200
wildcat strike

defined, 36, 51
willful
   defined, 208, 221
withholding taxes
   defined, 202, 222
Work Place Privacy Bill
   defined, 153
   generally, 139
work product
   defined, 187, 200
workers' compensation
   contributory negligence, 16
   defined, 25
   generally, 16
workers' compensation board
   defined, 16
workers' compensation statutes
   defined, 5
wrongful discharge
   defined, 8, 25